The Russo-Japanese War at Sea 1904–5 Volume 2

The Russo-Japanese War at Sea 1904–5 Volume 2

The Battle of Tsushima and the Aftermath

Vladimir Semenoff
Translated By L. A. B., Leonard Lewery
and F. R. Godfrey

LEONAUR

The Russo-Japanese War at Sea 1904-5
Volume 2
The Battle of Tsushima and the Aftermath
By Vladimir Semenoff
Translated By L. A. B., Leonard Lewery and F. R. Godfrey

First published under the titles
"Rasplata" ("the reckoning")
The Battle of Tushima
and
The Price of Blood

Leonaur is an imprint of Oakpast Ltd

Copyright in this form © 2014 Oakpast Ltd

ISBN: 978-1-78282-343-8 (hardcover)
ISBN: 978-1-78282-344-5 (softcover)

http://www.leonaur.com

Publisher's Notes

Contents

Part 3: The Price of Blood

CHAPTER 1

Ill Omen

On January 1 and 2 a fresh breeze from the S.S.E. caused such a heavy sea that not only were we forced to interrupt our coaling, but communication by boat between the ships became very difficult. A curious-looking native craft brought off the local "*administrateur*" (I hardly know how to translate this title) and the Collector of Customs, who came to call on the admiral. Amongst other things they gave us a very good piece of advice, namely, to move the squadron a few miles further north, and to anchor in Tang-Tang roads, at the mouth of the river of that name, where a spit of land reaching far into the straits would protect us against the sea and the swell coming in from the south at this season of the year.

Late on January 3 we again sent the *Russ* to Tamatave to collect intelligence, but chiefly to find out what Admiral Fölkersam was doing and intending to do. Next morning we moved the whole division, except the *Malay*, which was again suffering from machinery troubles, to the new anchorage, which under the prevailing conditions seemed indeed to be an excellent one, although the sailing directions make no mention of it.

The "master of the fleet"[1] rubbed his hands with delight. "We owe this entirely to those French settlers. It was an excellent piece of advice." Of course they did not give it without hopes of something in return. Well, the admiral submitted their names for the Order of St Stanislas "round the neck," (commander). May they duly appreciate it!

The men-of-war successfully completed their coaling, in part from the German colliers, in part from our collier transports.

January 4 passed in painful suspense. The *Russ* did not return, nor did we get any news whatever from Diego Suarez. In consequence of

1. Navigating officer on the admiral's staff.—Trans.

the prohibition to use the latter port, and thanks to the high-handed and autocratic action of the general staff, the whole of our calculations had been upset, and the greatest confusion prevailed.

On the assumption that perhaps the colliers dared not leave Diego Suarez for fear of being captured by Japanese mercantile auxiliaries, as to the presence of which in these waters there were constant rumours, the admiral decided to send Admiral Enquist with the cruisers *Nakimoff*, *Aurora*, and *Donskoi* for their protection to Diego Suarez, and from there to Nossi-Bé, to transmit to Admiral Fölkersam the order to rejoin the flag here at once.

On January 5, at 5 a.m., the cruisers sailed in accordance with the above instructions. About noon on the same day the first collier arrived from Diego Suarez. She brought a letter from Commander W—— and a report from Admiral Fölkersam. The former wrote that up to date only one of our five armed merchant cruisers, the *Kuban*, had arrived at Diego Suarez; the whereabouts of the remainder was not known. There was also no news of the division consisting of the cruisers *Oleg* and *Isumrud*, and the destroyers *Grosny* and *Gromky*, which was to overtake us. Admiral Fölkersam reported that after having proceeded to Nossi-Bé in compliance with orders from the general staff, he had commenced overhauling machinery, cleaning boilers, etc.—in naval language: "opened up everything." Nearly all his destroyers required a thorough refit. It would be impossible for him to make a move under a fortnight.

The admiral developed a perfectly feverish activity at this time. When he ate or when he slept, I do not know. Nobody got a chance of discussing anything with him; he only issued orders or called for information on some point or other. Once when I nearly ran into him on the ladder, he growled out: "Oh well, after a long passage,—the well deserved rest, that is our tradition."

"They are old ships, your Excellency," I tried to put in; "the passage was indeed a long one."

"And the one before us is still longer! If they are so old that they can't steam, then they may go to the devil. We have no use for rubbish here. But no, it is simply the old custom! However, I'll go there myself—I'll dig them out fast enough!"

The departure of our division for Nossi-Bé was fixed for the following day, January 6. It meant going 600 miles out of our way, but what was to be done ?—We had to "dig out" the others.

During the night the *Russ* arrived (from Tamatave); she brought the news of the fall of Port Arthur. It was bitter, humiliating for our pride, but since the destruction of the First Squadron this fact did not in reality make any change in our situation.

At 6 a.m. we received a message by wireless to the effect that the *Svetlana*, with the destroyers *Byedovy* and *Bodry*, was coming to meet us, detached by Admiral Fölkersam with a detailed report on the progress of the repairs, having apparently missed Admiral Enquist's division. All this was the result of the confusion occasioned by four independent departments issuing orders at the same time, *viz.*, the Admiral (Rojëstvensky), the Naval General Staff, those who directed the operations of the armed merchant cruisers, and the Ministry of Marine.

At 8 a.m. we weighed in accordance with the orders issued the evening before and proceeded towards Nossi-Bé. We did not meet the *Svetlana* and the destroyers until 11.30 a.m. We were astonished at their being so late, but it turned out that of the two only destroyers with Admiral Fölkersam, which had held out so far, the *Bodry* had had a breakdown on the way, in consequence of which she could only steam with one engine, that is, not more than 7 knots. The *Russ* was ordered to take her in tow; then we proceeded. Whilst this operation was being carried out (taking in tow), we communicated with the *Svetlana*. The admiral received a detailed report of the voyage of the second division. (Later on I read it in the original.) As regarded the ships it contained nothing new, beyond a long list of every conceivable breakdown, and of repairs which could not be put off.

On the other hand, it cited some interesting incidents, which indicated the attitude of the local authorities, an attitude which clearly reflected the views of the home authorities. It would seem that St Petersburg had allowed itself to be too much intimidated; in Paris it had in no way been anticipated that we would relinquish so lightly the rights which were given us by the French declaration of neutrality, and though it had been suggested to us that we might go to Nossi-Bé, everyone had been quite prepared to see the squadron steaming into Diego Suarez. Buoys had, in fact, been already laid out there to indicate the anchor berths of the different ships; fresh provisions (including 1,000 bullocks) had been prepared, the local workshops of the "Messageries Maritimes" had increased their staff of workmen to enable extensive repairs to be dealt with expeditiously, etc. It looked as though the protest had been merely a matter of form, but from the

9

moment that our diplomacy had shown how ready it was to give in, and that the General Staff had instantly ordered Admiral Fölkersam to go to Nossi-Bé— they were all the more pleased.

On January 7, (Russian Christmas Day), we remained stopped from 8.30 a.m. till noon, as the destroyers had to be coaled. About this time we called up the *Kuban* violently by wireless, she being in Diego Suarez, 30 miles off; but in vain.

After mass and the prescribed parade, the admiral assembled all hands on the quarter-deck, and, glass in hand, made them a short, but very impressive speech. It is noted in my diary, almost *verbatim*:—

> God grant that, after serving your country well and faithfully, you may be vouchsafed a safe return and a happy meeting with the families you have left behind. On this high feast day we out here have to work and do our duty. Yes, we shall have to work often yet, and hard. This can't be helped—it is war. It is not for me to thank you for your services. You as well as I serve our country side by side. But it is my right and my duty to report to the emperor how you are doing your duty, what fine fellows you are, and he himself will thank you in the name of Russia. Our task is heavy—our goal is far distant, and our enemy is strong. But always remember that '*the whole of Russia is looking upon you with confidence and in firm hope.*' May God help us to serve her honourably, to justify her confidence, not to deceive her hopes. To you, whom I trust! To Russia!"—and with a rapid movement he raised the glass to his lips, emptied it, and held it high over his bared head.

The admiral had commenced in his usual quiet manner of speaking, but as he proceeded he became more and more excited, and there was an uncertain ring in his voice—not blind confidence, not set determination. The ship's company, which at first remained standing in their appointed places, fell completely under the spell of this oration. So as to be able to hear and see better, the men soon began to climb on each other's shoulders; like cats they climbed up by any handy rope on to the bridges, boats, turrets, hammock nettings—preserving dead silence all the time. The concluding words, which were pronounced in almost a broken voice, were drowned in cheers, which were even louder than the salute the guns were then firing. The front ranks could hardly keep back those in rear. It looked as if this avalanche of human beings were about to overwhelm the admiral. Caps were thrown in the air, arms were raised as if in the act of taking an oath; many crossed themselves, there were tears in the eyes of many, but they were not ashamed of them. And—quite contrary to the rules of the service— loud voices were heard everywhere, calling out: "We'll do it!" "We won't give in!" "Lead us! Lead us!"

The ship's company did not calm down for a long time. Even when their special allowance of grog was being served out, they only came up hesitatingly. Their dinners were almost entirely forgotten.

I could not help thinking: "Oh, if we could go into action now!"

Alas, alas! there was still an entire ocean between us and the enemy.

About 5 p.m. the *Orel* had a breakdown in her machinery. We had to ease down to 6 knots. As this would make us very late, we sent the *Svetlana* on ahead to inform Admiral Fölkersam as to the probable time of our arrival.

Just before sunset we observed several columns of smoke on the horizon to the south-east. The *Borodino* reported that she could make out clearly four ships steaming in line ahead. We possessed no means whatever for scouting. We had not a single cruiser in company. They might very well be Japanese. Not far from Madagascar are the Seychelles, and still nearer Mauritius, a British colony, connected up with cables which were entirely in the hands of the British. No agents could send us any information which might not suit the allies of Japan.

There was no moon that night, but it was clear overhead. Every one was at action stations. Officers and men, except those actually on watch or on look-out, were sleeping at their guns fully dressed.

The remaining portion of the passage to Nossi-Bé passed uneventfully, but the difficult navigating conditions caused anxiety. The chart was simply covered with such ominous markings as "uncertain" near the soundings, and "P.D." (position doubtful) on the shoals and reefs.

"It doesn't matter; we are not coming here of our own free-will. Nicolai Ugodnic will therefore pull us through," the admiral said jokingly, but he never left the bridge. Turning to the captain, he added: "Have you got reliable signalmen aloft? Are they keeping a sharp look-out ahead?"[2]

About 11 a.m. on January 9 we arrived at Nossi-Bé, where Fölkersam's and Enquist's divisions were awaiting us, as well as the supply ships under the command of Captain Radloff (Imperial Navy).

2. Owing to the wonderful clearness and transparency of the waters of the ocean, it is often possible to discover shoal water by the change of colour of the surface. Of course only by day.

On the same day the *Ural* arrived, and on January 13, the *Terek*—both armed merchant cruisers.

The general spirit in Admiral Fölkersam's division differed markedly from that which permeated ours, influenced as it was by Admiral Rojëstvensky's presence, by the example which his restless activity, his boundless energy, gave us. With them there was none of that; they were all convinced that after the destruction of the First Squadron and the fall of Port Arthur any further advance was impossible. With the overhauling of engines and cleaning of boilers they were preparing their ships for—the return journey. They spoke of this as openly as if the question had been definitely settled, and naturally this affected the whole life on board, and the manner of carrying out the work. Why should we worry ourselves, if it is all for nothing, and we are returning home?—It was the general demoralisation which is the characteristic consequence of a retreat without fighting. If it is to no purpose, then why work? And therefore they indulge in a little distraction, on shore they kill time, they bemuddle their brains to stifle that ugly thought which has already taken deep root: to turn back without having accomplished anything.

Admiral Fölkersam, who was already suffering from the illness which caused his death, either paid no attention to this dangerous mood, or was himself under its influence, weakened as he was by his complaint. The work on board went its usual course; the crews were given leave every day (and not only by watches); the officers spent the whole of their time off watch on shore; it is hardly necessary to mention the crews of the auxiliaries, both the chartered supply steamers and the ships of the Volunteer Fleet—these simply behaved like free people, for whom there exist no war regulations. In that wretched hole Nossi-Bé there was a busy life—but an unwholesome life, such as is only found at Port Said, that thoroughfare for the entire old world. Indigenous beauties, Frenchwomen (real or sham), who called themselves *artistes* or even "stars," streamed in from far and near; numerous hastily improvised *cafés chantants* opened their doors; countless public and secret gambling hells did a roaring trade.

The local "*administrateur*" was in sheer despair; he obviously did not know what to do. On one side—the disorder; on the other—the *nation amie et alliée* and the undoubted enrichment of the poor colony.

The advent of Admiral Rojëstvensky drastically changed the course of affairs. The gambling hells were all closed. The crews of the mercantile auxiliaries were, as provided for in the war regulations, made amenable to all orders governing the Imperial Navy. Leave was given to the ships' companies only on high and feast days, and then only to men specially selected; the officers were only to consider themselves at liberty to go on shore when there was no work going on in their special branch or department, etc. And now work was begun at high pressure, not only in consequence of the threat of severe punishments, but also by reason of the influence of the idea, which brought every one to their senses, that Rojëstvensky was not going to turn back and meant to accept battle in any case. Was there anything not in order? Was there anything defective? Why had it not been made good before? So someone is to blame. You had better take very good care. . . .

Even at Sainte Marie the admiral had decided, though sorely against the grain, directly the news of the destruction of the First Squadron was received, to postpone the departure of the squadron to January 14, 1905; he did so in consequence of Admiral Fölkersam's report, stating that he needed a fortnight to carry out necessary repairs, and in consequence of all his calculations being upset by the dispositions made by the Foreign Office and General Staff, although he remained firmly convinced that the only chance of success lay in an immediate prosecution of the voyage.

The above-mentioned date the commander-in-chief rigidly adhered to. "That will give him, (Admiral Fölkersam), his two weeks, if he can't do it in less. But then he must be ready," he once said in his short, abrupt manner. But when on arrival in Nossi-Bé he saw for himself the general slackness prevailing there, even Rojëstvensky's personality had to bow to this *force majeure*.

With all his stubbornness, all the energy with which he stirred up the crews and incited all hands to renewed work, it was quite obvious that it would not be possible to sail on January 14. The departure was therefore fixed for the 18th.

The following had already been drawn up and issued:—Orders as to the cruising formation; instructions as to coaling at sea from our own collier transports, and as to filling up these again from the German colliers, which were to meet us at certain sea rendezvous fixed by latitude and longitude; confidential instructions for the masters of these steamers had already been drafted, giving them their several rendezvous—everything had been thought of, the parts in the play had already been distributed as it were, when suddenly—the Hamburg-

Amerika Line declined to carry out the contract, which had already been signed. The first supercargo (a species of commander-in-chief of the collier fleet) declared that his company could not, in face of the new declaration of neutrality, undertake to deliver coal anywhere outside neutral waters (in which it was prohibited), and that therefore there could be no question of coaling at any rendezvous in the open sea.

This explanation was totally unexpected. Up to that moment we could not bestow sufficient praise on the punctuality with which the Hamburg-Amerika Line had fulfilled the contract it had undertaken.

Active telegraphic negotiations commenced with St Petersburg.

Meanwhile, time was slipping by.

Every day lost could never be made good.—"We can't wait, we can't indeed," the admiral broke out every now and then.

He still adhered to the plan he had decided upon at Sainte Marie: the coal carried by our own collier transports was amply sufficient for the passage to Vladivostok of the nine battleships (to which *Aurora* and *Svetlana* were added), therefore these vessels should proceed at once, without the loss of an hour; the whole of the rubbish must be left behind.

It would seem that this view was not shared at St Petersburg. Without having recourse to the information which S—— (the flag-lieutenant) found it possible to give me (this would really amount to a betrayal of official secrets), I can say that it was quite obvious from the admiral's whole demeanour, from his remarks and his general dispositions, that we had received orders to await reinforcements, that St Petersburg had closed its eyes to facts, and was trusting blindly to some miracle, to something we could not possibly carry out.

These were bad times. In my diary there is not a line between January 18 and 30—the only (but very significant) interruption during the entire war. For this period I must rely upon my memory, strengthened, however, by the orders and circulars, by which the chief events of our daily life were regulated.

What can I say as to the general state of feeling in the squadron? When it was thoroughly realised that no junction was possible with any South American cruisers or the Black Sea Fleet, there no longer existed in the squadron the three different views I have mentioned before, but only the two: either forward at once, or—back. No one thought of any reinforcements which might be sent to us from the

Baltic. The representatives of these two views agreed on one point—that was the unanimous verdict: either forward or back—waiting was impossible.

The first words of my diary when I resumed it on January 30 were:—

A month yesterday since our arrival in Madagascar. The heat, the damp, the closeness are unbearable. Our stay in this climate, and not only the climate itself, but the mere fact of waiting here, this fatal delay, depresses everyone. Complete demoralisation is not—I venture to say—far off. I write this very reluctantly. We must get on as quickly as possible, so as to put an end to it somehow.

Strange ideas come into one's head now and then in this heat. I thought: if we are not allowed to go on, won't the Japanese send some one to deal with us here? Officially we were outside territorial waters, where everything was possible. Why should they not attack us one night with torpedo-boats, and settle the remnants with submarines?

What an obsession! . . . one's mind a blank. . . .

Still, there was one man in the squadron who did not give in to this mood, who made up his mind that for him, since "they" did not, or would not, understand his reports, ordered him to await reinforcements which he called a "superfluous burden," and hoped for a miracle to be wrought by the dispensation of heaven—there was now nothing left but to do his duty as a soldier to the bitter end.

That man was Zenobius Rojëstvensky .

To await reinforcements and then forward to victory and glory! Those are their orders ?—Very well.—Although he had renounced all idea of victory, yet he would at least make use of the time of waiting to train and weld together this heterogeneous armada, though the effort was belated.

He knew how to make people work, how to cheer up men who were on the verge of complete apathy. Alternating with coaling and refitting at anchor, we commenced a series of energetic exercises at sea—tactical as well as firing. Unhappily, the latter could not be indulged in as often as was desirable, since after every day of tactical exercises, which necessitated frequent changes of speed, two or three days had to be given up to making good machinery defects, directly due to the above, whilst as regarded target practice—there was the want of ammunition.

15

I could not help being reminded over and over again of the classical anecdote: "Why don't you fire?"

"For eighteen reasons: firstly, I have not got any powder—"

"You need not say more, and can keep the other seventeen reasons to yourself."

How bitter and painful was it to read in a General Order [3] evidently issued with a view to raising the drooping spirits of the men:—

> We must work hard, not sit still with our hands in our laps. We cannot afford much ammunition for target practice. . . . Everyone must become familiar with the telescopic sights. . . . If God grant us a meeting with the enemy on the field of battle, we must husband our ammunition.

And that at a time when, according to our information, the Japanese gun-layers had been familiar with telescopic sights for years, and were carrying out target practice night and day, not only without economising in the very least their ammunition, which they possessed in plenty, but without any regard for the guns themselves,[4] for the replacement of which there were new ones all ready.

Simultaneously with this order another one appeared, which was evidently due to the reports of our agents. In it the admiral ordered ships to redouble their vigilance, any floating object which might be sighted in the roads by day to be kept constantly under observation, to watch for any movement on the water at night, not to throw overboard any casks or cases, and not to permit any floating object to approach the ship's side, for the Japanese had, so he informed us, prepared various measures for causing every possible damage to our squadron before it could come in contact with their naval forces in the Far East.

> According to reliable information the Japanese have assembled a number of cruisers, both regular and auxiliary, in the southern straits and narrow waters on the other side of the Indian Ocean, with a view to way-laying us. They are accompanied by torpedo craft, which are to search out the bays in which our squadron might be expected to be found. Rumour also says that the first of the Japanese submarines, bought in England

3. No. 29, of January 23, 1905.

4. With the high gas pressures and temperatures which are produced by the firing, especially of large calibre guns, under present conditions, the bores get quickly worn—the inner tubes become eroded.

and America, are stationed there. Our active opponents do not confine themselves to preparing for the meeting with us on the other side of the Indian Ocean.

Several scouts have been sent across to the waters surrounding this anchorage. The task of the latter consists in seizing any supply ships, which may have become separated from the squadron from any cause, or which may be met with in circumstances favourable to capture or destruction, and finally to attack our men-of-war also, if feasible. These cruisers and scouts are in telegraphic communication with agents stationed in Madagascar, even in Nossi-Bé,[5] through a colony belonging to an ally of Japan, not benevolently inclined towards us, and from these they receive accurate information of all our dispositions, the distribution and whereabouts, as well as movements, of all our ships.

This memorandum ended with a positively touching exhortation addressed to the several captains not to leave so serious and responsible a task as the safety of the squadron (such as is customary in times of peace) to young officers, who:

....are not capable of finding their way or their whereabouts on a chart. It is no use setting any one a task beyond his capabilities. Anyone inexperienced at patrol work, and hence dangerous to his own side, may yet find useful employment in another sphere, where less initiative and decision are required.

On January 24 the exercises of laying out countermines were commenced.

About this time (I do not remember the precise date) the armed merchant cruisers, *Kuban*, *Terek*, and *Ural*, went out for target practice. "Well, and how did you get on?" I asked the staff gunnery officer, who had been superintending the practice, when he returned to the flagship.

He made a deprecatory gesture with his hand.

"Aimed at the rook and hit—the cow. But what more do you expect?[6] They were firing for the first time. They all behaved as if they had lost their way in a wood, or tumbled out of the moon."[7]

---

5. Such a one, a Swede, who spoke Russian, was recognised and forced to quit Nossi-Bé, in consequence of the boycott which had been pronounced against him, as if by tacit agreement, both in the squadron and on shore by the better class French citizens; the latters' hair stood on end at the very mention of the word *espion*.

On January 26 the two battleship divisions (except the *Sissoi*, which once more had her machinery out of order) and the cruisers which had been placed in the line, went out to carry out target practice after a plan which had been previously issued.

As I had already, to a certain extent, become acquainted with the state of preparation for war in the squadron, I did not expect to see anything very brilliant, but the reality surpassed my expectations.

"Well, and what do you say?" the flag-lieutenant (S——) asked me with a somewhat embarrassed smile, after the squadron had returned to Nossi-Bé after a long day's work.

"What do I say? Makaroff's task at Port Arthur was easier. What he had to deal with was at least the semblance of a squadron. But this . . . the Lord knows what they are!"

However, I will let the admiral speak for himself.

The manner in which the battleships and cruisers weighed yesterday showed that after four months in the squadron the results which might have been expected have not been reached as yet. This operation took about one hour. But even at the end of a full hour the ships had not yet taken up their respective stations, notwithstanding the fact that the guide of the fleet was proceeding at a very slow speed. In the morning all ships were warned that at noon the signal would be made: 'Turn together 8 points, stop engines in line abreast, and drop targets.' Yet the captains lost their heads, and instead of forming single line abreast, the ships became a mere jumble, in which they were steaming about in every direction.

In the first division the *Borodino* and *Orel* were specially conspicuous owing to the inattention of their captains. In the second division, consisting of three ships, only the *Navarin* turned to port, abreast of the *Suvoroff*; the *Ossliabia* and *Nakimoff* continued their course on their own account. The cruisers made no attempt to get into position. The *Donskoi* was 1 mile astern of the rest. When line ahead was reformed for target practice, the ships were so scattered that the distance from the *Suvoroff* to the *Donskoi* was 55 cables (11,000 yards).[8]

It is a well-known fact that the fire of a single ship, even in the centre, when the line is so much extended, can be of no use to

---

6. Russian colloquialisms.—Trans.

7. General Order No. 42 of January 27, 1905.

8. It should not have been more than 26 cables (5,200 yards).

the whole. If we have not learnt to work together during the four months we have been in company, we are hardly likely to do so by the time we may, under God's will, expect to meet the enemy.[9] ... The firing yesterday was extremely slow, and it showed to my greatest regret that, with the sole exception of the *Aurora*, none of the ships have devoted sufficient attention to the rules concerning the proper employment of the gun armament during the execution of the schemes of exercise.

The expensive 12-inch shell were fired away without showing anything like the same proportion of hits as the guns of other calibres. . . . Practice with the 12-pounder Q.F. guns was very bad; apparently the telescopic sights worked 'admirably' during the preliminary aiming exercises, but had no effect in laying the gun accurately. . . . As regards the firing of the 6-pounder Q.F. guns, which are intended to repel torpedo attacks, one really feels ashamed to speak of it. We keep men at these guns every night for that express purpose, and by day the entire squadron did not score *one single hit* on the targets which represented the torpedo-boats, although these targets differed from the Japanese torpedo-boats to our advantage, inasmuch as that they were stationary. . . .

Thus wrote the admiral in his general orders.

On January 31 and February 1 we again went out for target practice and tactical exercises. After that, in view of the minor breakdowns and damages on board the different ships, it was necessary to make a pause, and the next day's exercise did not take place until February 7. This completed the gun-layers' practices, as we could not afford any more ammunition. We were hoping to see the supply ship *Irtysh* arrive soon, bringing us perhaps a number of practice projectiles and charges.

In truth, these were not really exercises, but—an examination. A man who, the day before his duel, fires a few shots at a target, is not learning anything, but only tests his skill as a marksman. Now, what were the results which we achieved?

I will spare the reader the bitter words I wrote in my diary at the time. Possibly I had expected too much. I will confine myself to short extracts from the General Orders, which appear to me to speak pretty

---

9. I omit here some technical details, which would be neither interesting nor intelligible to the public, which is not familiar with naval matters.

plainly.

On January 31 and February 1 the weighing of the several divisions was satisfactory; the single line ahead was kept well closed up, but the alterations, of course, even those made by turning together, were badly executed. The *Ossliabia* either did not keep in the line or extended her distance from the next ahead so far as to hamper the ships astern; by stopping one engine she forced the *Sissoi* and *Navarin* to raise their cones, [10] and it was a long time before these ships were able to resume their proper stations. Line abreast still seems to present the same difficulties. No line is formed, only a huddled-up mass. . . . Target practice on January 31 and February 1 was somewhat better than on January 26, but with the heavy guns there is still the same reprehensible carelessness: on January 26 the *Suvoroff* fired a shot at a target which showed up clear of the *Donskoi's* stern and 6 cables beyond her, the latter then being on an opposite course to the flagship.

The officer controlling the fire on board the *Suvoroff* had given the gun concerned a certain range; the projectile pitched half a cable short of the *Donskoi* and a good deal to the left, in consequence of which it ricocheted over that ship. On this the sights should have been raised at least by 7 cables, so as to clear the *Donskoi*, and the deflection should have been altered largely, so as to place the shot more to the right. Notwithstanding the warning given by the first shot, the sights were only raised half a cable, and the deflection was not touched. The second shot, therefore, pitched right on the *Donskoi's* bridge. . . . This, of course, was bad enough, but the effect produced by it was totally unexpected: on February 1, the *Suvoroff's* gun-layers were only induced with great difficulty to fire through the intervals between the ships, although the targets were 20 cables (4,000 yards) beyond the ships, which made it possible not only to fire through the intervals between the ships, but over these.

It must be borne in mind that with a long single line it may sometimes be very important to alter course 16 points in succession, so as to concentrate the fire on the rear of a hostile line steaming past on an opposite course, and that consequently it is absolutely necessary that the gun-layers should learn to fire

10. Raising the cone means reducing speed. The higher the cone the less he speed. When the cone is close up, it indicates that the engines are stopped.

through the intervals between their own ships, both when the two fleets are steaming in the same direction (which would generally be the case for cruisers) and on opposite courses. . . . The rate of fire was still more slow on January 31 and February 1 than on January 26. If the 6-pounder Q.F. guns are really to be considered any longer as anti-torpedo guns, it must be impressed on their officers and men, that only a *hail* of shell of that calibre is capable of damaging a destroyer.[11]

The manoeuvres of the squadron on February 7 were badly executed. Not a single ship succeeded in altering course correctly, even 2 or 3 points, in single line ahead: some turned inside, others outside the leader's wake, although the sea was smooth and the force of the wind not more than 3.

The turns together were especially badly executed. . . . The firing from the heavy guns on February 7 was a useless waste of ammunition. . . . The firing, from the light Q.F. guns, which represented the repelling of a torpedo attack, was somewhat better than on a former occasion, but only in the first division. The firing of the second division of battleships, and of the cruisers, on this occasion was inexcusably bad.[12]

Is this enough of documents? They are expressed in the usual restrained official language. But what were the thoughts and feelings of those who, with this "huddled-up mass of ships," had been employed in "uselessly throwing away ammunition," and were to meet a squadron, flushed with victory, stronger than themselves, well trained in times of peace, with a year's experience of war, and which, moreover, had had time to rest and refit?

Directly after our arrival at Nossi-Bé the admiral ordered the supply steamer Malay, which had caused us so much delay by repeated breakdowns, to return to Russia. There was another such tub with Admiral Fölkersam's division, the *Knias Gortchakoff*. It was decided to dispense with her services as well.

Who was it who had chartered these steamers? Would it not have been possible to get, not merely something tolerable, but even quite good, anywhere in Europe, for the enormous sums spent on them?

But with us it is always the rule not to go to the bottom of anything.

---

11. General Order No. 50 of February 2, 1905.
12. General Order No. 71 of February 7, 1905.

It will be recollected that I once mentioned the fact that employees of the firm Slaby-Arco had been embarked in several ships of the squadron to ensure the proper working of their wireless installations on board. These were only bound, by the terms of the contract, to accompany us as far as Angra Pequeña, but already at the outset of the voyage many of these, fired by professional ambition, applied to the admiral for permission to remain on longer, even at a reduced salary, declaring that it was at the seat of the war that their experience and knowledge would be of the greatest use. This permission had been granted to some. Now they had all thought better of it, and were hurrying home.

Similarly a number of stewards and mess waiters, who had been entered by private contract, now demanded their discharge, as they were not prepared to go any further, although they could very well have found out at Cronstadt what was before them. As a matter of fact, they then had expressed their ardent desire to take part in the fray.

On board our provision ship, the steamer *Espérance*, the refrigerating machinery began to give more and more trouble. The defects were always dealt with at once by the repair ship *Kamtchatka*, but the more frequently these breakdowns occurred, the more serious was their nature. A committee, under the presidency of the chief engineer of the fleet, did not find sufficient evidence to justify the assumption of wilful damage; all the same, there were suspicions, and rather grave ones. After every repair was effected, the machinery was started in the presence of this committee, and examined in all its parts. Everything appeared in order—when, suddenly, after a day or two, some inexplicable damage again made its appearance.

The steamer had been taken over direct from a company trading between Argentina and London, at the very time when she was carrying a cargo of frozen meat. She was by no means an old vessel, but she had been bought, neither by the Board of Trade nor by the Ministry of Marine, but simply by a merchant, who intended to exploit her for his personal interests. . . . Be this as it may, in consequence of the frequent stoppage of the refrigerating machinery the temperature rose steadily in the store-rooms. The meat began to thaw and to rot. Finally, the struggle with this evil proved to be hopeless. Over 700 tons of spoilt meat had to be thrown overboard, and the *Espérance* returned to France. Thus the rats and cockroaches leave the vessel which is doomed to destruction.

Not only in the circle of my friends, in the messes to which I was invited as a former messmate, but also at the admiral's table, I lost no opportunity of pointing out, and proving it by examples from our Port Arthur experience, how little the present type of destroyer was equal to the demands made upon these craft. It must be admitted that as an offensive flotilla they accomplished very little. Even the "surprise attack" on Februarys could hardly be characterised as really successful. Under exceptionally favourable conditions, which would lead one to expect the annihilation, if not of the entire squadron, at least of the greater part, only three ships were damaged.

When, however, these same destroyers, under the force of circumstances, were employed as guard and despatch boats, as scouts, minelayers and sweepers, they rendered by no means inconsiderable services to both sides. In the execution of the various tasks; which up to the outbreak of war had never been demanded of them in times of peace, they often found themselves fighting their "opposite numbers" with guns or torpedoes (surface runners), and many of these spirited actions brought honour and glory to those who took part in them.

I think I am not far wrong in assuming that it is precisely in the above sense that destroyers attached to sea-going fleets should be trained. Of course, such training was looked upon as unpardonable heresy by the "armchair strategists" and the Transund tacticians, so I had to be cautious. Still, I scored some successes. By the latter part of January the destroyers which had accompanied Admiral Fölkersam, and had arrived at Nossi-Bé lame and maimed, had been put to rights; on January 28 an exercise was carried out on the following lines:—

A squadron, represented only by its leader (*Svetlana*), leaves Nossi-Bé for the East. It has obtained information that hostile torpedo craft are hiding somewhere amongst the islands in the neighbourhood with the intention of attacking it at the first favourable opportunity. A detachment, consisting of the *Zemtchug* and the first destroyer division, is therefore sent ahead to the suspected localities, to reconnoitre and act as a screen. The second destroyer division (the enemy), which had left earlier, was lying in hiding at some suitable place whence the approaches to the anchorage could be watched—the intentions and time of sailing of the squadron being only known to the enemy approximately (by means of spies). The task of the squadron was to prevent a surprise attack, and to beat off by force an open one; of the enemy, to seize upon a favourable moment for attack.

I will not describe the manoeuvres themselves, nor criticise their execution, but merely state that they aroused the interest, not only of those directly concerned, but of the entire squadron. The matter was discussed in all its bearings, there was a general awakening out of the state of apathy which had gradually spread more and more.... Unhappily, these were the last as well as the first manoeuvres. Originally, it had been intended to carry out a whole series of similar exercises, but the idea had to be given up on account of the damages, the necessary repairs, and—chiefly—as this steaming at full speed was considered a "useless" strain on the machinery of the destroyers, already overtaxed as they had been.... My strength was not sufficient to swim against this stream.

As regarded mine-sweeping, I succeeded in getting my views accepted, notwithstanding the failure in the "Belt," which produced much in the way of jeering and benevolently ironical remarks. On December 15, at Angra Pequeña, general instructions had been issued as regarded the formation of a mine-sweeping detachment by destroyers, together with a minute description and drawings of the apparatus employed outside Port Arthur. The "sweeps" were to be prepared at once by the big ships from their own materials, assisted by the *Kamtchatka*, so that immediately on Admiral Fölkersam's division joining us, the training of the destroyers in this hitherto unknown branch of their service might be started upon. Still, even after our arrival at Nossi-Bé this order remained a paper one. Its execution was hung up, since nothing was allowed to sail under my flag, and it could only be started under a strong foreign one.

Indeed, no sooner had Admiral Fölkersam shown an interest in the idea, and had, by order of the commander-in-chief, taken charge of the entire organisation, and begun to order about the staff torpedo officers (without the slightest compunction, since he was invested with full powers), than all difficulties vanished, everything was settled in the shortest of time: not only the mine-sweeping, but the laying out of mine defences by destroyers, which had up to then been looked upon as one of the Port Arthur fancies.

The business ran its regular course, so far as the almost constant breakdowns and damages of the destroyers' machinery permitted.

Probably in view of their deplorable condition, and perhaps also influenced by my accounts of the importance which the Japanese attached to steamboats armed with torpedoes, the admiral ordered all the steamboats carried by the ships to be formed into two divisions: the first one to consist of six boats of the newest types, the second of eight of the older and slower kind. Both divisions were placed at my disposal.

"Give them plenty of exercise. Let us hope that they will be good for something," the admiral said to me. "They could also be used for exercising the ships in repelling torpedo attack. Our destroyers can't be used for this, as it is quite possible that they would be hopelessly damaged, and never reach their destination at all."

On February 6, I took my flotilla out for the first time; they had never before been worked together. This, our first day's exercise, was marked by an incident which would have been ludicrous, if it had not been so sad.

Shortly before the war, in the autumn of 1903, a new signal code was introduced in our navy. (A standing signal committee had worked at this for five years.) The new signal books never reached Port Arthur, as it was already invested, but they got to Vladivostok, and the Second Squadron was also equipped with them.

At the time of our sailing from Libau I drew the attention of those concerned to the fact that if we were to meet the Port Arthur Squadron we should be speaking different languages; but I was pacified by the assurance that a set of old signal books would be taken as well in any case. The fall of Port Arthur, of course, removed the possibility of such a dilemma in the most radical manner.

But in the Second Squadron this is what occurred. During the hurried equipment of the ships they received boats' signal books of the new edition (these are abbreviated and simplified signal codes, having nothing in common with the ships' signal books); but the appendix, which contains the so-called evolutionary signals (governing tactical movements) had been omitted in the new edition. It was then discovered that in the new signal book, and in the appendix to the old one, the same combinations of flags had totally different meanings.

As soon as my flotilla was assembled off the *Suvoroff*, at the appointed time, I stepped into my "flag-boat," and, using the evolutionary signals (appendix of the old boats' signal book) hoisted; "Single line ahead." Great was my astonishment when, on the signal being hauled down, all my boats, instead of taking up their proper stations in line, steamed off in every direction at full speed. They had looked out the signal in the new book and found that it meant: "Search the coast." I had some difficulty in collecting the company again.

On board the flagship there was at first much wonderment, but then as soon as the new book and the old appendix had been compared, they realised that it was a misunderstanding. Of course there was much merriment.

The result of this was that a general order was issued to the effect that the new, incomplete edition was to be locked up, and in future the old one with the appendix to be used.

A mere trifle!—perhaps, but characteristic all the same. And if such a thing had happened in the presence of the enemy!

During the following days there is again a gap in my diary, but this time not owing to a general depression of spirits, but simply owing to want of time, as I was manoeuvring my flotilla from morning till night. It was a glorious, happy time. In the first instance, we had an occupation which shook us up and helped to dispel our sad thoughts. Secondly, my young "captains"—I must render them justice—were admirable; they did not know what fatigue meant, they did not know the word "impossible," and if, with God's help, we had got at the enemy, they would assuredly have given a good account of themselves. Thirdly, not only did no one look at me askance, did no one imagine that I was interfering in his concerns, but, on the contrary, everybody was prepared to give me his assistance, since everybody was free to act as he pleased, and since no one forced us to comply strictly with the letter of some regulations elaborated at headquarters.

On February 14 we went to sea with the whole squadron, then separated into two detachments, which manoeuvred against each other, as in battle, but in accordance with a scheme which had been drawn up and issued beforehand. "No very marked results, but it was always something," as my diary has it, at the end of the description of the manoeuvres. Towards evening, on our way back to Nossi-Bé, we were joined by the cruisers *Oleg, Isumrud, Dniepr* and *Rion* (the last two, ex-*Petersburg* and *Smolensk*, armed merchant cruisers) and the destroyers *Gromky* and *Grosny*, which we had been expecting from day to day.

Just a few words on the subject of wireless telegraphy in the squadron. The following is an extract from General Order No. 83 of February 14:—

On board the fleet auxiliaries *Korea* and *Kitai* there are installed Marconi W.T. apparatuses with short topmast and single leads. On board all the other ships of the squadron (except destroyers) there are Slaby-Arco installations with tall topmasts and a big net. The *Ural* carries a specially powerful Slaby-Arco apparatus, which should be able to work up to 500 miles and more. Throughout the voyage the Koreans apparatus alone was able to take in messages at 90 miles, whilst not one of our ships has been able to take in anything over 65 miles. And today, February 14, at 6.30 a.m., the *Korea*, although she was lying behind a hill, was the first to receive the *Oleg's* message, which the *Ural's* powerful apparatus was unable to take in, although the latter had yesterday received orders to get into touch with the *Oleg*, and notwithstanding the fact that at the time there was not only no land, but not a single mast, between the *Oleg* and the *Ural*.

It only remained for us to thank the Technical Committee for having despised the well proved Marconi system and equipped us with the Slaby-Arco apparatus, which was supposed to work still better.

After incessant daily exercises for a week my little flotilla was sufficiently advanced to undertake more extended night manoeuvres, amongst which, of course, frequent attacks on the squadron played the principal part. The latter indeed stood in much need of practising the repelling of torpedo attacks, as the admiral had said. Nothing expressed this so clearly as his orders, where, based upon each of these exercises, the various rules and methods are called attention to, which are useful to remember when beating off a night attack by torpedo craft. Not as if these rules had been unknown to the crews—the crux of the matter lies in the conversion of the knowledge into practice. The most conscientious study in the seclusion of an office can never produce that mastership of a craft which actual practical handling of its tools alone can give.

In time things got somewhat better; it became increasingly difficult to approach the squadron undetected, to divert its attention by a feint.

February 18 was a day of great disappointment for me. Notwithstanding the assurance of the torpedo officers that everything in their department was in the best order, I insisted on the steam-boats carrying out target practice with their torpedoes. Of course it was to take place by day, in a calm, and only at 5 cables (1,000 yards). In all this I will not speak of the second division (here the whole apparatus was obsolete—may God forgive those responsible!), but with the first division, six new boats, built and equipped in accordance with the latest ideas of the Technical Committee, the result was as follows:—

Seven torpedoes were fired. One never ran at all. Another began describing a circle, occasionally coming to the surface and threatening the boats, which speedily sought safety in flight. Two went off to the right, one to the left; finally two ran satisfactorily. And that in broad daylight, free from any disturbing factors, and with a smooth sea. We should have been in a fine plight if we had gone for the enemy with such weapons, in the conditions of a regular night attack.

"Quite inexplicable. Perhaps it was the swell; the test runs before delivery, in the harbour of Reval, went off splendidly," was the somewhat doubtful comment of the staff-torpedoist.

"That's just it—always in harbour. A little swell, maybe? But then, perhaps, when we do attack, the sea will be tossing about to any extent. Compared with this kind of self-deception, the old spar torpedo even was better. Then, if by the grace of God, one got close up and touched the hostile ship, the business was done. But here—are we to tow the thing up, or fire a revolver at the battleship? Oh! these magicians and necromancers! . . . Transund is ruining us."

He appeared to be offended.

However the expression, "Transund is ruining us," does not emanate from me. It was used not long ago by the admiral in the presence of many witnesses, when commenting on a report that "everything was in perfect order," and that, although the result had been nil, yet the "prescribed rules had all been carefully complied with."

For five days—or, to be quite accurate, for five times twenty-four hours—we were occupied, not with evolutions at sea, but with a very unusual business. Fearless of the thunderbolts of the Technical Committee, without the consent of which not one iota of the fittings may be touched, the engineer and torpedo officers, together with those commanding the steam-boats (for it was these, after all, who were to make the attack with these weapons), began to devise, to discuss, even to quarrel—to file, to lengthen, to bend this way and that . . . with the result that the torpedoes ran straight, and that was all one could demand.

On February 21, we went out with the entire squadron, including the newly-joined ships, to manoeuvre against a "skeleton enemy." (The *Irtysh* had still not arrived, so we could not do any firing.)

We began to manoeuvre according to the prepared scheme, as last time, but when the admiral later on in the action decided "to make the attempt of permitting his two opponents, Admirals Fölkersam and Enquist, complete freedom of movements, subject to the "general idea" of the scheme, he was soon forced (and not without difficulty) to collect the scattered units of the squadron, and to spend the rest of the day in carrying out the simplest movements, in which, as on former occasions, the single line abreast and quarter-line (line of bearing), as well as "turns together," were the chief obstacles.

Almost on the eve of battle. . . . How bitter and terrible it all was!

"Well, my optimistic friend," Flag-Lieutenant S—— asked me, "you always manage to find a word of praise for everyone. . . . What do you say now?" I merely shrugged my shoulders.

CHAPTER 2

A Night in Nossi-Bé

When I gave the short review of the general progress of the exercises and practices with which the squadron tried to fill in the gaps in its training during its stay at Nossi-Bé, but which unfortunately merely disclosed its want of preparedness for war to its fullest extent, and once more demonstrated the hopelessness of its existence, I purposely refrained from speaking of its inner life, of the spirit of its crews, although the notes in my diary contain rich material for this. I believe that if I had adhered strictly to their chronological sequence in reproducing these notes, I could not have given the reader a clear picture of the outer as well as the inner life in the squadron, although for us who took part in the voyage both conceptions were so intimately connected that I can, for instance, read the following lines without being in the very least in doubt as to how they are connected.

All yesterday, from early morning, torpedo running from my boats. Bad fittings, etc." (Here follow precise details of the practice.) "From 3 to 9 a.m. it poured.—Thank God, the admiral was only slightly unwell, he is better today.—When at mass today the priest prayed: 'Grant us to die like Christians, without pain, without reproach, in peace. . . .' I should have liked to interrupt him, and to cry out: Don't pray for all that, we need only pray that we may die *without reproach*—that suffices. I was very glad to hear that Menshikoff's pamphlet, *Russia in the Hands of the Reorganisation Committee*, had been styled improper, fantastic, idiotic, etc., in the squadron. When 'Russia stretches out her wounded arms,' it is no use speaking of plaster and bandages suitable for slight hurts, but one must try and keep the heart from receiving a deadly wound.

I fancy, however, that for the general public the reading of such notes, even when worked up, would necessitate a special interpreter.

As soon as it had become known that we had received orders to wait, the momentary enthusiasm which had been brought about by the bold idea of advancing instantly, irrespective of what might happen, melted away without having been turned to account. The stimulus was gone, and under the pressure of the absolute uncertainty of the future, this enthusiasm gave place to a state bordering on apathy.

Evidently this dangerous mood did not escape the admiral's attention, and against it he employed the only means at his disposal: he kept the men so busily at work, that they had no time for much thinking. From the middle of January onwards the exercises and practices alternated with the taking in of coal and stores, and went on from morning to evening, even at night sometimes. This treatment proved to be wholesome. The general feeling improved. The irritating thought, "We are waiting here to no purpose," asserted itself less often. Still this expedient should not be abused; the forces of the human body are not unlimited, and in the relaxing climate of Madagascar these are more quickly used up than replaced. The reaction produced by physical exhaustion might easily have brought about utter demoralisation, if a pause had not been made at the right moment, to allow the mind and body to recover their strength.

The admiral did not speak to anyone of his intentions and plans for the future. Lieutenant S——, who carried on the admiral's secret correspondence, the only individual in the squadron who knew everything, was as mute as a fish.

"Look here," I said one day to S——, "I don't want to extract any secrets from you, but will you tell me one thing: why is he so silent? Would you also be as silent in similar circumstances? "

He reflected a while and then replied with a question.

"Have you ever received from superior authority an order, which you did not consider capable of execution, and did you in consequence make representations, so far as was permissible by law, in the hope of influencing the decision? "

"That has happened to me."

"But when the affair was being dragged on, when you had not yet lost all hope, did you then consider it necessary or expedient to keep your subordinates informed of the course of your negotiations with the superior authority? If you spoke to these you would presumably hide nothing from them (otherwise you might as well have held your tongue), you would explain your views, and no doubt the greater part, if not all, of your subordinates (if you are the right kind of superior and not 'tumbled out of the moon') would then be on your side. Is it not so?"

"Let us assume that it is so."

"And if the superior authority, none the less, gave such orders as seemed to it best, in what light would your confidential communications then appear, seeing that they would undoubtedly have had a certain influence on the spirit of the forces confided to you?—As a criminal agitation, as an attempt to bring about a movement against the intentions of the superior authority, still worse—as an attempt to exert pressure on them, to force them into abandoning the enterprise projected by them!"

"It may be, still . . ."

"That is why he is silent. He still hopes that 'they' will understand him. But in vain. Hope is in vain, but not silence. I am not disclosing you any secret, I am only speaking of my own knowledge. We left Russia under the constant pressure of Russian society, which accused the admiral of not wanting to start for the relief of Port Arthur. Do you remember? You yourself spoke of your conversation with Nelidoff on your way through Paris. Even he, who was well informed, spoke in a deprecatory manner, connecting the name Zenobius Rojëstvensky with the idea that the squadron could never sail. Do you recollect? You gave me his own words: 'Either he is ill, or he can't make up his mind!' The whole thing depended on his personal decision, for there was no one beside him capable of commanding the squadron. Dubassoff was too old. Tchooknin—the Black Sea Fleet rests on him alone. . . . We sailed. . . . I put my hands over my ears when you said that the commencement of the bombardment from the land side was the beginning of the end for the squadron.

"We were full of Stoessel's heroic reports. If we did not wholly believe them, at least we wanted to. In a word, we looked upon our squadron here as a strong strategical reserve, which was going out as a reinforcement for an active fleet, employed in the theatre of war, based upon a fortified, well-stocked naval port. . . . With the fall of Port Arthur the last illusions disappeared. Our armada—this haphazard collection of ships, part new, but badly built and never properly completed, part old, and barely put in order—the *armada* which under the most favourable view only deserves the title of 'Reserve fleet,' became the active service fleet, with the task of overthrowing a victorious, active, real battle-fleet. And what is more, the latter is based on numerous, admirably equipped ports, whilst we, before we can reach our only base, Vladivostok, must first vanquish our opponents. We, the weaker, both as regards numbers and armament, as well as equipment, and finally—what is the use of denying it ?—also as regards the spirit of its crews—we still dare to hope? . . . But 'they' don't understand, or won't understand; 'they' still believe in miracles. *That* is why he is silent."

But though the admiral was silent, though S—— only spoke in parables, we were soon informed by the newspapers, which began to arrive from Russia, why we were waiting, what we had been ordered to wait for.—We were to await reinforcements; and of what kind!—*Nikolai, Ushakoff, Senyavin, Apraxin, Monomak*—all the old tubs, old "war junks," which figured in the lists of the Baltic Fleet. The very same ships which Admiral Rojëstvensky had energetically refused when the Second Squadron was being got together, and when, with a bleeding heart, he decided, failing something better, to take the *Navarin, Nakimoff*, and *Donskoi*.

"That is not a reinforcement, it is simply so many logs tied to our legs!" exclaimed our hotspurs.

What appeared very strange to us all was the fact (quite incapable of any explanation) that the despatch of all these old "flat-irons and galoshes" did not appear to be due to an independent decision at headquarters, where so many were reposing themselves in peace, but as a concession to that mighty public opinion, which it now turned out was inspired by K——.

"Is it a case of the voice of Jacob?" S—— growled out. "There is something not quite right here."

"Surely he must know what the situation is," others were saying. "He has either gone off his head, or he is being paid for this. . . . But whom is he doing it for?"

"Don't ask Admiral Rojëstvensky!" cried K——, addressing himself to Russian society generally. "Send off at once everything you can get. Don't loose a minute, or it might be too late; understand me well—*too late*. . . . Can you conceive what terrible words these are, what disaster they spell?"

In the absurdity of his statements K—— went so far as actually to propose that absolutely useless, quite obsolete ships like the *Minin*, *Pojarsky*, even *Peter Veliki* should be sent out to the war.

He said: "... in the 'eighties' the floating battery *Kreml* was sent out to the Far East ... when it was a case of dire necessity, energetic men dared to do the seemingly impossible...."[1]

"Such examples could be cited by the thousand.—Awake, you dreamers! let yourselves be shaken up, and grasp the fact—there is no other way out of it. You must realise that failing this the possibility of losing the campaign will loom up dangerously near. Only dare to do it, and the seemingly impossible will be accomplished."

"What noble words! How full of true patriotism! How is it possible not to believe them, since they come out of the mouth of an experienced seaman?"—Russian society could not say less.

"What an unworthy game! What infamous deception on those poor confiding landsmen!"—It was thus that we of the Second Squadron gave vent to our indignation.

Is it necessary to repeat even briefly all that with which K—— filled the columns of the *Novoe Vremya?* These inspiring articles he even published in book form. (I am almost afraid of advertising it for him—however, it is all one now.) The Russian reader will surely still remember them, if not literally, still their sense. It is very remarkable, though true, that no one forgot their contents more quickly than the author himself, who two years later, without pretending to be a prophet, but still speaking as one in authority, wrote in a semi-official work:—

The squadron ought to have turned back from Madagascar. It was obvious that its further advance was more than risky. There were practically no chances of success.

Now it seems to me that the author of the article "After the Departure of the Second Squadron" ought not to have been permitted to write these words without some sort of explanation.

At that time, in the year of a bloody reckoning for the sins of several generations, when every honest, every truthful word was priceless, he prophesied something very different. Basing himself on the system of coefficients of fighting value, he proved that the Second Squadron, as then constituted, "had some chance of success," but that it was necessary to turn this chance into "certainty"; and he proceeded to show how

---

1. A serious blunder (or a clerical error) on the part of K——. The *Kreml.* was never sent to the Far East. It had been intended to do so, but "they" thought better of it in time.—The impossible was simply recognised as being impossible.

this "certainty" might be attained by sending out reinforcements, to be made up of all the old "crocks," such as were still to be found in the list of ships of the Baltic Fleet. He referred the public to the official data of the Naval Handbook and the traditional reports—"that everything was in excellent order," and that the fleet was "fully prepared for war."

Whilst he called upon Russian society to demand from the Ministry of Marine the immediate despatch of all this naval rubbish to the seat of war, he did not even insist on these ships being thoroughly overhauled. (This, it was maintained, was *not* essential.) He wrote: "Let them go with whatever defects they may have, provided these still permit them to steam and to fight to some purpose." I believe that not only the seaman, but even any one quite inexperienced in seamanship, must see how strange such a proposal was. What is it—a ship which is not in order? What is not in order on board her?—Either the machinery or the armament. How can a ship "fight to some purpose" if either the one or the other of these is not in order?

K—— knew full well, as did all the other officers, that Admiral Rojëstvensky had categorically refused to accept these very ships when he was forming the Second Squadron; that was why, in anticipation of a possible protest, he called out: "Don't ask Admiral Rojëstvensky! Send off at once everything you have got—don't lose a moment."

What was the object of this press campaign? Whom—in whose interests was K—— serving? These questions have never been answered to the present day. He can hardly plead ignorance, or want of proper appreciation of the situation in extenuation; if so, his responsibility before the country is surely a very heavy one.

So as to avoid any unintentional betrayal of war secrets all the officers of the squadron had undertaken not to send any information to the press without having previously submitted it to the admiral, and even to confine themselves in their letters home to purely personal matters, without touching on the situation of the moment or on future plans; and this was obtained, not by order (which might always have been circumvented), not under threat of heavy punishment (which could always have been easily avoided), but by their giving their word of honour to the admiral, through their captain.

Hitherto, apparently, it had never occurred to any one to impose the work of a censor on the admiral, overburdened as he already was with other work; now, however, articles poured in as if shaken out of a *cornucopia*. The contents of these were nearly all alike. They only differed in form, that is, in the more or less sharp criticism of K——'s productions, which were declared by some to be sheer nonsense, by others to be the outcome of ignorant conceit, whilst yet others stigmatised them as criminal, yes, even treasonable.

The admiral found time to read all these articles (for him the expression "I have no time" did not exist). I even think that this proof of the general agreement of his officers with his views gave him a certain amount of satisfaction. The verdict he pronounced on them was uniformly favourable, even appreciative; but coupled with this was always the request that the article should not leave the squadron—for one thing, because such replies, belated as they were (by three or four months), were now of no avail to arrest the agitation which had been started, and would only show up our hand to the Japanese, who were already so well informed; secondly, because in the present state of public feeling in St Petersburg probably not a single newspaper would be prepared to print the articles.[2]

Whilst K——'s articles provoked a unanimous outburst of anger against him, and those who inspired him, in the officers' messes, thus leading to still greater solidarity, the effect produced on the men was extremely unfavourable, not to say dangerous.

Newspapers were taken in in the squadron in great numbers. Any attempt at preventing the men from reading these articles, to keep them from reaching the "lower deck," would merely have enhanced their interest, would have meant pouring oil on the fire. The only thing was to try and combat the evil by friendly talks on suitable occasions, not by any service methods. But in doing so even the most popular officers ran up against that distrust, reared up through centuries, never dying, at most only slumbering, which the uneducated man feels towards the "gentle folk who are all in league with one another."—The ships' companies became deeply affected by all this. "What's the meaning of this? *Us* they sent out, whilst they themselves—sit snugly round the fire. They themselves do not want to go out there. They want to leave all these ships unused? But aren't we also human beings?—No, my friends, think of your oath,[3] prove that you are faithful and true. We also have kissed the Cross. We are also the followers of Christ."

---

2. The latter assumption was proved to be correct by the fate of an article written and signed by Admiral Fölkersam, which he had sent off without heeding the friendly advice of his older comrade. It was refused everywhere under various transparent pretexts.

3. Sworn by the recruit on entering the service.—Trans.

Such like remarks were often heard; of course not openly, but in the shadows of the night, when friends were discussing together in whispers.

These simple people could not help believing the words of a commander, who only a short time ago belonged to the staff of the Second Squadron, and who now furiously attacked the authorities who were able, but not willing, to send us "reinforcements." Since they looked upon him as belonging to the squadron, they believed that he had been sent home for the very purpose of demanding "reinforcements."

During my long, almost continuous service in close contact with our men I gained the conviction that, in some inscrutable but infallible manner they very quickly form an opinion on their admiral, and that—be it said in their honour—in doing so they rarely go wrong.

It was thus at Port Arthur, for instance, when they said of Stark: "What are we to do with this old man? We'll wait for the right sort to come along." Makaroff was spoken of as "Little Grandfather," "Beardy," the "Head," "the right man to do the business"; of Alexeieff they said that "he was only there for show,[4] and would not go into action himself"; of Vityeft that "he was brave when he met the Japanese, but did not hit it off with his own people." The most important moment in the gradual formation of this estimate is the one when they begin to speak of the admiral simply as "our man," or "he"—that is, as soon as the conviction is reached that "our man will do the business." From that moment "our man" and "we" are inseparable conceptions, and every one of his decisions is considered admirable and irrevocable, as representing "our" interests, as opposed to those of the "superior authority"—a far distant, mysterious, but always unfriendly power, which has its own aims and interests, different from "ours," and whom "our man" is permanently forced to fight.

In the present case K——'s articles produced amongst the crews the wholly erroneous, but firm conviction that "our man" had sent off the former to ask for reinforcements, but that "superior authority" was refusing them. At the same time, it was impossible for them, owing to that lack of clear conception which obtains in the masses, accustomed to judge by the tangible, rather than the intangible, to draw a sharp line between the partisans of "our man," for whom they would have gone through fire and water, and the followers of "superior authority,"

---

4. In the Russian text "for show" is in English.—Trans.

who did not deserve much confidence.

An officer to whom they had only just appealed in some personal matter of the most intimate nature, was suddenly suspected of being one of those who tried to justify the actions of that mysterious "superior authority," who was in agreement with the same, and they began to draw back from him and no longer believed his former explanations. There arose a certain feeling of unrest, of confusion. The men felt that somewhere something was not right, but they did not know where to expect friends and where enemies. This period was marked by outbreaks due to discontent on board several of our ships, even such, for instance, as the *Nakimoff*, which possessed a nucleus of older men (even men of the Naval Guards),[5] who had been serving on board since her last foreign cruise.

These disturbances were instantly put down by the admiral's personal intervention, but all the same something, as it were, had snapped—had given way. Offences against discipline were more frequent. The hoisting of the "Jack" at the fore, accompanied by one gun,[6] became one of almost daily occurrence, and ceased to attract attention. The offences became more serious; often they were of a nature for which by the laws of war the death sentence was prescribed. The admiral never confirmed a single one of these. Once the judge-advocate permitted himself to express the view that clemency which went too far might prove harmful, that once in a way an example should be made so as to deter the others. "Undue clemency? Oh, no; I don't belong to those who always feel compassion. I simply consider it an insane proceeding. How can I intimidate men ready to follow me to the death by condemning them to be hanged? Before going into action all prisoners are released from cells,[7] and—who can tell?—perhaps *they* will prove to be the heroes," the admiral replied hotly.

Somehow or other this conversation, at which no one else had been present, was known all over the squadron the same day, and,

---

5. A portion of the naval personnel of all ranks, the pick of the service, rank as "guards," analogous to those of the army, and wear distinctive badges.—Trans.
6. Hoisting the "Jack" (usually flown on the stem or bowsprit) at the fore truck and firing a gun signifies the assembling of a court-martial, the highest tribunal of an independent squadron.
This very old custom, which also still exists in the British Navy, dates from the time when all signalling was done by means of single flags, to which the firing of a gun drew attention.—Trans.
7. This is laid down in the regulations.

oddly enough, the offences against discipline not only did not increase, but actually decreased.

Of course the actual words of the conversation did not become known, but only the sense of it, and this, too, was so embellished as to give the whole thing the character of a legend.

"Is it true, your honour," my servant asked me in his most confidential manner, "that 'our man' is going to let off all punishments before the fight? If anyone who has done wrong wants to make up for it by shedding his blood, he is not to be stopped?"

"Where did you hear this?"

"The men all say it on the lower deck."

"And what do *you* think of it?"

"What can I say? It is well known that 'our man' is going to do it. He says it, and then it's done. His word is enough."

These lines of mine were already in print (in the newspaper *Russ*), when I received information from a reliable source that K——'s tirade had been unanimously condemned by the officers of the army (on the Manchurian battlefields), as it had been by those of the Second Squadron.

This letter proves so clearly the agreement in the views of the "food-for-guns" (equally at sea and on land), it marks so clearly "his" connection with the heroes who sat in soft armchairs and never heard the whistling of the enemy's projectiles, that I venture to reproduce some extracts for the benefit of my readers, irrespective of style.

(The letter had evidently been written very hurriedly, and not intended for publication.)

. . . The well-known articles by K—— produced indignation also in the army; many said they were treason against Russia, against our native country.

The St Petersburg Telegraph Agency was very active in circulating these articles by telegraph, and on all of us, his (K——'s) optimism, based on figures and coefficients, had a depressing effect. His hysterical shrieks for immediate reinforcements for the Second Squadron made us ask in wonderment what might be thought in St Petersburg of this unusually improper behaviour of K——'s.

The Head of the Intelligence Department on General Kuropatkin's staff (Colonel Linda of the General Staff) often spoke with the head of the Naval War Section on the same staff (Captain Russin, I.N.), "on the necessity of representing to the commander-in-chief that it was most desirable to prohibit the appearance in print of K——'s criminal articles, as these effusions, which described the condition of the Second Squadron, and proved by figures the Japanese superiority, had a discouraging effect on the troops, and (above all) opened the eyes of the Japanese. In collecting their intelligence the authoritative nature of the source whence the news emanated was of great significance, and however well the Japanese might be informed, K——'s indiscretions were simply a revelation to them."

Furthermore, the same Colonel Linda pointed out to Captain Russin that it was necessary "to hasten the voyage of the Second Squadron"; he considered that "the squadron remaining at Nossi-Bé and awaiting Nebogatoff's ships was simply criminal."

My esteemed correspondent ended his letter by saying:

I considered, and still consider, K——'s articles as a criminal offence.

I deem it my duty to cite here this voice from Manchuria, as a corroboration of my diary written in Madagascar.

On February 17 the admiral had suddenly been taken so ill that he had to go to bed. In the squadron it was rumoured that this was the result of a telegram announcing the departure of Nebogatoff's division from Libau. It seemed as if the admiral had had some kind of a stroke. Two days later he reappeared on deck, still thinner, with still more wrinkles in his face . . . and dragging his right foot. We looked at him anxiously, but felt reassured as soon as we heard his familiar, unchanged, powerful voice.

"He won't get ill. Perhaps . . . after the peace is signed." . . . That was the fleet surgeon's favourite dictum, which he now repeated.

Strictly in accordance with the terms of the orders on the subject Admiral Nebogatoff, who was sent out with his division to reinforce Admiral Rojëstvensky, was only to come under the latter's orders on joining his flag; up to that moment he was absolutely independent, communicating only with the Naval General Staff, and receiving all necessary instruction from that source.

It actually happened sometimes (when the St Petersburg people telegraphed too late, in the press of work), that the admiral learnt the movements and intentions of his future junior flag officer from the telegrams of—the "Agence Havas." Incredible, but true! What a triumph for our organisation!

After February 21, that is, after the *Oleg, Isumrud, Dniepr, Rion, Gromky,* and *Grosny* had joined us, the general irritation against this useless and, in the opinion of many, absolutely harmful waiting, became so pronounced that the admiral was forced into breaking his silence, and reading out at a meeting of flag officers and captains (not all of these, only the senior ones) the text of telegram No. 244, which he had received in the middle of January, and his reply to it.

As was to be expected, none of those present kept this information to themselves. They all realised only too well how much all under their orders were suffering under the pressure of the uncertainty.— Well, perhaps not quite. This statement is inaccurate. Havas and Reuter's Agencies, Russian and French papers, gave, in general, quite a truthful picture of the situation of the moment and predicted with hardly a mistake the immediate future, so that, strictly speaking, there was no uncertainty—it was faith which was lacking. It was felt that some dispute was being fought out, that the Admiral was representing a definite view, but that St Petersburg judged of the situation quite differently. When telegram No. 244 and the reply to it became known, this assumption was strengthened.

To my regret I am unable to give the actual text of the two telegrams. I can only give their general sense.

Telegram No. 244 pointed out that after the fall of Port Arthur and the destruction of the First Squadron, a task of the highest importance devolved upon the Second Squadron: to obtain the command of the sea, and thus to cut off the enemy's army from all communication with its home. If, in the opinion of its commander, the squadron as at present constituted was not strong enough to fulfil this task, then without the slightest delay, and as soon as circumstances permitted, all fighting ships left behind in the Baltic would be sent out as reinforcements. Finally, the admiral was asked for his plans and views.

Admiral Rojëstvensky replied: (1) With the forces at his disposal he had *no prospect of obtaining the command of the sea.* (2) The old ships, in need of repair, and which, in part, had already been failures from their first completion, which it was intended to send out to him as reinforcements, *would not serve to strengthen the squadron, but to hamper it.* (3) The only plan which appeared to him feasible was to attempt to get through to Vladivostok with the best ships, and thence to operate on the enemy's lines of communications.

So far as I recollect, there were added a few words as to the unfavourable effect of the long stay in Madagascar, both as regarded physical exhaustion and the spirit of the men.

These telegrams were of great and decisive importance, as they not merely represented an exchange of views between the admiral and the home authorities; they went much further—they contained a prescribed plan of operations and the straightforward reply of one thoroughly versed in naval warfare.

No further direct orders were received, but the final reply to the admiral's representations appeared to be the information that Nebogatoff's division had sailed from Libau—a piece of news which nearly floored our chief.[8]

This explanation produced outwardly a certain amount of calmness. The discussions in the messes ceased. The "cursed questions," on the solution of which our brains had been racked, disappeared of themselves. There were no more riddles and assumptions. Everything was clear and simple.—It was *ordered* to be done. The case was now settled. . . . I did not like this calmness. It was not calmness, but indifference. It was not the calmness of the warrior on the eve of battle, full of proud and bold determination, but the calmness of the innocent, unjustly condemned man on the eve of his execution—assuredly also full of proud and bold determination, but of a very different kind. . . . According to Lieutenant S——, who expressed himself in mysterious terms, the admiral was still hoping that "they" would yet understand his report, realise that either they should concur or recall the squadron, seeing that in the altered circumstances he himself no longer believed in the success of the enterprise, and had only thought it possible to suggest a desperate attempt—in the faint hope of later on carrying out a guerilla warfare—in the place of a regular plan of campaign.

The people at St Petersburg did not, or would not, understand this.

On March 11, the *Irtysh* arrived. The long-expected powder and shell she did not bring. Besides coal, the most important part of her cargo for us consisted of 12,000 pairs of boots. I beg the reader not to laugh. This is not meant as a joke. In our repeated coalings boots

8. It afterwards became known that about that time Admiral Rojëstvensky had requested by telegraph to be relieved of his command, in view of his illness, and suggesting the appointment of Admiral Tchooknin as a successor, the latter being in good health and in every way a suitable man.—No result.

and shoes had been worn out so rapidly that by this time the greater part of the men were going about in self-made shoes, plaited out of hemp yarns.

On March 12 the telegram of the Havas Agency brought us the first news of the Battle of Mukden—50,000 prisoners, 23 colours and 500 guns captured. Of course these telegrams were not accepted literally in the squadron. We were already accustomed to the Japanese, eager to acquaint the world with their successes, greatly exaggerating the results of their victories; still, we now felt that, even if these results had been magnified two or three times over, this was indeed a terrible defeat, almost meaning the annihilation of our army. . . . As is not to be wondered at, this event did not produce any very marked effect on the squadron—at least outwardly. The matter was hardly discussed. Generally speaking (I do not speak of individuals), everyone was so weary, that the mere act of thinking appeared too great an exertion.

One saw the consequences of our two months' stay here, so trying owing to the uncertainty of the situation, the continuous exertions, which overtaxed the strength, the incessant nerve tension in this climate, which Europeans cannot stand for more than two or three years, notwithstanding every comfort which is to be found, even in the barracks. The result of a longer stay is anaemia, or rather, as the local doctors express it, thinning of the blood. The only remedy for this is—moving to some place in the temperate zone.

People who have personal experience of the heat of Turkestan, Syria, Algeria, even the Sahara, may shrug their shoulders contemptuously and say: "What is a temperature of 90° F? Surely nothing excessive!" But these 90° have to be endured night and day, with a corresponding degree of moisture which rises up to 98 per cent. That is the terrible thing. And there is no relief. The perspiration which breaks out of the pores remains on the skin and runs down the body in drops. However much one rubs oneself down, one can never get dry. The worst is the sultriness, mugginess. One breathes air saturated with steam. One breathes hot fog, as in a Turkish bath.

On March 13 I went to bed in my cabin with the scuttle open. The electric fan was working at full speed. Towards midnight I woke up in consequence of a curious feeling, which I was already familiar with—want of breath. One can literally get no air. One opens one's mouth like a fish thrown up on the beach; one fills one's lungs to their utmost capacity; but all the same only gets little air. There is a violent throbbing at the temples. General weakness, lassitude, and the one idea: nothing really matters, only no movement, no additional exertion! The sky is completely overcast, and there is not the slightest movement in the air. Oh, if only a thunderstorm or shower of rain would clear the air. However, till then. . . . I snatch up anything at hand—a blanket, an india-rubber air-cushion (ordinary pillows, which are always damp, only give one a headache), and hurry on deck, on to the after-bridge, which is given up to the officers for the night.

It is a weary progress. One stumbles on the ladders; arms and legs do not seem under proper control; the head is heavy. Thank heaven! up on the bridge at last. A breath of air seems to come across from the port side. Over to that side then. Thick, heavy clouds are hanging low down. There is an impenetrable fog. Although familiar with the locality, one stumbles over something, which utters an angry exclamation. One pays no attention, and does not take it amiss to be sworn at, for who would not swear if trodden upon? Arrived at the place selected, the port foremost 6-pounder, I throw down my blanket, prop my cushion against the gun pedestal, and begin to settle down.

"Steady there—confound it all!"

"Beg pardon; afraid I kicked you."

"No, never mind, but just move along a bit."

I recognised Lieutenant S——'s voice.

"So you've come up too?"

"The cabin was unbearable; I was nearly suffocated."

"It's a little better up here."

When I had got somewhat accustomed to the darkness I saw that he was stretched out on his stomach, his head resting on his arms. There was a dead silence all round. But here it was better than in the cabin. I felt somewhat relieved. My eyelids dropped, and I was gradually nearing sleep and happy oblivion.

Suddenly S—— began to speak in his nervous, abrupt manner.

"Look here. . . . These people at St Petersburg seem to have made up their minds, and now they no longer take anything into consideration. We have to go on with the whole 'armada,' with all the lame ducks and the cripples who have joined us.—We are going out to our destruction—our inglorious destruction. Luck! Success! . . . That only happens in fairy tales. Fools are the lucky ones. And that because the wise ones are more stupid than they themselves. . . . Fairy tales always end like that. I know that in your Port Arthur time you hated

44

that maxim of '*being careful and risking nothing,*' but here there is something to risk, and a good deal more. What we are now supposed to undertake is not a question of risking, it is sheer madness. Worse than that—a crime."

"But if 'for us'—understand me well, 'for us'—there is no other way out of it? . . . Let us leave the squadron out of count. Let us consider yourself personally. Supposing it were left free to every one to return to Russia—would you be one of those to do this? Let us assume that you are right. It may be that the squadron is condemned to go to the bottom to no purpose. Its destruction may be held to prove to the world that we had not possessed a fleet, but something in the nature of stage 'property.' This collapse may be the ruin of Russia. . . . Those who refused to take part in this bloody atonement, those who acted with deliberation and thoroughly logically, who did not go to certain destruction, they—I don't know what they would do, but I ask you, if you were to return home now at once, would you have the moral courage by and by to face those who returned later, after escaping safe and sound from the great sacrifice, the holocaust, which, of course, they were unable to avert, but of which they were not prepared to be the victim? "

"Oh, for goodness sake, hold your tongue!"

"No, I won't hold my tongue. If in the course of a gambling game, which started unluckily for him, the player were to stake his last gold coin on a card, in hopes of still winning, could one expect it to disappear, to fall under the table? No, it must remain honestly on the card. It does not decide its own fate—the gambler does that. The responsibility rests with the gambler."

"Ha, ha!" S—— laughed nervously. "But our squadron is a base coin! You beat me in similes and plays upon words, but this time you must allow me to follow this up. If in these circumstances the gambler stakes again, and fortune turns his way and he begins to win, then—all right. But when the card is turned and the gold coin is found to be counterfeit, won't there be a great scandal? You say the gamblers are responsible? That may be so. But the worst of it is that in this case the gamblers will keep in the background. The bad coin will be trodden into the dirt, but not those who made it, not those who staked it on the card. The false-coiners will take care of that themselves. I know them well. If history ever occupies itself with this affair, then all the odium will be put upon us."

"That is all very well and quite logical," we suddenly heard in Lieutenant B——'s hoarse voice, "but to say so aloud is not only useless, but even harmful. The heroes who sit in their comfortable armchairs, the St Petersburg strategists, who elaborate the plan of operations for the squadron, *they* won't hear us. We are 'food-for-guns.' Let us become reconciled to our parts. There is nothing gained by wallowing in one's grief. Things are unbearable enough without this."

A pause. Then S—— began once more, but in a lower voice, without any excitement, in an almost listless tone:

"Do you remember your telling us that Makaroff had called after you: 'To go down is not hard and not bad, but to die uselessly is stupid'? Do you recollect that thirty-six years ago the well-known Lieutenant Semetchkin said in one of his lectures: 'That death in itself is nothing terrible, we need not waste any words about it. But to die for nothing is awful. For one's native country one gives one's life gladly and cheerfully, but to give it cheaply, uselessly, for an inadequate price, is intolerably hard.' Thus he spoke thirty-six years ago, and it exactly applies to our case now. During the general *mêlée* one gets knocked over by some cheap shell, uselessly, senselessly. . . . Either one clings for a few more hours with all one's remaining strength to a piece of floating wreckage, and waits to see if the victorious enemy is gracious enough to pick one up, or . . . even worse, one is gradually choked to death in the inside of the ship, which is bottom up. How hideous! How awful!"

It was hard to have to listen to this. I tried to joke.

"Well, if merely for the sake of appearances you prefer to die mounted on a war-horse, with a flag in your hand, you ought to have joined the cavalry instead of the navy."

"Naturally," called out Lieutenant W—— (gunnery officer) out of some corner. "It is simpler in our case. But as regards the unpleasant moments, there is always one means of hastening the solution of the problem, if in a tight place—a Browning (revolver) in one's pocket."

"You either cannot or will not understand me," S—— continued after a short silence. "There is no object in indulging in fine speeches. You are simply trying to shake off disagreeable thoughts. But one can't shake them off. Ten thousand Russian men—perhaps even more—between the ages of twenty and thirty are going to be led—not into battle, but to the sacrificial altar. They don't realise it, but *you* understand it. They trust us, but you—are you going to be quite open with them?

Of course not. . . . What good would it do? We lead them into the darkness. We—their guides—don't dare tell them the truth, for fear of demoralising them. . . . True, the majority of us will not be called upon to answer, either them or the country—for in this world they will not be asked any questions . . . but when they demand an answer from us on the day of reckoning . . . what shall we say then?"

"Tell them that they had to die just the same as we. But the culprits, the traitors—these will be judged by God," came in a young voice out of the darkness somewhere.

I at once recognised it as being that of young Prince Z——, a sub-lieutenant. Somewhere not far off there was a sound as if the butt-end of a rifle was being moved from one spot to another.

There was a sigh, something sounding like "O Lord, O Lord!"

"Stop, the sentry hears," called out B—— angrily in English.

Again a long silence. From the shore there came the penetrating smell of rotting plants. A thunderstorm was apparently approaching, but it seemed to hesitate, as if waiting for something. Only quite far off, on the horizon, the sheet lightning lit up the heavy clouds from time to time.

"Strange thoughts, foolish thoughts," S—— began once more, slowly, as if half asleep, the words coming out one by one.

"Possibly they may be due to the weather. . . . We have come 12,000 miles. . . . We have yet 6,000 to go. Whereto?—to the shambles. . . . Have you seen calves, with their legs tied together, piled in heaps on a cart being driven into the town? Well, they are no longer able to do anything of their own free will; they have no 'Browning' in their pockets, as W—— said. . . . On the other hand, I can understand that French *marquise* on the scaffold praying to the executioner for 'one minute more.' Evidently her life had been so beautiful that even minutes appeared precious to her. . . . But we? , . . We are neither calves nor *marquises*—we, for some reason or other, are made to bear this punishment, though, after all, it is all the same—only the end. . . . Sometimes it seems quite tempting. . . . But is it worth going so far? . . ."

A sudden flash of lightning lit up nearly the whole sky, and after a peal of thunder the long expected rain poured down in streams. There was movement everywhere on the upper deck. One heard restrained exclamations of joy, the tramp of many bare feet—the men were making the most of this fresh-water shower-bath, so anxiously hoped for. The flashes of lightning, which penetrated the rain awnings with a kind of bluish light, showed up in the darkness groups of men, who were crowding together clear of the awning, naked, half naked, standing, sitting, huddled together here, scattered there; some had their arms raised high, others stretched them out; the figures were in every variety of strange attitudes, like ghosts, suddenly seized upon by some wild, fantastic dance. . . . "A regular witches' Sabbath, isn't it?" W—— called out to me.

I turned round to the side from which the voice had come, and made him out in the next flash of lightning, in Adam's costume, but as important as ever, sitting on the gunwale of one of the steamboats.

"Very much so. You especially are excellent. May I ask what part you are playing?"

"Naturally not that of Faust," came in his mocking voice out of the darkness. "I assume that in the present circumstances Mephistopheles would not pay a *stiver* for my soul."

CHAPTER 3

We Fly from Nebogatoff

Although the *Irtysh* had gladdened our hearts with the supply of 12,000 pairs of boots and had, as it were, warded off the danger of a "boot famine," we were, quite apart from the question of ammunition, not particularly well off as regarded the remainder of our stores and provisions. On opening a considerable quantity of casks containing pickles and salt meat, which we had brought with us from Cronstadt and Libau, explosions took place, accompanied by an escape of evil-smelling gases, so that their contents had to be thrown overboard.

Moreover, the salt rations, which form the bulk of the men's food at sea, might have to be used, not only on the passage, but at Vladivostok as well, where, according to our latest information, provisions were not over plentiful, whilst it was no use relying on the railway, as "it was only satisfying the wants of the army with difficulty." Partly owing to these considerations, but chiefly in the interest of the health and of the due strengthening of the crews, the admiral took all possible steps to ensure the men being fed almost exclusively on fresh provisions during our stay at Nossi-Bé. But that was no easy matter.

Of course if the contractors had been able to foresee the length of our stay at Nossi-Bé they would not have hesitated to establish as many depots there as requisite; now, however, not only had everything to be scraped together that was to be had in the harbours of Madagascar and the East coast of Africa, but much had to be ordered in Europe, even at the risk of it arriving too late. There was no lack of fresh meat, for the north of Madagascar is the part of the island where there are immense prairies suitable for rearing cattle, and those employed in this industry were only too glad to sell their stock at good prices. On the other hand, vegetables were scarce. Pineapples, bananas and other tropical fruit are of no use for making vegetable soup (the staple dish of the Russian sailor). Cabbages, potatoes, also sorrel, onions, and spinach did not thrive in this climate. All of these were procured, part in a semi-preserved state (dried, roasted, soldered up in tins), from the ports of South Africa, where European vegetables are grown on the high table-land; part from Europe, as regular preserves. The prices were pretty stiff. But even at these prices it was often not possible to obtain the necessary supplies. Often what was missing had to be replaced by so-called "substitutes." The word "took on," and its use spread everywhere in the squadron.

If, for instance, two steamboats were sent in lieu of a defective torpedo-boat, they were called the "substitutes." If a sub-lieutenant went away in charge of a steamboat for torpedo attack in place of a lieutenant who was ill, he also became a substitute. Moreover, the substitutes were generally issued in larger quantities than the articles they replaced. As regarded provisions the proportion between the two was fixed by a committee of doctors in conjunction with the commander on the staff in charge of supplies. Thus, for example, cabbage was replaced by three times its weight of Manioka. Rice took the place of buckwheat (made into a kind of porridge).

From the beginning of February onwards, rye-meal and coarse biscuit were treasured up as delicacies, and eventually rolls and buns were made of them. Macaroni as a substitute for buckwheat porridge was very successfully introduced on the lower deck, where it counted as a lordly dish. On other days vegetable soup had to be prepared from preserved spinach, the very article so much used by cooks when preparing good dinners on shore. Once Commander W——, who had undertaken the wearisome business of fleet supplies at the admiral's personal request,[1] rushed out of the latter's cabin with his arms raised heavenwards, fell into an armchair in the wardroom and called for a glass of cold water.

"What's up? What has happened?" he was asked laughingly, though it was felt that he was merely acting a part.

"You may well laugh. But what am I to do? I say: 'Your Excellency, my belief in science is as firm as in the gospel. The doctors say that onions are urgently required. I agree. But if these onions are more

---

1. He only consented, as he had already commanded a small cruiser on foreign service, and since there were no vacancies in the commands of ships in the squadron going out to the seat of war. On the other hand, it was impossible for a man of his character to sit at home when others were fighting. He went down in the *Borodino*.

expensive than artichokes in St Petersburg? Then we might as well serve out pineapples, which are cheaper than turnips.'—He replies: 'That is a good idea. Ask the committee. Still onions are onions.' 'But what a price.' 'The health of the men is more precious than anything else.' What can one answer? It is easy enough for him to say that. He evidently hopes to be the first to fall, but if I survive then I shall be the one to answer for this to the 'superior authority.'"

When I returned towards 6 a.m. on March 15 from a night expedition with my steam-boats, I turned in and told my servant not to wake me for breakfast (midday meal). However, I woke towards ten o'clock of my own accord, with the uncertain feeling that there was something unusual going on in the ship. I listened. On deck the captain was giving orders himself in a high voice; from a steamboat which was passing someone was shouting something through a megaphone; the commander was chasing the servants out of the wardroom; in the steerage someone was calling out to various people as they were passing whether they had seen the engineer in charge of the coal bunkers; mingled with all this, there were sounds of men's feet running up and down ladders. . . . Apparently everything was as usual, but in the sound of the voices, in the trampling feet, there was a special note, something new—not like what one had heard yesterday. There was no more question of sleep. Dressing hurriedly, I rushed out of my cabin and nearly knocked down the chief engineer, who was tearing along.

"Hard a-port, full speed astern both! What on earth is up?"

"We're off."

"What?"

"I've no time," and escaping from my hands he disappeared.

I hurried to the wardroom. On the way I nearly collided with the commander, who was also cruising at top speed. First he swore, then apologised and called out something about "in the heat of action" "as he disappeared down the ladder.

In the mess I found Lieutenant B——, who was hurriedly smoking a very fat cigarette he had just rolled himself. I ran up to him.

"My dear fellow, do explain what is the matter. Everybody seems to have gone off his head."

"Isn't it enough to make one mad?" he cried joyfully. "We're running away from Nebogatoff."

"Tell me everything; I've only just turned out. I can't make it out."

"During the night the *Regina* arrived—a steamer full of provisions. It was hardly daybreak when the committee went on board to serve out the stuff, to say who was to get what and the exact amount, so that no one should get short measure—the normal business, in fact. Suddenly a telegram, signals, semaphores, orders, 30,000 messengers, boats from every ship to be sent at once, orders to empty the steamer in twenty-four hours. What could not be stowed was to be handed over to the auxiliaries. Prepare for sea. What the devil did it mean? We were all speechless—could not make it out. From the shore a Havas telegram: 'Nebogatoff hurriedly coaling in Crete; expected at Port Said today or tomorrow.' Suddenly we all understood; we were delighted. Our spirits rose mightily. Well, I can't stand chatting here any longer. I'm up to my neck in work."

"The deuce," I thought, "this is getting interesting. Last night there was no idea of so early a start."

I went up to the staff office. There I found a tremendous bustle. As B—— had expressed it, 30,000 messengers seemed to be hurrying in every direction. I cunningly awaited my chance to catch Lieutenant S—— alone in his cabin. (Latterly we had become more and more close friends.)

"I know you have no time, therefore no beating about the bush. Don't make a mystery of it. Tell me straight. Are we running away from Nebogatoff?"

He refused, as usual, to give me a straight answer, and only gave me his personal impression.

"The admiral has in no way initiated me into his plans. I know nothing, and if I knew anything I should not repeat it. You know the circumstances. The admiral is opposed to a junction with Nebogatoff, but he is powerless to send him back, even to stop him. He is not even in telegraphic communication with him. St Petersburg orders and directs everything, yet there exists no direct order to remain here and await reinforcements. Whether this is a lucky or an unlucky chance, I don't know. . . . I can explain to you what is going on to-day. There were other witnesses present besides me. This means that it is not a secret. When the admiral received the Havas telegram he took it as usual into his study,[2] but he came out again almost at once, visibly agitated, and gave the order that all coaling and provisioning was to be finished

---

2. Russian admirals are always provided with a special cabin in which to write and transact business, here called "study."—Trans.

and the squadron was to be ready for sea in twenty-four hours. At the first moment it occurred to me that he meant to save time by going out to meet Nebogatoff. I asked him whether a rendezvous or course was to be telegraphed to any one. He looked at me doubtfully and then said in a tone admitting of no discussion: 'Nothing, to no one.' I am now putting into cipher a telegram in which he reports quite shortly that the squadron has sailed East."

"Without any indication as to the course or by what straits?"

"Absolutely none."

"But what is to be the result? What is Nebogatoff to make for?"

"That's just it. That is the straw at which he is clutching. It seems to me that he is still hoping that in view of this step 'they' will give up their plan and either recall Nebogatoff, or stop him at Jibuti. Perhaps they may then sanction the admiral's original plan of pushing on with the best ships, and possibly (but I hardly dare to believe this) they may even grasp the senselessness of our whole enterprise."

It had been a long time since I had seen S—— so animated, so confident. The entire squadron awoke, as it were, out of its slumber.

"This is something like," said the youngsters. "The devil take all the flat-irons and galoshes! With God's help we'll get across the ocean, and then we shall see. We may yet stow away one or other of our old junks at Saigon, and then we go off full speed. [3] We'll get through all right when once we are rid of all our *impedimenta*."

Thus they spoke in the *Suvoroff's* wardroom, but I am quite sure the same thing was said in the other ships. This is why.—At 2 p.m., as had been arranged the day before, all the "substitute" captains (officers commanding steam-boats), that is to say, fourteen officers from the big ships, came on board to discuss with me the exercises of the previous night. Naturally, they brought with them indications of the feelings which animated their ships, and these completely coincided with those in ours.

At 1 p.m. on March 16 we began to weigh. The mass of fleet auxiliaries formed as great a jumble as at Tangier, only on a larger scale. Some kind of order was finally evolved, and we moved off—at 2.40 p.m.

At 6 p.m., when we were clear of the islands and the banks and reefs surrounding them, we shaped course for the passage at the northern extremity of Madagascar. Suddenly the *Orel's* port engine broke

---

3. The Russian text has "full speed" in English.—Trans.

down. Our delays were already beginning! Until eight o'clock we practically remained on the same spot. At eight we went on 5 knots; only at midnight were we able to increase to 8½.

A battle-fleet? . . . No, hardly. At night a fascinating sight—forty-five ships. A whole town afloat. . . . And how tempting for a torpedo attack!

I must observe here that already on our arrival at Madagascar we had received, both from our agents and from our "dear friends and allies," information as to numerous "ambuscades" planned on our line of advance not only in the style of the Durban scheme, but of a more serious nature. We were told quite positively that the auxiliary cruisers *Hong-Kong Maru* and *Nippon Maru* had been sent to meet us, both carrying submarines. The Seychelles, Diego Garcia, and the Straits of Sunda were named as the principal bases for these operations.

A few words as to our route eastwards. It was only just before sailing from Nossi-Bé that I was told that the original intention had been to take the squadron through the Straits of Sunda, and to make a more or less lengthy stay in Lampong Bay (Sumatra), for the purposes of rest and filling up with coal and stores. Needless to say, it had not been possible to keep this intention secret. Excepting myself and the majority of officers in the squadron, who had been left in ignorance, all the world (beginning, of course, with the Japanese) had learnt it from the most reliable sources. The result—an energetic protest on the part of Japan against this intended violation of neutrality, and even an open threat against Holland in the event of her permitting us the use of her territorial waters.

It was clear that in these circumstances the position of Holland was, to use mess slang, "deuced awkward," for on one side stood Japan, which possessed the might, and therefore the right, to demand the strict observance of the newly proclaimed rules of neutrality; on the other, a power which considered herself fully entitled to disregard these rules. If we had found it necessary to touch at Lampong Bay, we might have treated the demand of the Dutch authorities to leave the place with as much indifference as we had shown towards the protest of the indomitable little *Limpopo* in Great Fish Bay. The only difference—and a very material one—was that there was no Japanese Fleet anywhere near Great Fish Bay, whilst at Lampong Bay such a one might appear at any moment and attack us; in doing which it could declare to the whole world that we had been the first to violate the sacred principles of the laws of nations.

One may well claim that our position was also "deuced awkward," since Holland apparently possessed no means of protecting her territorial waters against an incursion, by us or the Japanese.

For all European newspapers (with the exception of the Russian, to which such discussions were forbidden), the question of the further route which the squadron might select formed a topic of burning interest. The views and opinions of well-known (and sometimes also quite unknown) admirals filled whole columns. In general, all these authorities were agreed that the passage through the Straits of Sunda spelt ruin; of the Straits of Malacca there was simply no mention; suggestions were made to go round Java, or between New Guinea and Australia, leaving the Sunda Archipelago on one side, as the lack of cable communication there, and the large number of passages between the islands, would make it extremely difficult to organise a proper scouting service for the safety of the squadron. Admiral Fremantle (who enjoys a good reputation in the British navy) went so far as to declare that if he were in Rojëstvensky's place he would go south about Australia, a long but safe route, which, moreover, permitted a stoppage at the Carolines, as these belonged to Germany, the only power which had up to now shown us open friendship.

On reaching the open sea, we heard that the admiral had chosen the passage through the Straits of Malacca.

On board the *Suvoroff* this decision was greeted with joy

"From one point of view it is, of course, a wholly unintelligible adventure, but on the other hand it may succeed precisely on account of its desperate character. Shrewd Japanese won't believe in such a venture. But if it does succeed—all honour and glory! And won't Fremantle & Co. stare open mouthed!" Thus the officers spoke of it.

I fully concurred in their views.

This twenty-eight days' passage of a fleet counting forty-five pendants stands unexampled in the history of steam navigation, and I therefore shall venture to describe it, however briefly, from day to day—as it were a "letter of proceedings," based on the notes of my diary. Before doing so, however, I should like to give my readers a general picture of the life in the squadron at that time.

Excepting on the days when we coaled, the exercises and practices, by means of which the gaps in our preparedness for battle were to be made good, took place continuously. The principal concern, of course, was the correct laying of the guns and the taking and estimating of distances. Every morning during general quarters the cruisers *Aurora*, *Donskoi*, *Zemtchug*, *Isumrud*, *Dniepr*, and *Rion* were sent out on both sides of the squadron with orders to move about continuously, altering course and speed, opening out or closing in, sometimes drawing ahead, at other times dropping astern. They were the objects on which the guns were laid for exercise. In the same way we utilised the movements of the scouting division, which had been trained in its special duties for days by its chief, Captain Schein. At the same time these ten cruisers, which were always manoeuvring in sight of the squadron, formed a tolerably reliable screen all round it.

The basis of each of these exercises was, as before, a scheme of battle which had previously been worked out by the senior officers—a scheme with which, according to the admiral's orders, "everybody, down to, and inclusive of, the sick-berth staff," had to be familiar.

Special orders had been issued as to the manner of assuming battle formation on the hoisting of the signal to that effect, if the enemy were sighted ahead, astern, to starboard, or to port; also directions as to what the fleet auxiliaries were to do in each case. It was clearly laid down by whom and to whom assistance and protection was to be given in case of damage in action by gun or torpedo. Whoever rendered such assistance was enjoined (1) to inform the admiral immediately, by every means in his power, of the condition of the vessel requiring help; (2) to take all necessary steps for saving her; (3) to take energetic measures for her destruction, if there should be any danger of her being captured by the enemy.[4]

The changing from cruising to battle formation, on the assumption that the enemy had been sighted in particular directions, the removal of the auxiliaries from the fighting zone and their protection, were actually carried out several times; but, unhappily, it was not possible to carry out exercises of this kind very often, since the fleet, whilst thus employed, had to neglect its chief task—to get forward. Target practice did not take place, "firstly," because we had no ammunition—it is not worthwhile enumerating the remaining reasons.

At dusk it was the admiral's chief concern to close up the squadron as much as ever possible; but this was by no means a simple matter, especially as regarded the auxiliaries, which were not accustomed to keeping station. At night the scouting division—*Svetlana*, *Kuban*,

---

4. Order No. 159 of March 27, 1905.

Terek, and *Ural*—steamed ahead of the squadron in two indented lines abreast, *Zemtchug* and *Isumrud* on either beam. This half-moon was to protect the head of the squadron against any sudden attack.

Almost every night, sometimes even two or three times in the same night, the ships' companies were called to their fighting stations on the admiral's personal order, so as to test the alertness of those on watch, and to ensure the proper working of the searchlights, as well as exercising night signalling. It also happened that such "calls to arms" were caused by the chance incidents of a sea cruise, thus becoming very realistic: for instance, when suspicious vessels were sighted and were approaching the squadron on the same or opposite courses. Judging by their behaviour, it would appear as if the fame of the squadron had spread far and wide after the Hull affair. It was quite sufficient for one of the cruisers to head for the "stranger" and turn her searchlights on him; the latter instantly, without a moment's hesitation and without waiting for any signal or other demand, put his helm over and steamed away from so dangerous a neighbourhood at best speed.

The moments of the highest tension, of a feverish activity, were, of course, the days on which we coaled.

Coaling from a steamer alongside did not succeed once. On the high seas there is always, even in a perfect calm, a certain amount of swell from somewhere—perhaps hundreds or thousands of miles off. Coaling was carried out by transporting the coal from the collier transports in sacks, stowed in the ships' launches or specially constructed lighters, towed by steamboats. For the purpose of filling the sacks and hoisting them into the boats, considerable working parties (one hundred men and more from each big ship), with officers, were sent to the transports; a goodly number of men were also employed in the lighters, launches, and steamboats. Of course it was not possible to maintain any formation during this operation, as the transports and men-of-war were all mixed up so as to ensure rapid coaling. Moreover, the guns were all run in and secured, and covered up carefully, so as to keep the coal-dust out of the delicate parts of their complicated mechanisms and mountings.

In a word—the squadron was not only not prepared for action, but could not even be rapidly prepared for it in case of a sudden alarm. It was true that the armed merchant cruisers (*Kuban*, *Terek*, *Ural*, *Dniepr*, and *Rion*), which, owing to their enormous coal capacity did not require replenishing, acted as look-outs during the time;

they were posted on the circumference of a circle, of which the centre was taken by the huddled-up mass of fighting ships and their attendants, but unfortunately this ring could not be pushed out far enough. They had to keep within distant-signal range, as we could not rely for one moment on the working of our wireless telegraphy (Slaby-Arco patent—Technical Committee). In an atmosphere almost sodden with moisture distant signals could not be worked at more than 5 to 7 miles, and an approaching ship could not be made out beyond 18 or 20 miles. Therefore in these atmospheric conditions we could only get notice of any approaching danger when it was not more than 20 miles off, that is, forty to fifty minutes up to the moment when the enemy could fire his first aimed round. And we could not possibly, as was proved by experience, get cleared for action within that time, even if we left the boats in the water and only re-embarked the men.

One should not criticise the victor, but it must be confessed that the Japanese lost many a favourable opportunity for hindering the advance of our squadron. If their auxiliary cruisers had followed us steadily, then the mere appearance of one of these, even if, after exchanging a few shots with our look-outs, she had fled, would have caused us to interrupt our coaling and to clear for action. I maintain that they could absolutely have prevented our coaling at sea. They made no use of this opportunity—perhaps they credited the Slaby-Arco apparatus with being better than Marconi's.

CHAPTER 4

Details of the Ocean Passage

I now come to the description of the passage. I must begin by stating that I have only noted in my diary the serious breakdowns in boilers and machinery which delayed the squadron several hours; minor defects which only necessitated the ships affected hauling out of the line and which could be made good whilst keeping company, are not noted down by me; they happened too often. In part 2, the Battle of Tsushima I have said:

> . . . our long voyage was an uninterrupted series of breakdowns in boilers and machinery, as well as an incessant martyrdom for our engineers, who had an exceedingly hard time, since they were expected to do wonders with bad material.

On one day I have a note that, steaming with ten boilers, we changed nineteen in twenty-four hours, that is, almost the whole of them.

March 17.—The night was quiet (as regards the Japanese). The admiral never closed an eye. He tried, by means of signals, to get some sort of order into the crowd of ships, which could not possibly be described as being in any formation. Above all, some of the ships keep on dropping astern, stretching out the columns, and the distance between the columns, to an enormous extent. Less frequently they run on top of their next ahead, only to sheer out of the line and disturb their neighbours. At 8 a.m., when we reached the open sea to the northward of Madagascar, we shaped course to pass to the southward of the Seychelles. At 2 p.m. we lost sight of the coast. Light N.E. wind. Frequent breakdowns of machinery (especially in the fleet auxiliaries), cause great delays. It is true they are only trifles. It is to be hoped

59

that it only means that the engines, after having been at rest so long, require a little time again for smooth running, and that things will go better in a day or two. Before sunset we observed on the horizon on the port quarter several columns of smoke. We sent some destroyers to reconnoitre the first of these, which was evidently gaining on us. It turned out to be—a German merchantman.

March 18 (2.30 a.m.).—I was sleeping soundly in the relatively cool temperature. I was awakened by a shower-bath, which poured in through the open scuttle. I had therefore to clear out of the cabin and wait until its traces had been removed. Pity! I had now to stew in my own juice, for it was no good going on deck. In the first place, the deck was covered with "stokers" and hot ashes which the draught of the furnaces drove up the funnel; secondly, it was raining.

At 6 a.m. orders were given for the destroyers to be taken in tow by the auxiliaries, in accordance with a plan which had already been issued. The first time this operation took an hour and a half, during which time we remained stopped. Soon after eight o'clock the formation had been opened out so far—the ships were practically going off in every direction—that the admiral made the leading ships of columns stop engines, and then tried by means of much signalling to collect those that had gone astray.

Towards nine o'clock order had been re-established to a certain extent, and we once more went ahead. Suddenly the towing hawser of the *Irtysh* parted. We again stopped. Another hour. Between ten and eleven we had just increased to 8 knots, when the steering engine on board the *Sissoi* broke down. She sheered out of the line. She went on as best she could, steering with her engines. On her account we were only able to go 5 knots. But it proved too fast for the *Sissoi*. From 1 to 2 p.m. we all stopped engines to wait for her. Then once more—5 knots. By 4 p.m. the *Sissoi* was repaired. We increased to 8 knots. I notice with joy that (at least on board the *Suvoroff*) the men, though they are somewhat anxious, show no signs whatever of fear. The general mood is good. It is just as well that we are cut off from the rest of the world, that we get no news. Latterly, the news we got was very bad. If so, it is better to get none. We'll do our duty, and then—as God wills!

March 20.—A good day. We only stopped once, when the *Blest-yashtchi's* towing hawser parted, but then only for a short while. The distance made in the last twenty-four hours is 187 miles, that is, 7.8

knots per hour.

March 21.—At 5.45 a.m. the signal: "Commence coaling." At 7.15 the first launch load came alongside the *Suvoroff*. At 4 p.m. the signal: "Stop coaling." We hoisted in boats and took a long time taking up our formation. It was 7 p.m. before we moved ahead. We were stopped altogether for thirteen and a quarter hours, of which eight and three-quarters were devoted to coaling, whilst four and a half were taken up with preparations and the opposite. *Suvoroff* took in 206 tons, which makes an average of 24 tons per working hour.

This is not brilliant, especially when one considers that the conditions were very favourable: light, westerly wind and an insignificant swell. But was it to be done? Everything has to be learnt. It was the first time. Let us hope that it will be better in future. Towards 10 p.m. we sighted to port and astern some lights, which, however, quickly disappeared. The torpedo officers pretended that they were getting wireless messages, but were unable to make them out. Could they have been discharges of atmospheric electricity? But who can tell?

March 22.—No special news. Only the towing hawsers seem to part very frequently.

March 24.—All in order. In the evening before moonrise the *Oleg* reported that she could distinctly see several vessels without lights, which were overhauling the squadron; could even make out the flames which were coming out of the funnels of a destroyer. Until moonrise all hands remained at their fighting stations. However, nothing suspicious was sighted. One must assume that it was only a case of imagination.

March 25.—During the night the *Kamtchatka* had a breakdown in her machinery, but only for a short while. On board the *Sissoi* and *Nakimoff* the condenser tubes are leaking badly. Our mean speed for twenty-four hours was only 7½ knots. On the other hand, Nikolai Ugodnic gave us 22 miles of current in our favour (apparently a special gift for us, since the sailing directions made no mention of it). Calm, overcast.

March 26.—Towards noon we were 200 miles south of Peros Banos (Chagos Archipelago). Tomorrow morning we shall be passing Addu Atoll, at a distance of only 60 miles. It is a very likely spot for anything in the way of torpedo work on the part of the Japanese.

Evening.—It is blowing quite fresh. Is not this a gift of heaven? In weather like this no torpedo attacks against ships under weigh could be carried out.

March 27.—The wind has dropped, but there is still a heavy swell. We performed evolutions the whole forenoon. Assuming battle formation and several other (quite elementary) movements were not badly performed. There was no confusion. Apparently they have learnt something. Only 165 miles made good, as we had no current with us. In the evening we sighted some lights ahead.

March 28.—Absolute calm. Only a very slight swell. At 6 a.m. we commenced coaling. Some progress was noticeable. Both the rigging up and the unrigging went quicker. The rate of coaling has been nearly doubled, thanks to numerous improvements, but chiefly thanks to the practice. *Suvoroff* took in 43 tons per hour. Run 144 miles. Contrary to the sailing directions, 14 miles of northerly current. Disagreeable. This is by no means helpful.

March 29.—All quiet. Calm. Swell, not high, but very steep (short). We coaled. A steamboat of the *Sissoi* foundered, happily without loss of life. The thing happened as follows: after several trips with boats in tow, the steamboat went alongside her own ship to fill up with coal and water; here, by clumsy handling, she got her gunwale caught under the heel of one of the torpedo-net booms. The ship, which was rolling in the swell, was just heeling towards that side; the boat was forced over to one side, the water ran in until she filled and sank. The crew managed to save themselves. Towards evening the breeze from the south began to freshen.—It is seven years ago to-day since the Grand Duke Cyril Wladimirovitch, (son of Wladimir), personally hoisted the Russian flag on Golden Hill at Port Arthur. . . . A melancholy anniversary! Has Nicolas I.'s proud saying: "*Where the Russian flag has once been hoisted, it will never be struck,*" been quite forgotten?— How painful and sad!

March 30—At 9 a.m. we crossed "the line." It was as well that we made good use of the fine weather and took in coal "over our ears," for it came on to blow from the north-west, force 5, in the afternoon, and the sea got up.

April 5.—At 6 a.m. we sighted Great Nikobar and shaped course to pass between the Nikobars and Pulo Brass. We were nearing the

Straits of Malacca. I am very curious to know: Have the Japanese got touch with us or not? There was plenty of opportunity for it. About noon we entered the straits and took the course along the coast of Sumatra. One notices the proximity of the land. The temperature rose about 4° F. and the moisture increased greatly. A close, unpleasant heat. Even if the Japanese should have touch with us, one can hardly expect to meet their main fighting force and to have the decisive battle here. For them it would not be advantageous to get so far away from their base, whilst we are going there in any case.

What is more likely here are surprise attacks—guerilla warfare. Consequently, we decided upon the following formation for the passage of the straits:—in the centre the auxiliaries in two columns; ahead the look-outs *Zemtchug* and *Isumrud*, the two battleship divisions on either side, the cruisers bringing up the rear. The destroyers have cast off tow, are steaming with their own engines, and have taken station according to the plan. A bold, somewhat risky formation, intended, like a bold move on the chessboard, to bluff the adversary. From 8.30 to 10.30 p.m. we stopped engines, as a steam-pipe had burst on board the *Orel*.

April 6.—The night passed quietly. It was hazy in the morning. About 8 a.m., rain and thunderstorm. Until noon thick and rainy weather. It then cleared up. During the night we met a steamer. She quickly altered course when the *Zemtchug* lit her up with the search-light. At daybreak we saw several others. Where may they be bound for? How soon will they reach the next port? In other words: How soon will the telegraph be proclaiming to the world that we are passing through the Straits of Malacca? If up to now the Japanese were in ignorance, will they still have time to undertake something?

April 7.—The night was calm. Foggy weather. We meet more and more ships. The more nervous of our ships behave as if they had sighted the enemy.

From the *Almas* we got a signal that the admiral, captain, and officers, who had been on the bridge, as well as the signalmen, had all seen quite plainly twelve destroyers or torpedo-boats, which had hidden behind a steamer of the British India Company, and then steamed away to the north-east. A strange report. Presumably the Japanese came to inform us that they were here, so that we should be more careful during the night. In no other way can such a manoeuvre be explained. The *Oleg* observes suspicious indications more frequently than the rest. She has already reported submarines in sight.

At 2 a.m. we passed One Fathom Bank—in my opinion the most favourable spot for a night attack of the whole voyage. Until dawn we shall be in waters which occasionally narrow down to 5 miles. A risky night!

April 8.—Everything all right. We met many vessels, but no suspicious ones. All the same, let us avoid deductions. What has the next night in store for us? The narrows are passed. We get to Singapore. All around—deep sea passages, heaps of islands. There is room here for any battle manoeuvres. Therefore the sudden appearance of the hostile battleships is possible. At 11 a.m. we resume the former cruising formation, which is more suitable for assuming battle formation, that is, the auxiliaries are astern and independent. At 2 p.m. we pass the lighthouse on Raffles Island. Singapore lies before us like a panorama. In the roads are two English cruisers. Up to our full numbers we solemnly steam past, without a single ship falling out, and enter the Pacific. An impressive moment! On board there is absolute silence. . . .

"In a few minutes the telegraph will report this to the whole world," the admiral said, speaking, as it seemed to me, with a slight tremor of the voice, as he stood on the port side of the bridge and looked searchingly into the far distance in the direction of the town.

The flag-captain, J——, unexpectedly caused general hilarity by laughing cheerfully, and exclaiming: "As to that fellow Fremantle, won't he just be in rage! He believes us to be to the southward of Australia now, the sly old fox!"

And suddenly every one also became wonderfully cheerful. Even the signalmen laughed, but out of respect for their chief they hid their faces behind their binoculars.

A small steamer, flying the Russian consular flag, came out of Singapore, steering to cut us off. It was certainly tempting to receive the consul personally and to hear all the news, but to do that we should have been obliged to stop. We therefore confined ourselves to sending a destroyer to fetch the despatches and hand them over to us, whilst moving ahead—a case which had been provided for. After having handed the packets to the destroyer the steamer caught us up and steamed for some time alongside the *Suvoroff*. The consul called across that he had scraped together all the newspapers he could lay his hands on in a hurry—there might be some missing numbers; consequently, he gave us the principal items of news by megaphone.

Amongst these it turned out that Japanese cruisers called at Singapore three days ago, and that their squadron had now gone to North Borneo. This looked as if they had missed us.

At 7 p.m. we passed the lighthouse on Pedro Branco Island. The South China Sea was before us.

April 9.—The night was quiet. We stopped at 6 a.m. The destroyers, which were no longer being towed, took in coal. At 11 a.m. we proceeded once more,

April 10 (2 a.m.).—Yesterday I slept so much in the daytime that I can't sleep now. I believe that even if the Japanese are trying to find us, they won't sight us before tomorrow; we are 600 miles from Labuan. It is possible that a battle is before us. I carefully note my own thoughts, listen to the conversation amongst the officers, endeavour to picture to myself the general state of feeling. It is courageous and calm. There is really too much calmness, almost indifference as to our own fate; and with this the fate of our cause is after all closely bound up. Apparently it is the result of over-exertion. We are all weary. Our nerves are unstrung. There is no breathing time possible. Well, the end will come all the quicker. . . . Our sudden departure from Madagascar had brightened up all hands.

The successful passage of the Straits of Malacca had raised our spirits and courage. This excessive calmness, almost indifference, resignation, which is noticeable, appears to be due to purely physical causes. In action they will all pull themselves together and the proper spirit will once more assert itself. It will last us out for the battle. Still, one must not overestimate one's strength; it is about spent. So as to kill time I was reading a translation of a novel called *Abraham's Sacrifice*, dealing with the time of the Boer war, by a certain Johnson, who must have taken part in it. Strange, but I came across many a thought which had also occurred to me at Port Arthur, especially after the first collision with the enemy. For example, the pitying "Ohs" and "Ahs" over the fate of the wounded.

I am not speaking of the officers who have voluntarily and of their own initiative chosen as their profession the business of war, and therefore also war itself with all its consequences—no, I am only speaking of the rank and file, who are called up for service, who are bound to serve, although it may not agree with their inclinations (conscripts). The sound and healthy lad is taken away from his family, carried 10,000 miles, forced to fight some unknown enemy without his knowing why, and when he lies wounded in hospital, nurses give him tea and load him with sweets and "feel so very sorry for the poor boy." I have nothing to say against the tea and the sweets, against any such pleasant things, in fact, but this pitying seems to me rank hypocrisy. This pity is almost an insult to the wounded. Their sufferings entitle them to be judged more seriously. One sends the man to his death, one allows him to be mutilated, and when this is done, then— one pities him. Is he not justified in saying:

"Spare me your belated plaints. You should have thought of this *beforehand*. If instead of me, those who are now shedding tears had themselves been obliged to go out to the war, if they did not always possess a fresh supply of 'food-for-guns,' they would be more careful."

That is true, "they would be more careful"; but no care is able to exterminate the possibility of war, that is the death and mutilation of hundreds of thousands.

And thus we stand once more face to face with the eternal, unfathomable secret, that curtain which hides from man's inquisitive spirit the true significance of war as decreed by fate. I have no faith in those who hope that in time wars will cease. War is quite as much an elemental factor in organic life as an earthquake in inorganic life. The author of this novel tries honestly to solve the riddle, he leaves it an open question. But it is strange that he considers another, similar question as being also incapable of solution: "*May a sincere Christian go into war for the purpose of killing his neighbour?*" This idea permeates the entire book, it is elucidated by numerous quotations from the Scriptures, but no answer is given, although, in my opinion, such a one exists. At first sight, what a violent contradiction!

On the one side we have Christian churches (of all confessions), which recognise the validity of the oath of fealty taken by the soldier; they read prayers laid down according to canonical rules, they even hold special church services for "vanquishing and destroying" the enemy.

On the other hand, every person bearing arms for the State must divest himself of his arms, not only previous to taking the Holy Communion, not only when he takes an immediate part in the Easter procession, but even when he wishes to enter the space outside the altar, for the purpose of making his obeisance to the holy shroud (laymen have no right of access to the sanctuary enclosing the altar). [5] Does this mean that arms are not permitted in a holy place? If so, how can one then call down on them the blessings of heaven? I think that the contradiction is removed and the answer becomes quite self-evident, if only it is put differently: "May a sincere Christian go into war for the purpose of protecting his neighbour at the sacrifice of his own life, against the enemy from without?"

The answer is clear: "Not only may he do so, but it is his sacred duty to do so, since '*Greater love hath no man than this, that a man lay down his life for his friend.*'" An aggressive war, which has for aim the extermination of peoples and the robbery of their property, violates Christian doctrine, but the defence of one's native country, sacrificing one's own life for its good, is a sanctified act of love and devotion. But enough of philosophy.

April 10 (2 p.m.).—This morning I was quite unexpectedly (and indeed for the first time) summoned to a conference by the admiral. Besides me there were only present the chief of the staff and Flag-Lieutenant S——. I believe I owe my summons to the latter. The admiral began with the statement that those present were in possession of all the facts and were requested to give their opinion quite openly. As regarded myself this was not quite the case, as I was not numbered amongst those who were initiated into the secrets of the staff, and if I knew more than the other officers of the *Suvoroff*, it was only thanks to the short and often reluctantly given replies of Lieutenant S——, as well as to the conversations at the admiral's table.

The chief of the staff spoke rather discursively and vaguely. So far as I understood his meaning, he was pointing out the necessity of the squadron first taking up its strategical position, and then acting according to the news at hand as to the distribution of the hostile forces. On my asking what was to be understood by the phrase of "the squadron first taking up its strategical position," I was told that on April 7 Admiral Nebogatoff had sailed from Jibuti with his detachment. It turned out that this information had been transmitted by the Consul on our passing Singapore.

I could not help exclaiming: "So they have sent him on all the same! Without giving him a rendezvous? Just simply at haphazard!" The admiral said nothing, only frowned and bent forward still more; S—— whispered in my ear: "It's all over. We've not managed to es-

5. This, of course, refers to the "Orthodox Church."—Trans.

cape them. They are the stronger. One has to bow to the stronger. We 'report' to them and they 'order' us about."

This news affected me profoundly, and I confess quite frankly I was beside myself at first. So Nebogatoff had been ordered to go on all the same. . . . We had succeeded in eluding the watchful enemy. One move in the game we had won, but we dared not hope to win the next one. Moreover, we were still a respectable force: five good battleships, one armoured and three light cruisers, if the old vessels were not counted. But he, Nebogatoff, he had only rubbish. What were we to do? Wait? Impossible! To go on, leaving him to his fate, to the attempt at getting through as best he could?

That was not acting as good comrades. And yet, if we were to go on, would the Japanese then divide their forces and leave behind here in the south a detachment of sufficient strength to annihilate Nebogatoff? Hardly. They like playing for safety, and any success, however incomplete, which we might then possibly gain in the Sea of Japan, would still be a heavy blow for them. Now if they were to leave something behind here, and, let us assume, were to beat Nebogatoff under favourable circumstances, he would then hide somewhere in neutral waters and would disarm his ships if it came to the worst. Well, then may God be with him! Naturally—forward!

All this flashed through my brain in the short pause during which the admiral was drawing something with a pencil on a piece of paper, looking up at me every now and then, as if waiting for my reply.

I openly expressed what was in my thoughts, and proved the impossibility of waiting by the considerations which I entered in my diary that evening: "We should make full use of the fact that the spirits of all had been raised by the successful passage of the Straits of Malacca; this mental condition overcame all fatigue, made every one bold, strong, and healthy. We must not deceive ourselves, this state would not last long; bodily exhaustion would demand its rights; the higher the spirits had been raised, the more violent would be the reaction when it set in; we dared not wait. Forward, and let come what may!"

Lieutenant S—— spoke after me. He expressed himself very decidedly.

On our way to Vladivostok we undoubtedly had before us the decisive battle with the victorious Japanese Fleet, which had already destroyed the First Squadron, superior to ours in strength. We on our side, exhausted by the long sea passage and the continuous strain, were going into battle with ships which had never been in action before, which had never experienced the destructive effect of the enemy's accurate fire. In this battle (we must not hide it from ourselves) we should suffer heavy losses, if we were not completely annihilated. . . . We might hope to push through, we might hope for favourable weather, for some failure on the part of the enemy, but could we hope for any success? . . . Was this possible when throughout the war fortune had been persistently on the side of Japan? It might perhaps be conceded that the remnant of the squadron could fight its way through to Vladivostok.

What would the ships do there?—Wait, each in her turn, to go into the only existing dock? And where were they to replenish their ammunition and other stores, seeing that the Siberian railway "was only with difficulty satisfying the wants of the army"? And all this time what would our auxiliaries be doing, and Nebogatoff with his archaeological collection of naval architecture? Who would in these circumstances be "in command of the sea"?—the task laid down in telegram No. 244. "What should we do?" I reply unhesitatingly. "Make full use of the effect which our appearance in complete strength in the South China Seas has undoubtedly produced, and hasten to conclude an honourable peace.—To count on the success of further sea operations. . . . To believe in miracles. . . . Unhappily though such a decision does not depend on us! Pity! . . ."

The admiral did not give us his personal views, he did not even reply to our suggestions. Still, it seemed to me (though I may quite possibly have been mistaken) that he was in sympathy with my proposal; also that he was closely watching S—— with a strange expression in his eyes, whilst the latter was pronouncing the concluding sentences of his speech. Evidently the secret of the "most secret correspondence," only known to these two, was here at stake.

The remainder of the day passed uneventfully.

April 11.—At 6 a.m. the *Cressy,* an English armoured cruiser, passed us on an opposite course on our starboard side and saluted the admiral's flag. We returned this with the same number of guns.

About 8 a.m. another English cruiser was sighted to port, she never approached nearer than 5 miles from us.

We saw no more Englishmen, but we took in some of their wireless communications between several of their ships. (Our torpedo officers had become well acquainted with their wireless system during

69

our passage from Vigo to Tangier and Dakar.) It was quite clear. The English cruisers had undertaken to do the scouting for the Japanese.

We came across many vessels steaming both in the same and in the opposite directions. This was not to be wondered at, for we were on the great ocean highway between Singapore and Hong Kong.

We were steaming in semi-battle formation, ready to complete it at the first intimation of an enemy being sighted. The look-outs, under Captain Schein (*Svetlana, Kuban, Terek, Ural, Dniepr,* and *Rion*) were spread ahead.

At 11 a.m. we detached the hospital ship *Orel* to Saigon to replenish her stores. Her captain had been given Kamranh Bay as a secret rendezvous. If he did not find us there, he was to do his best to rejoin the flag, making use of any news he might collect, or otherwise to ask for orders from St Petersburg.

At 5 p.m. the *Svetlana* made by wireless: "Enemy in sight." Cleared for action. *Zemtchug* and *Isumrud* sent out to her. It was nothing. Evidently a mistake.

At nightfall the look-outs were drawn in and ordered to take up as usual the two indented lines abreast, ahead of the main body, with *Zemtchug* and *Isumrud* on the flanks.

Terek reported that towards evening a friendly merchantman had informed her that she had seen a flotilla of torpedo craft to the eastward of our course. Possibly this was what *Svetlana* had sighted.

Soon after ten o'clock the *Navarin's* starboard engine broke down. We crawled along at 4 to 5 knots, and yet the *Navarin* dropped astern. At the end of an hour she was ready again. We increased to 8 knots. The *Navarin* was still astern, about 2 miles from the rear ship.

April 12.—The *Navarin* made an effort to prove her recovery, for by 2 a.m. she was once more in station. We increased to the normal speed of 9½ knots.

The night passed quietly. At daybreak we stopped and commenced coaling. I was astonished at this. We were only 60 miles from Kamranh. Why?—Strange. And the admiral is so odd today, so restless, so taciturn and irritable. . . . He is running about nervously, dragging his leg, appearing first on one bridge, then on the other, then disappearing for a short time in his cabin; after that he moves about again on deck, looks through his note-book, notes down something in it; now he is frowning, now again smiling (but the former more frequently), and finally he starts talking to himself.

"What's up with 'our man'? Has he been stung by a fly, or has a louse run over his liver?"[6] W——, the assistant torpedo lieutenant, asked me.

The same day (before lunch), the admiral had a long talk with the "master of the fleet." What about, is not known. Meanwhile, the navigator ran into the charthouse and fetched the general sheet, "Hong Kong to Vladivostok." Then there was a very animated discussion with the chief engineer. The collier transports were ordered to report how much coal each one had on board for the use of the squadron. Further signal (general): "Are boilers and machinery in good order for a long passage?" In reply nearly every ship asked permission to overhaul something or other, but only for a few hours; the *Navarin* required the most time, but she would be ready by 3 p.m. It seems to me that the fate of the squadron will also decide our fate. . . .

Lieutenant S—— thought the same.

"What do you think?" I asked him. "It looks as if 'our man' had decided to go straight to Vladivostok. There is something in this idea. The Japanese have missed us—an indisputable fact. Let us admit that they have picked up our trail. But what then? Suppose the English tell them tomorrow that they have sighted us on the coast of Annam; the hospital ship *Orel* arrives at Saigon—a further sign that we are in the neighbourhood. Before they can take further steps we shall be past Formosa."

"You know my view of the situation," S—— replied. "If it should prove wrong, then I naturally join hands with you. Forward! Let us fight! To wait still longer—no! One gets embittered, gets slack. And above all—straight from here, from the open sea, without first calling in anywhere, without first communicating with any one by telegraph"— and he shook his fist in the direction of Saigon. "Probably there are already awaiting us there further directions in high-flown language, in which the appeal to the Heavenly Hosts forms the principal item. So far they have not reached us yet—our hands are not yet tied. If we anchor—then all will go to the devil. Then we shall be tied to the telegraph cable."[7]

---

6. Russian colloquialisms.—Trans.

7. As was afterwards proved, Lieutenant S—— was absolutely right. On April 16 the Havas Agency sent out into the world the following telegram from St Petersburg :—"Rojëstvensky will await Nebogatoff." Obviously this could not be the admiral's decision, but was the decision come to at St Petersburg immediately after the reception of the news that the squadron bad arrived at Kamranh Bay. Not to speak of the decision itself, what criminal indiscretion!

At table the admiral, quite contrary to his habit, spoke with no one. Directly after lunch he went into his study. About one o'clock he suddenly appeared on the upper bridge, and ordered a general signal to be made that all ships, after a careful computation of the contents of the coal-bunkers, were to report the exact amount of coal on board. This was a very unusual order, and apparently even superfluous.[8]

"Well," I thought, "he is evidently determined. Good luck to him!"

As was to have been expected, all ships reported from 100 to 150 tons more than in the morning report. Only the *Alexander* hesitated in making the reply. She got a reminder. At last she hoists her numbers. We see it, but can't understand it. The semaphore asks:—"Is not there a mistake in your signal? You are showing 300 tons less than this morning."—Alas! It turns out that the signal is quite correct, that there was no error. On the contrary, by means of this signal a whole string of errors were corrected, which the morning report had contained. The "coal remaining" for the purposes of this report was generally arrived at, not by any estimate of the contents of the bunkers, but by subtracting the amount of the daily expenditure from the amount on charge, which had been replenished (both at Nossi-Bé and at sea) five times, not counting today's coaling; the result: a clerical error, that is, 400 tons less than at first stated! (See note following).

★★★★★★

Note:—Of course errors were possible, both in noting down the amount expended and in estimating the amount received; but not to this extent. The coal burnt is noted hour by hour. In the Second Squadron, where coal was a question of life or death, it had been particularly prescribed that the coal was not merely to be transferred from the bunkers to the stokeholds, but that it was to be weighed out carefully, for which service a sub-lieutenant (active service or naval reserve) was attached to the engine-room department. The object of this measure was to account for every pound of coal. In these circumstances the chief engineer had the means of exercising a rigid supervision over his subordinates. If the amount of coal burnt in one

---

8. All ships made their "morning report" by signal every morning at eight o'clock. This contained information as to the amount of coal and fresh water, the number sick and in cells, the temperature of magazines, etc. A repeated enquiry as to the above could only mean a check on the first report.

watch was in marked contrast to that of another, he had to satisfy himself personally whether this was due to ignorance or carelessness of the firemen, whether, may be, they tried to make up for incomplete combustion (which depends upon the manner of tending the fires) by putting on more coal. In a word, though the methods of recording consumption were perhaps no masterpieces, yet they could hardly produce *such* results. It was rather different with the records of coal received, as they had to be made during a "hands-evolution," when work was at high pressure, everyone trying to distinguish himself, to beat all others....

To avoid misunderstandings I must observe here that in this case there could be no question of any pecuniary advantages to either the one who supplied or to the one who received the coal. The coal was ours, the property of the State, paid for long ago at St Petersburg. Whether it was on board a transport or on board a man-of-war was quite immaterial; any percentages of its money value could not possibly be pocketed by any one in the squadron. If those who kept the *Alexander's* coal accounts were inclined, when estimating the weight of the sacks, to add the doubtful pounds instead of subtracting them, this was due to the (certainly short-sighted) endeavours to present favourable figures, but in no way from selfish motives.

★★★★★★

"*Four hundred tons short!* Here we are catching them out, these fellows in the *Alexander*, who were always first at coaling! Eighty tons for every coaling.... 400 tons.... If she were to take these in now at sea, we should lose two or three days. And would this be possible? Where are the Japanese? Perhaps quite near. Who can tell? Shall we now be obliged to go to Kamranh and tie ourselves to the telegraph cable?"

It was pitiful to see the admiral. He who even in trifling matters could get quite beside himself, who used to shake his fist at a ship performing an evolution badly, launching out into the most uncomplimentary remarks about her (it was as well that at the distance he could neither be heard nor seen), now could hardly get out a word.

Stooping slightly, his hands grasping the bridge rails nervously, he stood on the bridge and stared with a frown at the signal flying from the *Alexander's* foreyard-arm—he could hardly believe his own eyes.

The explanation which followed by semaphore admitted of no

doubt. We replied: "Understood," and the *Alexander* hauled down the signal.

The admiral recovered his composure, waved his hand, and went below.

"*Et tu Brute!*" said Lieutenant S—— with a bitter smile, looking at the *Alexander*, which he as well as many others (myself included) had always looked upon as the pattern ship of the squadron. "Well, and what do you say?" he added, turning round to me.

"What can I say ?—He won't be able to go on now."

It was clear that the scheme of steaming straight to Vladivostok had now come to nought.

As I know the admiral's character to a certain extent, and know that, with all his energy, he is not quite free from fatalism, I fancied I had guessed his view—"not a mere chance."

Soon after two o'clock we began to receive wireless messages. Judging by the system they were unlike the English. The sender was approaching.[9] We at once ceased coaling, embarked the working parties, hoisted in the boats, and assumed the day cruising formation which was specially adapted for changing over into battle formation. Soon after 3 p.m. the sender of the wireless messages began to move away from us. At 4.30 we shaped course for Pandaran Light, at the entrance of Kamranh Bay.

April 13.—The night passed quietly. By 7 a.m. we were off the entrance to the bay. We stopped engines. We sent the destroyers ahead to search the intended anchorage for mines (one can never be too careful), and the picket boats to lay down buoys for anchoring on, to avoid mistakes and consequent shifting of berths afterwards, which were not only possible, but even probable with the feeble organisation of the *armada*. Whilst these tasks were being executed we coaled, the *Alexander* being enjoined to bestir herself specially.

From 1 p.m. on, the auxiliaries began to enter the bay in order of their numbers. Notwithstanding the buoys and the most elaborate instructions, the business dragged on so much that it was no longer possible for the men-of-war to go in before dark. The latter had therefore to spend another night at sea.

At 4 p.m., when we had finished coaling, certain precautionary measures in Kamranh Bay and its approaches were taken to guard against a sudden attack on the part of the enemy. The groups into

9. It is easy to tell at the apparatus whether the sender is approaching or receding.

which we now broke up steered S. 10° E.; the cruisers formed the group furthest south and to starboard; in rear of these, and more to port, were the battleships; finally, to the eastward of all these came the group of scouts. The distance between the nearest ships of two adjoining groups was 2 to 3 miles. Until 6 p.m. we went slow, then we stopped engines and turned head to sea. The current was weak and setting to the northward, so that towards morning our centre would be again off the entrance of the bay. The entrance itself was guarded by the destroyers.

The night was calm and clear. The range of vision was good, and any attempt at torpedo attack could have been detected at once; all ships had ample room for independent movement.

April 14.—The night passed quietly. Only between one and two o'clock a small steamer was seen, running from north to south and keeping between us and the shore. The destroyers and the *Zemtchug* at once steamed towards her, lit her up with searchlights, and made her out. It was a passenger and cargo steamer on coasting service under the Chinese flag. They accompanied her until she was out of sight from us and kept their searchlights on her—the best way of preventing her people from seeing anything.

At 11.30 a.m. we entered Kamranh Bay and anchored according to plan.

In all we had done 4,560 miles from Nossi-Bé here, without touching anywhere—an unprecedented performance. Wouldn't the English burst with envy! We arrived all well, in full numbers and without any losses on the way. And if it had not been for the *Alexander*, we might similarly in another fortnight have reached . . . Vladivostok. . . . Most annoying!—Our spirits had become markedly elated. I went into the ward-room, B—— (the torpedo lieutenant) was delivering an oration.

Whether it was a good thing to do or not, from Cronstadt here is 16,628 miles. Not a bad performance! And up to our full numbers. All honour to Zenobius (the admiral's Christian name). Who else would have done it? Dubasoff and Tchooknin, but that exhausts the list.

It was indeed no mean performance. But when the thing is treated arithmetically we get, after deducting the time spent in coaling, an average of 180 miles per day (including current), that is, 7½ knots per

75

hour; deducting the current—7 knots. That is our sea speed.[10] Hopeless. . . .

As soon as we had anchored, the torpedo nets were got out (at sea they were kept stowed away).

Four colliers of the Hamburg-Amerika Line arrived in the bay about the same time as we did. That meant close on 30,000 tons of coal. Oh, if we could only have taken these on board and then sailed, without getting into communication with St Petersburg!

A fresh breeze was blowing by day. It dropped towards evening. During the night there was a flat calm. Two cruisers were on guard at the entrance and formed a bar of light across it with their searchlights; four destroyers were patrolling in the offing and six picket-boats formed a line of vedettes.

Herewith I end the textual reproduction of the notes in my diary on the ocean passage, and will continue now again my narrative. In doing so I shall omit the less interesting technical details, whilst completing and elucidating more fully the short notes, which tell me so much, but which would be hardly intelligible to the wider circle of my readers.

---

10. The reader may ask here: "Why? The worst of the fleet auxiliaries (and those were the ones working by contract) always could do their 10 knots." I reply: "It was the breakdowns, damages, and insufficient preparation for such a voyage which caused the endless delays."

CHAPTER 5

The Death-Struggle of the "Armada"

On April 15, 16, and 17 we coaled as fast as we could, first the men-of-war and then the fleet auxiliaries, from the German colliers.

On April 15 the hospital ship *Orel* arrived from Saigon. A curious incident took place about this time.

During the passage of the Straits of Malacca a man disappeared from the *Nakimoff*. It was assumed that he had fallen overboard and had been drowned. However, it turned out differently. He did, in fact, disappear overboard, but whether accidentally or intentionally it is hard to say. Probably the latter. A man who falls off from anywhere immediately cries out, and although the man in question may not have had sufficient breath left and may therefore have been unable to cry out, the entire watch on deck was, at the moment of his disappearance, devoting its closest attention to what was going on outboard, the bulwarks were lined with men who were watching for every sound, for everything, in fact, so that the falling overboard of a man could only remain unnoticed if he had chosen a specially secluded spot and a specially favourable moment.

Probably when he saw the lights of the town of Malacca and believed the shore to be quite near (at night one often misjudges distances) he made up his mind to desert, in hopes of either reaching the shore or of being picked up by a fishing-boat or a passing steamer. Moreover, it turned out that when he was discovered he was keeping himself above water by means of a life-belt, which, according to his statement, had accidentally fallen into his hands. . . .

This incident is not a solitary one in the experience of war. Very often a man deliberately exposes his life, even commits suicide, so as to escape from that fear of death which he knows he will feel on some future occasion. In connection with this I cannot help being reminded of a case at Port Arthur, where an officer was sent back to Russia as, after taking part in several engagements, his nerves were so shattered that, with a wild look in his eyes, he assured both the doctors and his superiors ' ' that he could not wait any longer," and would in the next engagement commit suicide at the sound of the first gun.—This time fate played a trick upon the unhappy deserter. He was unable to swim to the shore (it was about 6 miles off), sharks did not devour him, but, on the other hand, he was not picked up by any fishing-boat.

Now, whether he reached Malacca or got on board any steamer—provided she was bound for any other port, *except* Saigon—he would in any case escape the fate of the Second Squadron. I must here point out that the Straits of Malacca is a much frequented part of the sea, many steamers traverse it. It was ordained that after having been eleven hours in the water a Messageries Maritimes steamer, which only passed here twice a month, picked him up and brought him to Saigon, where he was handed over to our Consul. With the next steamer which brought us provisions he rejoined the squadron and was handed back to the *Nakimoff*. Of course he was not tried by court-martial, as he gave the assurance that he had fallen overboard accidentally: he was evidently not to escape his fate!

On the same day (April 15) there arrived in Kamranh Bay on board the cruiser *Descartes* the second-in-command of the French Squadron in Chinese waters, Rear-Admiral de Jonquières, whose acquaintance I had already made six months ago at Saigon when there in the *Diana*. He was of medium height, spare, quite grey, but uncommonly alert and as lively as quicksilver. His age?—Well on in the "forties," perhaps even fifty, but as energetic as if still a lieutenant. He was very decidedly of the opinion that Japan's attack on Russia was only the first step towards the total expulsion of all Europeans from Asia, in any case towards replacing the domination of the white races by the hegemony of a pan-Asiatic league, the common banner of which would be the flag of the "Rising Sun."

"Sometimes I don't understand the Japanese," he said, "but I am of opinion that their forward movement is justified even by their geographical position alone, but chiefly by the fact that their advance towards Korea is something like yours towards Constantinople—matters which go back many centuries, but which are quite understood by their educated people. This is a chord, by the striking of which they could produce an outburst of enthusiasm, as with you at the times of the Turkish wars. With you it was Oleg who knocked at the gates of Constantinople with his sword; here it was Hideyoshi.

"From the point of view of war, pure and simple, it would have been more correct if they had attacked the line at the point of least resistance—here in the Far East we are much weaker than you. And close to us is Siam, where the heir to the throne is married to a Japanese princess; where amongst the ministers there are two Japanese (one of them Minister of War); where the troops are armed with the Japanese rifle and trained by Japanese instructors according to Japanese methods; where the stores of munitions of war can serve equally well the native troops and those of an expeditionary corps, which would have been received with acclamation. "What means do we possess here for defending the colony?—It is simply laughable.

"I felt quite sure that the first blow would be aimed at us. Though possibly the Japanese, who follow the wise rule of taking into account the psychology of their possible adversaries, and who knew you as incorrigible idealists, thought, and not without reason, that you would not act as our government have done, but would, on seeing a good ally in danger, throw yourselves on them from the north with all your might. That is quite possible, and I can understand it. What I can never understand is the irresolute, irresponsive attitude of our government.

"Can it be that they are unable clearly to appreciate the fact that after you, it will be our turn? That in repudiating our original declaration of neutrality and in concurring, in part at least, in the new supplementary rules, all to please England, we are simply digging a pitfall for ourselves? In case we should find ourselves at war, and these principles were to be upheld, we should be as houseless and homeless as you. In any case, pray believe that we, who are working on the spot, and who are able to take in the situation, are your true allies—not only in the sense of the friendship of which there was so much talk before the alliance was concluded (do you recollect—first, the *entente cordiale*, then the *nations amies,* and finally the *nations allies?*) but sincerely so—and with calculated deliberation."

On April 16 the *Eridan* arrived from Saigon, the first steamer to bring us fresh provisions and vegetables. Fresh cabbage soup![1] One

1. The favourite dish of the Russian sailor.—Trans.

can appreciate that after a whole month of "hermeticals," as they were called in the mess. Lieutenants K—— and M——, as well as a ballooning expert, came also in the steamer.

These had been at Port Arthur up to the end. Being ill, they were not made prisoners, but sent to Shanghai at the disposal of the Russian Government. As soon as they were convalescent, they felt drawn towards the Second Squadron. Their accounts were bad, so that we "begged" them (a prohibition would in our situation have been a sham) not to relate too many details, so as not to depress still more the general spirits, which were bad enough as it was.

According to their accounts Stoessel's attitude had been far from heroic. Unanimity, solidarity, there was none. The feeling in the masses, which I had personally observed even in July—that distrust of what the authorities said and promised—had got worse. With Kondratenko's death the last person really in authority disappeared. The conviction that the game was only kept up at the cost of the rank and file, that "nothing mattered, that it was not worthwhile," took root and spread more and more. During the last days there were not more than 5,000 men in the fighting line, yet 23,000 in all surrendered. Terrible scenes were enacted, men came to blows, were even killed—always arising out of the question: "Where have you been hiding, you scoundrel?"

The real defenders of the forts, when they returned to the town, suffering the pangs of hunger, clad in rags, could not be indifferent to the sight of the stores of uniforms and provisions which were being mustered in readiness for being handed over to the Japanese. Much was destroyed or stolen.

On the same day Jonquières went to Nhatrang Bay (about 20 miles north of Kamranh) in the *Descartes*, and returned the following day.

April 18 passed quietly and undisturbed. The weather was quite settled: by day—fresh breeze; by night—calm. I went to see Jonquières by order of the admiral, to inform him that we meant to go out the next day for a trial of the engines which had been overhauled after the long sea passage.

I had dressed myself as was demanded for such a visit. On my coat I wore the "Legion of Honour," in place of the Russian Order of St Wladimir, which generally adorned it. I began by explaining that I had myself asked to be sent with this message, as I had been anxious to see once more the man who had given such friendly assistance to our ill-fated cruiser (here he interrupted me with the words: "*Ce n'est pas la fatalité—c'est de la diplomatie*"), who had rendered to myself and the other officers of the *Diana*, and eventually to the ship herself, so kindly services. If he had not succeeded in carrying out his intentions, it had not been his fault . . . (Here he made a deprecatory gesture with his hand, saying: "Hush, hush! if they were to hear us in Paris.")

When I had finally reported to him respectfully the official object of my visit, he asked me, with an enormous expenditure of amiable words, to thank the admiral for his message, which he had not dared to expect, as in time of war the causes for sailing were a secret, and if these were being confided to him, he could only be proud of the confidence placed in him, etc., etc. He added casually that he was in direct communication with the central authorities vtd Nhatrang, and intended to act in accordance with the declaration of neutrality which had been made at the commencement of the war, "until. ..." According to his opinion we were acting in a thoroughly correct manner, and the object of his presence was to protect the French territorial waters, chiefly against the Japanese, who had already violated neutral waters at Chemulpo and Chefoo.

"I know how to do it. *Qu'on tire, qu'on vise même sur mon croiseur.* Without firing a shot I will carry the French flag (*les couleurs de France*) up to the limits of our territorial waters."

Why do I love this Frenchman, who was an utter stranger to me, and why shall I never forget his acquaintance, which, measured by the clock in the ordinary manner, does not represent more than a few hours of conversation? Perhaps because for the outcast, the hunted creature, a word of sympathy said sincerely and honestly is so precious.

"*Enchanté de vous voir et au plaisir de vous revoir,*" he said as I took leave of him. "But if you should succeed, if . . . but I won't prophesy. Then our declaration, which (*Dieu soit béni*) we have not yet repudiated officially, will recover its full force, and your *Diana* will join up with your squadron. *Vous y reviendrez, mon commandant, hein?*"

"*Pour sur, mon Amiral,*" I replied, and gave his hand a hearty squeeze.

On April 18, at 8 a.m., we went out with the two battleship divisions, only taking the *Aurora* of the cruisers. We regulated our compasses and carried out a few evolutions. The real object of the whole manoeuvre was to cover the departure of our collier transports *Kieff, Kitai, Jupiter,* and *Knias Gortchakoff* for Saigon; we had pretty well emptied them, and they would only have been a burden if we had taken them any further with us. When after arrival at Saigon they had filled up with Cardiff coal from the local stores, they were to form floating depots for our cruisers, which they were to meet at certain rendezvous to be communicated by telegraph. The *Kuban*, *Terek*, and *Ural* were to escort them to the entrance of Saigon in case any of the Japanese armed merchant cruisers were to put in an appearance.

April 20.—We coaled. At 6.30 p.m. the *Kuban*, *Terek*, and *Ural* got back safely. They did not see anything of the enemy. The collier transports were at Saigon.

April 21.—About noon Jonquières came on board very sad. He declared that on the demand of the French Government (our allies) we had to quit their territorial waters at once. He could only give us a respite of twenty-four hours. What was to be done? The vanquished are always in the wrong. If Oyama had been annihilated at Mukden, we should now be living here "in peace and plenty," awaiting Nebogatoff's arrival.

Oh, this detachment of Nebogatoff! We know it now: the orders are that we are to await its arrival. "To complete our strategical dispositions," and—to trust to the Heavenly Hosts for the rest. If this detachment did not exist we should now be halfway to Vladivostok, whilst the Japanese had lost our trail. Whose fault is it? Theirs, those strategists, who had never yet heard the shriek of a hostile shell, who had even shrunk back in fear and trembling from the possibility of finding themselves in such a position! His, that K——'s who had whined: "Don't ask Rojëstvensky! Send off everything you possess! Don't lose a minute, or it might be too late! Out there every ship, every gun is of value!" Truly, every ship is of value out there, but not galoshes. Valuable, too, is every gun, but not a hole surrounded by iron. It was bitter and vile to have to write these lines in my diary; it is still more bitter to read them again.

"Well, and what did I tell you?" Lieutenant S—— asked me in connection with this. "K—— won't return!—He is not such a fool! Do you recollect my words? Sitting in a comfortable armchair he will criticise us. Well, that need not trouble us. The terrible thing is the want of principle. That public opinion is so blind to it is humiliating. I have kept up my correspondence with St Petersburg the whole time, I therefore know their innermost secrets. Do you know that K—— is sacrificing the whole of his convictions for 'filthy lucre'? All his tirades are a hymn of praise on (Admiral) Birileff's report of October (or November) 1904? The report in which our 'fighting admiral'[2] (where was it that he fought?) proves the possibility, even the necessity, of sending out reinforcements in the shape of all our old rubbish? K——'s opposition was not directed against the thing itself, but against the individual. Avelan (Minister of Marine) is overthrown, Birileff takes his place—and K—— rises. He has all his expenses and losses made good. . . . Ha, ha! . . . "

I never saw him so excited before.

April 22.—Throughout the night we were employed in clearing the *Tamboff* and *Mercury*, as well as the German colliers and the steamers which had come from Saigon with provisions.

At 1 p.m. (exactly at the expiration of the twenty-four hours' respite) the whole of the men-of-war went to sea. In the bay were only left the auxiliaries and the *Almas*,[3] which even the most rabid enemy could not consider as belonging to the class of fighting ships.

On board the *Suvoroff* a meeting of flag officers and captains took place.

In the Indian Ocean (on April 3 and 4 in the General Orders Nos. 170 and 171) the admiral had requested the commanding officers to point out daily to the officers and gun-layers how necessary it was on meeting the enemy to fire away the ammunition with deliberation and without haste; to explain to them that a senseless production of a hail of "overs" and "shorts" only pleased the enemy, and showed him how not to shoot; that loading should be very rapid, but laying had to be done with great care. But the best laying was useless if the sights were set wrong.

This order was to be read out in the presence of the officers and gun-layers, but captains were not merely to confine themselves to the reading out, but were to assemble the above daily for the purpose of making it clear to them, to inculcate the idea, in fact, of how important it was to fire deliberately and without haste. In repelling a torpedo attack at night it was necessary to keep calm, so as not to fire into our own ships. The cruisers which were covering the flanks of the fleet were not to fire inwards, except in the intervals between the ships and with the guns duly depressed. So long as a ship was under

2. In English in the Russian original.—Trans.
3. She had been built as a yacht for the viceroy.—Trans.

control she should never sheer out of the line, and thus cause confusion amongst the ships astern of her, as this was very favourable for the attacker. Only a damaged ship, which was no longer able to keep up the speed of the fleet, might fall out, and in such a case the ships as laid down in General Order No. 159 were to come to the assistance of the damaged ships.

(I have already mentioned this order in the introductory remarks to the report on the passage across the Indian Ocean.)

Amongst numerous other orders, that of April 15 (No. 178), which deals with the measures for repelling an attack by sub-marines, is worthy of notice, as well as No. 182 of April 16, in which directions were given in the event of considerable hostile forces appearing off Kamranh Bay:—

> ... I shall then go out ... with the main body, that is, with the two divisions of battleships, the cruisers *Zemtchug* and *Isumrud*, and the first destroyer division, as well as the cruiser division consisting of the *Oleg, Aurora*, and *Donskoi*. The positions of the *Zemtchug* and *Isumrud* and the destroyers are those given on the plan of battle formation in case of meeting the enemy at sea. Their task is to cover the flanks of the battle squadron against torpedo attacks. The position of the cruiser division is abreast of the centre of the battle squadron on its disengaged side, and out of range of the enemy.
>
> Their task is to attack the enemy's cruisers, should they attempt to work round the battle squadron, so as to get it between two fires; besides this they are to cover any battleships which may have been damaged by the enemy, or are otherwise in difficulties. In such a case the *Oleg* and *Aurora* may also join in the attack, if a suitable opponent be found; the *Donskoi*, however, which is not fast enough, must not allow herself to be drawn off by such an attack, and must always keep at such a distance from the battleships that she can at all times be covered by these and cannot be cut off from them.

For the defence of the fleet auxiliaries against an attack by hostile cruisers and destroyers the *Svetlana, Kuban, Terek, Ural, Dniepr*, and *Rion*, the second destroyer division, all picket-boats armed with torpedoes, and the *Almas*, were told off. On the main body going out, all ships except supply ships were to weigh. (This was necessary on account of Jonquières, so that he could report "they have all gone.")

The *Almas*, which was also to weigh, was to remain in the inner bay with the supply ships (Jonquières said "*they* can't fight"). All the above-named armed merchant cruisers were to go out into the outer roads, under the command of Captain Schein, the commander of the look-outs, and to extend in single line between Cape Kamranh and De la Prise Island. Between them and the shore would come the second destroyer division; the picket-boats were to take station on the north side of Tange Island.

> According to circumstances and the strength of the enemy, the commander of the look-outs (Captain Schein) will either await the enemy's approach, or he will stand out to sea to engage him outside the bay; in the latter case, however, he must manoeuvre so as to make it impossible for the enemy to get round him and to break through to the anchorage of the supply ships. Single ships which may attempt this will be attacked by the destroyers of the second division, which are to follow out the cruisers, and at the entrance of the bay itself the picket-boats will attack, taking care not to divulge their presence until the last moment.[4]
> All steamboats of the squadron will be hoisted out, and are to spread themselves at the entrance to the inner bay, where they are to watch for the possible appearance of submarines, which they are to attempt to destroy by ramming. If the adversary should reach the entrance to the inner anchorage, notwithstanding all these dispositions, the *Almas, Kamtchatka, Anadyr,* and Irtysh are to open fire on them. The three last named are to be ready to slip their cables and to advance for the purpose of attacking the enemy with the ram, if he should penetrate into the inner bay.

Besides this, in anticipation of possible damage from Whitehead torpedoes, the Fleet Constructor P—— and his colleagues K——, S——, and L—— were directed by General Order No. 183 of April 16:

> To inspect all water-tight compartments and wing passages, and to satisfy themselves that the manhole doors are tight, and that all other appliances for ensuring the buoyancy of the ships are

---

4. There could be no question here of a violation of neutrality on our side, for this violation would already be carried out by the enemy by the feet of his attack on the supply ships lying in the territorial waters of a neutral power.

in good working order.[5]

All these orders, as well as others which I have already mentioned, and which contained directions as to action to be taken if the enemy were sighted on different bearings, were discussed and elucidated at this meeting. Then the admiral communicated the hard decision of the French Government received through Jonquières.

> To judge how far they are justified in making such demands upon us is not our business. If the *Descartes* were an English cruiser the thing might be considered . . . in case of need we might employ force. The English could then assemble a squadron strong enough to force me to leave. But here it is the case of our allies. And they—'beg' us to leave. I shall keep at sea, outside territorial waters, in the neighbourhood of Kamranh Bay, where I am leaving behind the supply ships and non-fighting vessels. My orders are to wait for Nebogatoff. I shall wait. I will endeavour to keep up telegraphic communication with St Petersburg through Saigon. I shall wait until we have just coal enough left to take us to Vladivostok. If Nebogatoff has not arrived by then, there is no help for it—we go on without him. Forward! Always forward! Pray keep this always before you."

The admiral spoke without any excitement, in a cold, business-like tone, which was not usual in him. The effect was depressing.

And now began our wanderings on the coast of Annam, the slow, wasting away of that heterogeneous collection of ships called officially "the Second Squadron."

In these sad days I used up much space in my diary. I had much, too much leisure, which was relaxing in its effect. I am afraid the reader would find it difficult to follow my notes from day to day. I will endeavour to shorten my narrative as much as possible.

First for a chronological enumeration of the events of our wanderings.

As already stated, on April 22 all men-of-war went to sea before Jonquières' eyes; in the bay there only remained the fleet auxiliaries to which the draconic rules of neutrality could not, according to our view, be made to apply. Besides this the promise was given on our

---

5. About this time the Fleet Constructor P—— visited all ships by order of the admiral to see to the removal of all inflammable material from the upper parts of the ships, and to give, in connection with this, not only advice but orders in the name of the admiral.

side that so long as these vessels enjoyed the protection of France's neutrality, and so long as the squadron, which would be cruising outside territorial waters, was in communication with them, we would not carry out any cruiser operations, neither confiscate ships carrying contraband of war, nor reconnoitre in any way, so as to give no cause for saying that we were using the territorial waters of our ally as a base of operations. It is surely not possible to act more correctly? We certainly thought so—so did Jonquières and the local authorities. St Petersburg and Paris thought differently.

As I have no proofs, I will not decide whether the French were specially pressing in their demands, under the threats of England, or whether our authorities were specially ready to yield—anyhow, the decision was come to that no trace of any ship of war or commerce flying the Russian flag could be allowed to remain in French territorial waters. The news of this decision reached us on April 25, and next morning the entire armada went to sea. Jonquières, on board the *Descartes*, was a witness of this. He accompanied us up to the limits of the territorial waters, and watched us until we were out of sight; he then steamed to Saigon with the report that "the Russian squadron had left the coast of Annam in an easterly direction; its destination was not known."

To cruise about at sea waiting for Nebogatoff, to cruise about with the entire armada and at the same time to protect the auxiliaries when our own protection was highly problematical, was simply an impossibility. The admiral therefore came to the decision—the only one which was still open in our hopeless situation: as soon as the *Descartes*, which was going to Saigon, and the coast of Kamranh, from where one could follow our movements and report them by telegraph, were out of sight, we turned to the northward, and entered, the same evening, Van-Phong Bay. We went in with our full numbers, auxiliaries as well as warships, and anchored. It was a disagreeable place, but at least we were at anchor, and this was necessary, for though it did not permit any relaxation, it at least gave the weary crews a certain breathing time. Here, at least, the attack could only come from one side. But of that I will speak later.

The only advantage of this bay was the absence of telegraphic communication, and of any authorities. And yet—even that did not help us. Once a month a small coasting steamer comes here and buys up the catches of the local fishermen, and supplies them with all they need. Unfortunately, she reached Van-Phong Bay on the very day of our arrival, and on April 27 she sailed for Saigon, calling in at the various bays along her route.

It was therefore all up: as soon as she arrived the authorities would hasten to "request us to leave the bay."

As a matter of fact, the telegraph cables had by April 29 informed the world of our presence in Van-Phong Bay. The *administrateur*, who resided at Nhàtrang (20 miles as the crow flies South of Van-Phong) immediately received orders to transmit to us the request to leave within twenty four hours. The honoured *administrateur* was apparently of the same opinion as Jonquières, but as regarded the ethical aspect of his duties he took the same view as the "Major" of Angra Pequeña, who will be in the reader's recollection. Not being prepared to undertake a sea voyage (as not suitable to his nature), he brought us his stern ultimatum by the land route, and owing to defective means of communication he only reached the *Suvoroff* on May 2, utterly exhausted, as he had travelled night and day in the execution of his duty;

There was nothing to be done. On May 3 we once more went to sea with the entire "*armada*" before witnesses, Jonquières having been sent from Saigon, but no longer in the *Descartes* but in the *Guichen*. Again he was able to report that we "had sailed in an easterly direction, destination unknown." However, he informed us he would cruise for fully twenty-four hours along the coast to see if by chance we were to enter another bay not joined up by cable.

On May 4 we returned to our old anchorage. It was all so hateful (but of that later), that we did not care what happened; they were welcome to accuse us of having broken our word.

On May 5 the "Master of the Fleet," Colonel F——, and I started off in the steamer *Russ*[6] to inspect the neighbouring bays which might be suitable as anchorages, but which were outside telegraphic communication, and so formed that passing steamers could not see the squadron from seaward, and would, therefore, not be able to give away the secret of our asylum.

We visited Vung Ro and Port Dayotte; the latter was very suitable. The only drawback was that it was badly surveyed and charted. There might be unpleasant surprises in the shape of coral reefs rising up

---

6. By an order from the Admiralty, which reached us at Madagascar, my position in the squadron had been "legalised" by appointing me navigating officer on the admiral's staff—a mere matter of form, seeing that there were already three navigating officers on the staff, who were all senior to me and more experienced.

sheer from the bottom. We hesitated before going there in view of the news received from Nhàtrang (to which place a destroyer had been sent, as it were, coming from sea) that a typhoon was approaching and expected to pass in our neighbourhood. It was therefore a case of *force majeure.* The right of taking refuge on the approach of a typhoon cannot be curtailed by any supplementary paragraphs of the declaration of neutrality. In fact, a heavy swell was already coming into the bay, and the cruisers on look-out had a bad time of it, although the typhoon passed some way off, much further north.

Still, our present anchorage was openly in view of all passing vessels. Although the local authorities were full of benevolence towards us, we received, on May 7, the confidential information that our return to the neutral waters of Annam was being discussed in every newspaper in the world. Japan, it was said, was incensed, and making protests; England was supporting her energetically; Paris, totally intimidated, was launching thunderbolts against the local authorities; St Petersburg, still more intimidated, had said: "It is not my fault! The horse is no longer under my control! I am powerless, and know nothing. Rojëstvensky is acting independently. This is his affair. Fetch him out if you like—we wash our hands in innocence."

At the same time—"strategic dispositions . . ." Nikolai Ugodnic . . . . . Seraphim Sarovsky . . .

How hard this was to bear! How heavy was one's heart!

On May 8 we despatched two pairs of cruisers—*Rion* and *Zemtchug,* and *Dniepr* and *Isumrud*—to meet Nebogatoff, as it became known that he had passed Singapore at 4 a.m. on May 5.

On the morning of May 9 we again went to sea. Jonquières in the *Guichen* again watched our departure.

Oh, Heavens! Why was this disgrace brought on us? We were not allowed to rest anywhere. We were hunted out of every place. The veritable "wandering Jews."

Jonquières, our sincere well-wisher, looked on, then cruised up the coast so as to be able to report at the end of twenty-four hours: "They sailed to the eastward—destination unknown."

During the forenoon our scouts came back without bringing any news of Nebogatoff.

About 11 a.m. we took in a wireless message from the *Monomak* which was reporting something to the *Nikolai.*[7] About noon we were

---

7. Two of Nebogatoff's ships, the latter his flagship.—Trans.

in wireless touch, and at 3 p.m. we joined hands with the "flatirons and galoshes," which bore the sonorous title of "Special Division of the Second Squadron of the Pacific Fleet." Of the impression produced by this meeting I will speak later. Here I only give the chronological narrative of events.

At 5 p.m. Nebogatoff came on board the *Suvoroff*. He discussed the further dispositions with the commander-in chief. We were ready, but Nebogatoff had to coal, overhaul his ships after the long sea passage, to study the numerous orders which had been issued in the squadron in the event of meeting the enemy. He was directed to the secluded Port Dayotte, already mentioned. He went there. We remained at sea.

On May 11 we tried to fill up with coal, having expended much of it. But we could not manage it, the swell being too heavy. We therefore decided to make for Van-Phong. We were in hopes of being able to fill up with coal before we were requested to leave. We worked like mad all night. Early on May 12 we left the bay. It had all been done in one night. Without boasting one may well say that it was not a bad performance.

Cruising about at sea we waited until May 14, on which day Nebogatoff's division rejoined after having replenished stores and prepared generally for a continuation of the voyage.

At last! Heaven be praised!

It would appear that this was the unanimous sentiment.

Having now described the events, I will endeavour to indicate briefly the general feeling on board the ships at the time of their involuntary wanderings on the coast of Annam.

What I had dreaded most was that the chord which had been stretched too taut would not hold out, and if it did not snap, would at least give. This dread proved to be well founded on the very day on which it became known that we had "received orders to wait."

One had the feeling that after working at such extreme pressure the whole organisation only just pieced together would collapse, and that in the place of the squadron welded together at last we should once more have only an "*armada*" to deal with. We had exhausted our strength. This was what we felt. Of course I may be met with the reply: Do not judge others by your own feelings; give us facts for the statement that the orders to wait for Nebogatoff caused all the remaining energy to evaporate; prove to us that the exhortation to trust above all in the Heavenly Hosts instead of raising our spirits depressed them.

Very well, here are some facts.

Even on April 16 the admiral found himself obliged to modify the dispositions he had made for the safety of the squadron at anchor—not with a view of protecting it still more efficiently, but simply because it had been proved to be impossible to adhere to the very suitable arrangements he had made.[8] It turned out that the cruisers, destroyers, and picket-boats could not be made to carry out their duties in two reliefs only. The captains reported that the crews were exhausted, and that there were frequent breakdowns of machinery, chiefly due to carelessness. And only a week ago they did this work unflinchingly and declared their readiness to continue it until Vladivostok was reached!

On April 17 (General Order No. 204) the number of destroyers to be sent out on patrol duty were reduced to two.

It would appear that even Admiral Rojëstvensky had now realised that the dictionary contained the word "impossible."

It is difficult to give the reader a clear picture of the mood which prevailed among the men of the squadron. It seemed to me that it might perhaps be expressed as follows: We are not allowed to carry out now at once what we are able to do; by the time we get permission for it, it will be too late. Those at the other end of the old world, blinded by their own conceit, want to direct us, believing themselves to be better able to judge than we, who have penetrated to the very borders of the Land of the Rising Sun. And we are powerless in the face of their decision! But our duty as sailors comes first. When the order comes we shall not hesitate to stake our lives. We are without fear, but also without hope. It is false to say that fate is blind; fate sees very clearly, and when it compares our "*armada*" with the battle fleets of Japan, it will come to its decision very speedily.

All were so weary that they began to lose heart, and were only kept up by the strong will and the firm determination of a few individuals.

On April 20 (in General Order No. 194) the admiral said:—

The strenuous work of eight months spent in perfecting the wireless telegraphy in the squadron ended with the following results: Yesterday, April 19, whilst the battleships were at sea, a special order was to be transmitted to the commander of the fleet auxiliaries. The flagship called up the *Almas*, then 15 miles

8. General Order No, 201 of April 16.

off, for one and a half hours, without getting any response; then the flagship called up the Oleg, also without any result. Apparently the *Zemtchug, Isumrud, Dniepr,* and *Rion* were equally inattentive as regarded the wireless service, as they should have informed the ship concerned by signal that she was being called up, and have reported the fact that her apparatus was not working properly. Today, at 2 p.m., there should have been wireless messages from the cruisers *Kuban, Terek,* and *Ural,* which were approaching the squadron.

The flagship did her utmost to take in the prearranged messages, but got nothing. This condition of the *Suvoroff's* apparatus is a very sad fact, but still more sad is the fact that not a single apparatus in the whole squadron took in the *Kuban's* message and communicated it to the flagship. Today the *Suvoroff* tried in vain to call up the *Rion,* which was out patrolling. Is the captain of the *Rion* quite clear in his mind as to how useless his patrolling service is if his wireless apparatus is not in working order?—Admirals and captains! it is time to take the most energetic steps!

Of course the admiral was not only justified, but in duty bound to issue orders like these, but did he himself believe in the possibility of his demands being complied with? That is the question. I do not think he did.

Again insubordination showed itself, discontent began to break out over the most trifling matters; offences against discipline (which had almost ceased for a time) became more frequent. Whilst clearing steamers which had brought provisions from Saigon, there were scenes which bordered on open robbery; the working parties stove in wine-casks, broke open cases with liquor, became drunk and uproarious, and insulted even the officers who tried to restore order.

Notwithstanding the original assurance that the word "impossible" did not exist, its effect became more and more apparent.

On April 20 the admiral said in General Order No. 196:

So as to ease the work of the destroyers, and to give the captains the possibility of keeping their vessels in a complete state of readiness, two patrol-boats will be withdrawn. . . . Yesterday a destroyer on patrol duty lost an anchor; that means that she was either at anchor, or had the intention of anchoring, which is quite incompatible with the duty confided to her. . . .

With the commencement of our "wanderings" matters went downhill at a daily increasing rate.

By day we lay with engines stopped and watched the horizon unceasingly (for any smoke which might appear), as well as the surface of the water in our vicinity (for the periscope of any submarine which might be approaching). At night we steamed at 3 knots, a speed just sufficient to maintain our formation, and in the event of a torpedo attack we were to increase to the speed necessary for handling the squadron. Throughout the twenty-four hours the personnel was kept at the highest tension; watchfulness, resourcefulness, coolness, resolution—all these were demanded. And that from men who had already done six months' cruising through the tropics under war conditions.

The exercises were continued automatically. I remember it very distinctly, but in my diary I cannot find any notes on the subject. They were lifeless exercises, carried out according to rule, as a part of the weekly routine of drills. The war game, which had been so engrossing, the solving of tactical problems in the mess (on paper), which had taken place throughout the voyage without interruption, tacitly came to an end. The naval handbooks, the essays on questions of naval tactics and strategy, works on naval history, which were formally so much in request that it was hardly possible to get hold of them, now remained untouched.

In their free time the officers read chiefly—do you know what?—cheap novels of the fantastic kind. . . . Especial favourites were the publications of Fr, Kryanovsky (Rochester), which were written in the manner of spiritist revelations. How pleasant it was to forget, even if only for a while, the realities of life, and to allow oneself to be engrossed by the wonders of the *Magician,* of the *Elixir of Life,* of *Life in Mars,* of the *Adventures of the Hungarian Count* (I forget his name)—a *Vampire,* etc., etc. Laugh if you will and can, but facts remain facts; it shows that such an existence will reduce grown up and thoroughly sensible men to a condition in which they have only one desire, one idea: to get away as far as possible from the actualities of their surroundings.

In the midst of this deep demoralisation, the one thought shone out ever like a beacon: The admiral is always the same! He's not weary! He'll get us along! He'll pull it off! He still has confidence!

This our people believed. But were they right? Could they say that they had searched the innermost recesses of his heart—that they knew him? They were at least willing to believe it, and they placed their fate completely into his keeping.

It was like a half black, half red mist, a fever, this death-struggle of the squadron, as 1 have called it before. From time to time (it seemed to me and not to me alone) that even the admiral gave himself up to that fatal power of attraction of the open abyss. . . . Only shut the eyes . . . . a false step . . . . and the end is reached. How good! And over so quickly!!. . . .

Can one find any other explanation for these night alarms—these exercises "in repelling torpedo attack at night"—which used to be suddenly carried out on his personal order in the depth of the dark nights, when we were crawling along the coast of Annam at 3 knots? The searchlights of the squadron produced an illumination which could be seen at least 50 miles off, and which would indicate our presence and whereabouts very clearly to the enemy, if any happened to be in the neighbourhood.

"What is the matter with him? Surely this is provoking our fate!" I said to Lieutenant S———. "For all one can tell the Japanese destroyers will find us by this illumination. In fact, we are showing them the way ourselves. We are regularly calling them up!"

"And what if we do call them up?" he replied, giving my hand a nervous squeeze. "How the end comes is a matter of indifference. Possibly it is better so. . . . They won't sink the entire squadron. Something will be left over. Ha, ha, ha! but the hope of beating and annihilating the enemy with the kind assistance of the Heavenly Hosts will now have to be given up whether we like it or not. But no! It is quite clear—the Japanese are acting deliberately. They are not going to trouble themselves about trifles; they go in for the whole. They only deal 'wholesale.'"

One should not criticise the victor. Yet I venture to maintain that if this "wholesale" business had not succeeded, if a continuation of bad weather (such as seemed quite probable at this time of the year) had prevented a decisive battle from being fought in the Sea of Japan, or if fog (also very frequent during this season) had enabled the squadron to get through to Vladivostok, undetected by the enemy, Admiral Togo would have been severely reproached for not having made use of the time of our wanderings on the coast of Annam for torpedo attacks, for not having even made an attempt in that direction.

What considerations were, in truth, hampering at that moment the famous spirit of enterprise of the Japanese?

I could have wished that our patent strategists at headquarters, who were so fond of prophesying after the event, had solved this riddle.

These strategists accused Admiral Rojëstvensky of neglecting his scouting service. I will not give an opinion on this point, which History alone will be able to answer without bias, provided those who write it have had access to all the secret archives. Were these gentlemen so badly informed, or were they deliberately deceiving public opinion so as to throw the whole responsibility on Admiral Rojëstvensky, whilst they, the instigators, were cleared? I cannot judge of this with certainty. I only wish to point out that in accordance with the promise we had given, we were unable to carry out cruiser operations during our stay off the coast of Annam. Paris feared above all that the suspicion, or even a shadow of one, might arise that we were using the territorial waters of France as a base of operations. From St Petersburg *we* received directions, the *French* the assurance, that nothing of the kind was permissible. We had to obtain all our intelligence by means of secret agents who were sent here and there in specially chartered steamers. We did all that was possible.

I may say not without results. We found out for certain that during the ten days or fortnight preceding our arrival in Japanese waters, Japanese cruisers, accompanied by destroyers, had carefully searched the bays along the coast, not only of Annam, Tongkin, and Cambodia, but also of Siam. The uninhabited, almost virgin islands of the Gulf of Siam, amongst which there are numerous suitable anchorages, were also visited by them. After that they seemed to have disappeared off the face of the earth. A vague trace of them was discovered not far from Singapore, in the Rio Straits, off the coast of Borneo. They were probably waiting for us in the Straits of Sunda.

After our successful passage of the Straits of Malacca, they commenced moving about again in various directions. They went to North Borneo, and in the first days of April they assembled in the roads of Mopo (Pescadores), the only anchorage belonging to them in these waters, as there is not a single bay in Formosa suitable as an anchorage for a large fleet. It became known that at Mopo troops and siege artillery had been landed, fortifications thrown up in haste, the approaches to the anchorages blocked by mines—in a word, that a temporary base had been created there. Then again all news ceased—naturally not without the friendly co-operation of that good ally, England, who has nearly all cables in the East in her hands.

It was once more as if they had disappeared into space. They only reappeared within the ken of our agents after Nebogatoff had passed Singapore. Were they by chance just a little too cunning on this occasion? As regarded us, everything spoke in favour of our going through the Straits of Sunda; diplomatic negotiations with the Dutch Government, the despatch of the colliers to Lampong, etc., etc.—all this, though done in secret, could not remain unknown to the world at large, how much less to the Japanese. The admiral had not communicated his intention to go through the Straits of Malacca to any one, not even in the most secret cipher telegrams. The secret was preserved. Nebogatoff, on the other hand, reported, on starting from Jibuti, to the Naval General Staff (of course in secret cipher) that he intended going through the Straits of Malacca.

The result was that all newspapers (in the English colonies) reported the route with certainty, and even competed with one another in their calculations as to the precise date on which he would pass Singapore. Possibly a *pari-mutuel* was set up for the purpose. These noisy manifestations looked so much like a challenge, that the Japanese were justified in not attaching any credence to them. They argued quite correctly. Rojëstvensky himself spread the report that he was going through the Straits of Sunda, but went through the Straits of Malacca. Nebogatoff, in trying to reproduce the same trick (but less skilfully), almost openly advertises this intention of going through the Straits of Malacca, but naturally he will go through the Straits of Sunda. There we shall find him. The calculation in itself was quite correct. But— even the cleverest can make a mistake. No doubt in this case Nebogatoff had been one too many for them.

These two failures, one close on the other, seemed to hit the Japanese hard. After Nebogatoff had passed Singapore they hurriedly showed themselves once more at the Pescadores, but did not remain there long, gave up the whole business, and made off to the northward. The latest information received by us placed their main body, almost their entire fleet, at Masampo (25 miles to the westward of Fusan—an excellent anchorage). A certain number of destroyers, as well as the armed merchant cruisers *Hong-Kong* and *Nippon*, carrying submarines, were in southern waters. As to that our information was such as not to admit of any doubt. And yet they undertook nothing against us, who were playing the "wandering Jew" on the coast of Annam. Why? I do not think that we shall find out the true causes of their decision for a good while. But if it is permissible to admit that they really believed in our strength, that they dreaded us. . . . How singularly favourable was that moment for concluding an honourable peace! By whose fault was it missed? History will answer this.

It was so easy at that time to damage our squadron, if not to annihilate it completely.

As I have already said, with the commencement of our wanderings matters went downhill at a daily increasing rate. In proof of this I propose giving extracts from some of the general orders of the time.

Last night (General Order No. 219 of May 3), when the squadron was steaming at a speed which was half what the boilers in use were capable of developing, the cruiser *Admiral Nakimoff* and the battleships *Imperator Alexander III, Orel,* and *Sissoi Veliki,* increased their distances from the next ahead to twice, even three times those prescribed. I request the captains of these ships not to overlook the fact that by acting thus in action they might place the whole of the ships astern of them in a very awkward predicament.

Yesterday during the night alarm the searchlights of the battleships *Sissoi Veliki* and *Navarin,* as well as of the cruiser *Admiral Nakimoff,* did not project any beams of light, but merely a kind of luminous mist, which enveloped the whole neighbourhood. This shows how little attention is paid towards keeping the searchlights in working order and adjusting them properly. The entire cruiser division continued to work their searchlights, and consequently to fire their guns, after the flagship had made the signal to cease fire and to extinguish searchlights, by raising one of her beams vertically. In this way one usually fires on one's own ships."

On May 5 (General Order No. 223 of May 6) the *Kuban,* whilst on patrolling duties, sighted two destroyers, which, on discovering the cruiser, hoisted French colours and steamed away at high speed. The captain of the *Kuban* did not consider it necessary to make sure whether they were really French destroyers. On the evening of the same day the captain of the cruiser *Dimitri Donskoi,* on the same service, reported by wireless that he could see a searchlight beam to seaward of him; as a matter of fact, searchlight beams were observed from the flagship in the bay, over the high land, against the sky, and the direction in which these were seen coincided with the bearing of the station of the look-out cruiser *Ural*.

From this it can be concluded that the *Ural* (unless she was working her searchlights herself) was in a better position to observe these strange lights than the flagship, and also the *Donskoi*, as she was nearer to the source of the light than the latter. The captain of the *Donskoi* did not make up his mind to ask the Ural whether she could see the light in question, and the *Ural* herself made no report on it by wireless. When the flagship ordered the *Donskoi* to enquire from the *Ural*, the latter never took in the call of the *Donskoi*. The *Donskoi* did not think of using the searchlight for communicating with the *Ural*, but left her station for the purpose.

After she had thus moved away she was no longer able to take in the flagship's wireless messages, and thus ceased to act as linking ship between the *Ural*, the picket-boats, the destroyers, and the squadron at anchor. It therefore took nine hours (from 8 p.m. to 5 a.m.) to get an answer from the *Ural*. The impression produced by this manner of carrying out the look-out and patrol service by our cruisers on May 5 is very bad; it proves that there is a complete lack of initiative, and that there is no just appreciation of the situation and its requirements. What makes this bad impression still worse is the fact that on May 5 there was no chance combination of unfavourable conditions. Incidents like the above are of almost daily occurrence.

Thus the admiral wrote, and thus he unquestionably had to write in his General Orders. But in this case I consider it to be my duty to say a word in defence of the personnel.

"Lack of initiative, of appreciation of the situation, of knowledge"— all these were facts. But whence could any one have obtained all this if he had not been trained up to it? In individual cases, though never for any length of time, it had been possible to make up for this lack of previous training, to a certain extent, by high enthusiasm, by the personnel being made to exert itself to its utmost—often to an excessive, or even senseless, extent. But human power of endurance is not unlimited. In ancient times, when firearms were still unknown, the bow was only bent just before battle, and afterwards it was eased up again, allowed to rest. But in the Second Squadron there was no rest.

Those high spirits which prevailed in the early days after our arrival in Madagascar vanished again during that two months' stay in Nossi-Bé.

A second, if possible still more powerful wave of enthusiasm, which was the result of the successful passage of the Straits of Malacca, was also not utilised.

If I may use a simile, I would say that it was perhaps still higher and more steep than the first one, but precisely on account of its strength it melted away still faster, still easier. It melted away as it met with no obstacle against which it could have hurled itself with all its might; it melted away like every wave which, after having lost its crest of foam, becomes merged in the gentle, powerless, dead swell. . . .

CHAPTER 6

Hurried Preparations for the Last Stage

The junction with the division of Nebogatoff's "autosinkers" (as they were called by the men who were not serving in them) did not give rise to any fresh enthusiasm, gave no new impulse towards a victory of the mind over physical weariness. In my diary, this meeting is described in great detail. It was solemn. We were moved almost to tears. Every one was rejoicing, jubilating. But what was the cause of it? "We are stronger now, we can now hope to destroy the enemy." Was it that? No, not that! Thus thought, perhaps, those heroes who sat in comfortable armchairs at St Petersburg, and whose sea-cruises were limited to the stretch of water between that place and Cronstadt.

It was not this, that the squadron concerned itself with. No; at 3 p.m. on May 9, when Nebogatoff's division joined up with us, every one rejoiced and congratulated his neighbour, but . . . not over this addition to our strength, these increased chances of smashing the enemy, but because of the prospects of a speedy termination of that enervating period of waiting.

"At last!"

If in place of Nebogatoff's ships the Japanese Fleet had hove in sight, we might perhaps have received it with no less, if with no greater joy.

That was the mood we were in.

The admiral issued a general order, drawn up by himself, which was intended duly to appreciate the happy event, and to raise our spirits. But how artificial, how insincere this order (No. 229 of May 9) read; how little did it resemble those fiery words flung out at Vigo, when a collision with the twenty-eight English battleships seemed imminent, or that stirring speech which he made on Christmas Day off the coast of Madagascar!

During the four days which Nebogatoff spent in seclusion in Port Dayotte, whilst we cruised about at sea, he not only had to replenish his ships with coal, provisions, etc., but he also had (and that was the chief thing) to make himself acquainted with the general orders and circulars which had been issued in the squadron and which contained various directions for assuming battle formation, and making preparations for action, according to the bearing on which the enemy was sighted; and, further, the orders as to the employment of the armament, etc., etc. The whole of this literature was supplemented by the orders which had been previously worked out and had now been issued, in which was laid down the part the "Third Division of Battleships" (as Nebogatoff's division was now called) was to play. The *Monomak* was removed from his command to that of the cruiser division under Admiral Enquist.

I need hardly mention that as a matter of course, on the same day, May 9, complete sets of all these documents, which had been prepared beforehand, were handed not only to Admiral Nebogatoff and his staff, but to the captains, seconds-in-command, and the officers' messes of the newly joined ships. It was out of the question to assemble these officers and to explain all this verbally to them, as there was no time. Above all, it was imperative to fill up these ships with coal, stores, and provisions, for Jonquières might arrive any moment and ask the division to leave, however sincere his regrets might be. Indeed, this actually happened.

On May 14 the *Guichen* was a witness of our final departure from these waters; she hove in sight (intentionally or accidently) just at the moment when the whole *armada* was already outside and taking up its cruising formation. Our sincere friend was thus relieved from the disagreeable necessity of "having the honour to request." On the contrary, he was able (with all his heart, I believe) to send us by wireless his best wishes for a good passage and every success in the battle which was before us.

There could be no question of carrying out any tactical exercises or target practice in conjunction with the "Third Division of Battleships." As regarded the latter, there were "firstly no shell. . . ." As regarded the former, it was intended to carry them out *en route,* if opportunity arose. It was too late for lessons; we might have to go into action tomorrow, if not today.

A few words about the general state of health (a strange subject!). Thanks to the steps which had been taken to carry through both the best system of feeding and of living generally, and as to which the admiral had given stringent orders, the general state of health in the fleet was satisfactory. Ten thousand men shut up in iron boxes, six months in the tropics—and no epidemic of any kind. Of one malady, however, I have spoken—exhaustion due to over-exertion. Of this there were pretty frequent cases. I have no statistics at hand, and can, therefore, only cite examples such as came under my personal observation on board the *Suvoroff*, as I do not trust my memory concerning information from other ships, as to which my diary does not contain any notes.

The admiral, as I have already related, was taken ill in Madagascar. He spent two days in bed, then he got up again, not so much thanks to the doctor's treatment as to his own strength of will; all the same, he generally looked ill, and on the days immediately following upon periods of special excitement or exertion he dragged his bad leg very markedly. Outwardly he was literally reduced to skin and bones. The chief of the staff had a slight infusion of blood into the brain during the passage to Annam, resulting in partial paralysis, which, however, did not prevent him from doing his work. (I am afraid the doctors will accuse me of using inaccurate terms.

I beg their pardon. I did not enter in my diary the Latin terms which those of the flagship gave me.) The "Master of the Fleet"(Colonel F——) latterly only partook of liquid, or soft, carefully chopped-up food. He was personally convinced, from his own observations, that he was suffering from cancer in the alimentary canal; the doctors assured him in the course of friendly talks that it was a case of aneurism, which produces the effect of a swelling and contracting of the alimentary canal.[1]

The second flag lieutenant, S—— (not to be confounded with the senior flag-lieutenant, also S——, my friend), whose constitution was generally feeble, was obliged, on the doctor's advice, to take refuge in opium and morphia. So far as I recollect, the staff torpedo officer. Lieutenant L——, was in a similar condition.

---

1. The same illness attacked the senior torpedo lieutenant, B——, a veteran of previous wars, who had been seriously wounded during the attack on the Taku forts.

Flag Lieutenant N——,[2] who was outwardly in robust health, also went to the doctor, and when asked: "What is the stuff you are always swallowing?" replied: "The local doctor prescribed me something containing bromide to calm my nerves and to counteract my sleeplessness." Of the ship's officers, a good third were patients, and they were all suffering from illnesses with such learned Latin names, that, since I did not at once enter them in my diary, I must decline trusting to my memory.

An astounding capacity for living—if I may use the expression—was exhibited by the captain of the *Suvoroff*, Captain J——. Firmly convinced that we were going to our certain destruction, he closed his eyes to the future, after he had once irrevocably decided this question, and lived entirely for the present, wholly absorbed in the care for his ship and her crew.

How is it all to end? Whether we are going to capsize or not, or be killed by shell, torpedo, poisonous gases, wounds, by suffocation or drowning?—that all depends on God Almighty—and the 'superior authorities.' We shall certainly do our duty. No doubt the whole fire will be concentrated on the *Suvoroff*. It will be simply a hail of shot. But I have already given all necessary orders, and impressed upon the commander and the more senior lieutenants who would succeed to the command in turn after the captain had fallen, that they are always to bear this in mind: If the *Suvoroff* is nearing her end, let her go down, but before that transfer the admiral to an undamaged ship. Without 'him' it will be all up. I am only afraid of one thing—he will expose himself to the fire, and they will kill him with the first shot. Then all will be lost.

Thus spoke the man whom, notwithstanding the many accusations which have been brought against him as regards his carelessness, even frivolity, I cannot help looking upon as the type of the ideal fighting sailor.

A very serious loss for the fleet was the death of Admiral Fölkersam, a cultured, experienced, and active seaman, and—what was still more important—a friend, loyal comrade, and co-operator of Admiral Rojëstvensky, whose views he fully shared.

He was still alive at the time of our junction with Nebogatoff, but his condition was already hopeless and his days were numbered.

2. Apparently a third.—Trans.

He was not called upon to suffer any longer. Fate was kinder to him than to his elder colleague. He did not witness the collapse of the squadron, and, his coffin, placed under the ship's Holy Image (on the upper deck amidships), now rests on the bottom of the Sea of Japan together with the battleship *Ossliabia*, perhaps still flying his flag, which had been kept up after his death, to avoid depressing the spirits in the fleet by striking it.

During our "wanderings" (which, by the way, cost us 20,000 tons of coal, not to mention the expenditure of lubricating and other material) in the long hours of enforced idleness, which was so relaxing. Lieutenant S—— and I mostly foregathered. In the situation in which we found ourselves we both recalled with pleasure the half-forgotten time of our common experiences during the five years we sat on the same bench at the Naval College. In the course of these talks with him I learnt much which up to then had been unknown to me, since I was considered an "outsider" by the staff. Possibly I learnt even more than other "real" members of the staff, for amongst these S—— undoubtedly counted as the one who was the most initiated.

Naturally I am not even now able to make public much of this, since at the time of writing it might have some influence on the march of events; on the other hand, it seems to me absolutely necessary to place on record the truth as regards certain events, about which our "strategists," who give themselves the appearance of well-informed men, have already written so much nonsense. But this is only possible on the supposition that mere office secrets are disregarded so far as they refer exclusively to the past, and so far as their divulgence now does no harm.

I heard now that, according to the admiral's original plan (at the time when the Second Squadron was being got together), the objective of its voyage was the freeing of the First Squadron from its blockade (in Port Arthur), and then co-operating with it. Moreover, it had been decided, since the Japanese had grossly violated the neutrality of Chifoo at the time of the *Reshitelny* affair,[3] and had already, previously to that, acted in a similar objectionable manner at Chemulpo, not to pay any attention to the neutrality of these ports, and to enter into communication with Port Arthur, whilst using Chifoo as a base. The distance between these two ports is 70 miles, and therefore the fleet auxiliaries of all kinds would have been protected in the latter place by

---

3. *I.e.,* the capture of that destroyer.—Trans.

the fleet, which would be operating in so restricted an area.

For the command of the sea, the Japanese, with four battleships and eight armoured cruisers at their disposal, would have had to fight the decisive battle with the First Squadron—six battleships and one armoured cruiser—and with the Second Squadron—seven battleships (*Nakimoff* and *Donskoi* were not counted in)—whilst the co-operation of the Vladivostok cruisers was perfectly feasible. The issue of the whole war would have depended on the result of this battle.

If the Japanese (which, however, was not very probable) had decided not to engage in such a game of *va-banque*, and had retired, even only temporarily, into their ports, then the siege of Port Arthur, also perhaps only temporarily, would have been raised, the place could have been supplied with all it required, and then our combined fleet would have acted in accordance with the progress of the land operations— that is, would either have assisted at the liberation of Port Arthur, in which besieged and besiegers would have exchanged parts, or would have left Port Arthur, once more fully supplied with provisions and munition of war, to itself, and proceeded to Vladivostok. In this case it would have had to base itself on the latter place and to endeavour to bring about a decisive battle, which would give it the command of the sea and cut off the Japanese Army from its home ports.

Under our institutions this plan, which was kept secret from the officers of the Second Squadron, could hardly remain unknown to the unfriendly foreign powers. Did not the new supplementary rules to the declaration of neutrality, the celebrated "Hull-affair" and all the noise which was made on its account, look like desperate efforts to prevent this plan from being executed? This question can be answered in the affirmative almost with certainty.

With the fall of Port Arthur (and even before), with the destruction of the First Squadron of the Pacific Fleet, this plan collapsed of itself. The admiral worked out a second one, in his view the only practical one—*viz.*, an immediate advance with picked ships, with Vladivostok as the objective, counting upon the temporary weakening of the Japanese Fleet, due to the exigencies of a prolonged war. Once there, since the available forces would be insufficient for a decisive blow, their object would be to open a guerilla war against the enemy's lines of communication. For this task our forces would suffice.

This proposal was not approved of. It was decided to send out reinforcements to the Second Squadron, which were intended to make up for the failure of the co-operation of the First Squadron, and the *"armada"* retained its original task of (with the help of God) obtaining the command of the sea, that is, of beating the Japanese in a decisive battle. In vain the admiral reported quite openly and in so many words that he looked upon the junction of these old, defective ships with his squadron as a "burden"; that with the forces at his disposal (even with the co-operation of the "burden") he had *no prospect* of obtaining the command of the sea. The St Petersburg' strategists found that, based on a careful calculation of the sum total which was made up of the "coefficients of fighting value "of the several ships of the squadron, the latter already possessed "prospects of success," but that if a certain addition were made to this sum, the mere "prospect" would be turned into "certainty."

It is difficult to say whether the Japanese were informed of these negotiations. Perhaps they were. But perhaps also, after having received reliable information as to the real fighting value of the "Third Squadron," which the Baltic yards were able to put together, they read with sincere pleasure K——'s inspiring articles, which led astray not only Russian society, but what was more, the persons who held the power in their hands. Be this as it may, it is certainly worthy of note that the Japanese took no steps whatever, either directly or indirectly, through their good ally (England) to shorten our stay in Nossi-Bé, which lasted over two months.

At that time the admiral also received purely business instructions: To bear in mind that during his presence at Vladivostok he should not make too great demands on its slender resources both as regarded stores and means of repair (they had not had time to equip the place properly when the war broke out); and also that he should not count too much on the Siberian railway, "which only managed to satisfy the requirements of the army with difficulty." In other words, he was not only required to beat the enemy and force his way through Vladivostok, but he was given yet another task: If he should really have no prospects of obtaining the command of the sea, he was, in forcing his way through to Vladivostok, to bring with him all the means of carrying on guerilla warfare.

I have already said that the admiral did what he could—he submitted the plans which he considered to be the only ones capable of execution, and declared quite openly that he saw no chance of accomplishing the task, set him—of obtaining the command of the sea. None the less, he was ordered to carry out this task, with the help of— God, and the reinforcements which were to be sent to him. After that how was it possible not to be successful?

It is true, a desperate effort was made to get away from the "burden." But alas! it miscarried. This is really an occasion on which one may with a clear conscience call the telegraph a damnable invention.

While we were suffering and were being used up, our strategists at St Petersburg were working out plans in the seclusion of their offices. Seamen only as regarded their uniform (which somehow had been conferred on them), they unhesitatingly threw dust in the eyes of people who had no conception of naval war, drafted plans of operations and opened up perspectives which had no other basis than the conceit of their authors and the simple faith of their audience.

To lead a fleet of auxiliaries past Japan, to set the squadron the task not only of being ready at any moment for the decisive battle with a superior enemy, but also of convoying the above auxiliaries, was stupid to such a degree, that even the worst strategists should not have dared to suggest such a thing. Apparently there was a way out of this and they chose it too with joy; they spoke of it then and also after the war. It consisted in this: At some suitable spot we were to establish ourselves, create a temporary base, leave behind there all auxiliaries and other superfluities, and, clear of these *impedimenta*, endeavour to bring about the decisive battle; in the event of success—even only the clearing of the way for a short time—this was to be utilised to push through to Vladivostok with the entire "*armada*"; in the case of failure we were to fall back on the temporary base, replenish with stores and—act according to circumstances.

I do not propose to enumerate here all the plans of these freshwater sailors, which included such ridiculous ones as the one referring to Petropavlovsk (Kamtchatka), which is cut off from the rest of the world not only as regards telegraph, post, and means of communication, but also as regards climatic conditions (there are constant fogs there in spring), or the seizing of the Bonin Islands, where there is no suitable anchorage for even a small number of ships, leave alone an entire fleet. These makers of projects amply proved their gross ignorance as regarded sailing directions and their incapacity as regards chart reading. It became quite clear that when deciding upon questions of naval war they had obtained their knowledge from the text-book of geography by Smirnoff (for the lower classes of the public schools), and only supplemented this by a rapid glance into Ilyin's *Atlas*.

As I have already said, this plan of working, if only for a short time, from a temporary base appeared to offer to a certain extent a way out of the desperate situation in which the squadron found itself, but a speedy solution of its task depended almost entirely on the assistance of the Heavenly Hosts, and was, judged by the standard of common sense, almost impossible.

This plan was much discussed in the squadron, and, of course, still more pondered over. The admiral, anticipating that the business might take such a turn, and in the feeling that notwithstanding all his reports the authorities at St Petersburg would obstinately stick to the rule "we know better as to the how and the when," long ago had fixed his eye on a place in the Chusan Archipelago, which lies on the road to Shanghai from the south, at a distance of 500 miles from Japan.

The anchorages of this archipelago could easily hold a fleet twice as large as ours, and were, above all, very suitable from a tactical point of view, as it was easy to organise a defence against a sudden attack.[4] There were also other suitable localities on the Chinese coast, for example, Nimrod Sound.

All these plans which referred to Chinese waters had to be dropped, as the admiral had received official intimation that England, which had apparently forgiven and forgotten Chemulpo and Chifoo, had undertaken the protection of the neutrality of Chinese territorial waters, and was prepared, in case of their being violated, to use force in upholding this protection. This was neither more nor less than a threat of war, and Admiral Rojëstvensky was perfectly right when he pointed out at the end of his letter, which appeared in the *Novoe Vremya* (of January 3, 1906), that behind the Japanese Fleet there had stood the British Fleet.

In this manner the Chinese waters were closed to us.

The French Government took, as is known, every possible measure for driving the squadron definitely and as quickly as possible out of its territorial waters; of the English and American waters there could be no question; it only remained to search for some suitable spot in Japanese waters, of course provided it were possible to reach it without too great losses.

---

4. I beg the reader not to confound the Chusan Archipelago with the group of the Saddle Islands, as people often do who are not well up in geography. The Saddle Islands were quite unsuitable for our purposes.

The Bonin Islands, Liu-Kiu, Miyako, the harbours in Formosa—only those who were unable to read charts, who had never seen the sailing directions of the Pacific, could contemplate these places. The only suitable spot was the roadstead of Mopo in the Pescadores (in the Formosa Channel). But as I have already mentioned, the Japanese had not neglected it: the approaches had been blocked with mines; on the surrounding islands temporary fortifications had been erected, which were armed with siege guns and provided with garrisons. This base could therefore only be taken by force. Assuming that the Heavenly Hosts, who left us in the lurch at Tsu-shima, had given us in this case their entire support, and that we had established ourselves at Mopo without losing a ship and without serious losses in our landing parties, which would have to be disembarked for the purpose of occupying the coast: in any case a certain, perhaps very considerable proportion of our ammunition would have been expended without the possibility of replenishing it.

Now to go into action against a superior enemy without a full allowance of ammunition is tolerably risky (of course the paper strategists pay no attention to trifles like these). However, let us assume that we could get over even this objection. What would be the next procedure? From Mopo to Vladivostok it is a matter of nearly 1,500 miles, and up to the Straits of Korea nearly 1,000. Could our fleet, which was depending on this base, on its departure for the battle in the Sea of Japan, have left the place without any protection, without anyone to man the coast batteries, which had to be armed with guns taken from the ships, without a detachment of ships to watch the approaches? Of course not! Otherwise, on the day after the fleet had gone, the newly established base would have, fallen into the hands of the Japanese, together with all its stores; and to accomplish this it would have sufficed to bring over one battalion of troops from Formosa, together with a few destroyers, or even armed merchant cruisers.

On its return from an expedition which had miscarried, the fleet would have found, not friends, but enemies, and it would have been utterly houseless and homeless, robbed even of its floating base—the fleet auxiliaries. Adequate protection should therefore have been left behind. What should be employed for this service? Of course the old ships. But if the commander-in-chief had already reported that with his full force he saw no prospect of obtaining the command of the sea, that is, of winning a victory in the decisive battle, then this task appeared still less capable of accomplishment when the forces were divided. Surely this is clear!

The patent strategists, who were not concerned for the honour of the Russian name, but only with the one idea of how they could manage, by means of their pseudoscientific arguments, to justify the decisions already come to by their protectors, thought differently. Anyhow, they had already provided a loophole of escape:

> If in truth you see no prospect of obtaining a victory on the high seas, and are not merely in a funk, you might leave behind what you designate as a 'burden,' and push on to Vladivostok yourself. The 'burden' would then play the part of drawing the Japanese forces away from you.

But this plan— getting through to Vladivostok—had already been put forward *four months ago*, when the Japanese Fleet had been weakened by nearly twelve months of strenuous war, whilst our fleet was "burning for the fray."

Then why this wearying delay of two months at Madagascar, followed by another month of aimless wanderings on the coast of Annam, which was still more enervating and used up all our remaining strength? Why were these "reinforcements" sent out which were destined to become a cheap prey of the Japanese, yet more prizes to be added to those provided by the First Squadron at Port Arthur? Was this ever thought of by those whose fundamental idea was to be accommodating, not to irritate anyone, and whose chief concern it was to be able, if need be, to get out of the water without having got wet, as the phrase goes.

Now that things have come about worse than could have been expected; when every other expedient which might not have spelt such utter ruin appears almost successful, they use their loophole; but I can well picture to myself the reproaches which would have arisen from them had the admiral come to such a decision! How they would have raged against the criminal division of forces, and the atrocious treatment of his comrades, who had been abandoned, who had been singled out as the victims, etc., etc.

However, enough of all this! History will pass its unbiased judgment.

What was there left for us to do in these circumstances? Only one thing—to do our duty to the last, to comply with our orders "to obtain the mastery of the sea," to continue the voyage, even without the prospect of gaining any success with our own forces. The only hope we had was the help of God. Perhaps a fog, a fresh breeze, might help us to slip through unobserved. Perhaps God might strike confusion into the ranks of our bold and active enemy.

In this war, however, God's blessing was with the Japanese at every step. Independently of their admirable preparations, their organisation, equipment, etc., fortune was ever on their side. The *Petropavlovsk* struck the same kind of mine as the *Pobieda*, but the former was hit abreast of the mining room which exploded, the latter abreast of a full coal bunker; the former went to the bottom, the latter only heeled over 4° and steamed with her own engines into port to be repaired. Eventually several officers were also saved from the *Petropavlovsk*, including the Grand Duke Cyril and the captain of the ship, who had both been close to the admiral just before the catastrophe, but Makaroff went down. . . . And on August 10 was not the shell which killed Admiral Vityeft a chance shot? Certainly the *Mikasa* suffered also, and even considerably, hardly less than the *Tsesarevitch*, but Togo never got a scratch!

And in the same battle both topmasts of the *Peresviet* were shot away, so that Admiral Prince Uktomsky was unable to hoist any signal visible to the whole squadron. Is not that also a piece of luck? Or can one say that these were especially good shots, that it was all intentional? No; in this war the old Russian cry of "God is with us!" did not come true. God was with "them." The hopes of a lucky chance, of favourable weather conditions, which might permit us to slip past unobserved, of inattention on the part of the enemy, were very slender. And there was nothing else. I think I can confidently assert that in the fleet there was hardly anyone (except, perhaps, the quite inexperienced youths) who counted upon success in an open, decisive battle.

On the contrary, there were some who maintained that the Japanese, who were perfectly convinced of their own superiority, would not only not disturb us, but would even assist us in reaching Vladivostok, as they intended blockading us there, so that when that fortress was taken the ships of the Second Squadron would become gratuitous prizes, in the same manner as had been so brilliantly successful at Port Arthur with the First Squadron. Taking this standpoint, the captain of the *Oleg*, at a conference with the admiral, offered to bet a large sum of money that if we went on to Vladivostok and the Japanese had realised our intentions, they would not fight us, even if we met accidentally.

The admiral did not take up the challenge, as he said it would be sheer robbery on his part. He strongly held the opposite view. He believed that the Japanese would do everything in their power to prevent our reaching our only base, where we should be able to rest, to effect repairs, and put everything to rights, and where we could leave behind all impedimenta and reorganise the fighting fleet, after which the struggle with us would be far more dangerous. As they were far superior to us in fighting strength and organisation, a decisive battle on the way to Vladivostok seemed inevitable. It only remained to choose the route by which it would be easiest, with the help of God, to get through, and where, in the event of such help not being forthcoming, we should find ourselves in the least unfavourable situation.

I beg my readers' pardon, but I am obliged to dwell a little longer on this point, and to go into it yet more fully. Too much nonsense has already been written on this subject by gentlemen who have autocratically proclaimed themselves authorities in the art of naval warfare.

The route to Vladivostok lay in any case through the Sea of Japan, which at that time was entirely in the hands of the enemy, since the Vladivostok ships gave no sign of life, and could not give any. This was known to us for certain. Four roads lead into the Sea of Japan (if Tartar Sound, with its insufficient depth, is not counted): the Straits of Korea—between the southern extremity of Korea and the Japanese Archipelago, divided into two parts, eastern and western, by the island of Tsu-shima; the Tsugaru Straits—between the islands of Nippon and Yezo; and the Straits of La Pérouse—between the islands of Yezo and Sagalien.

The only prospect of success lay in the following chances: *viz.*, either our appearing suddenly or bad weather coming on, which we might use either to hide our movements (fog) or to avoid battle (gale of wind, heavy sea or swell). Which road were we to choose?

The Tsugaru Straits could not be considered at all. Evidently (I will be honest) even the foolish "strategists" did not take it into consideration. It is a strait which is only 9 to 10 miles wide at either entrance, measured from point to point, and if one only takes the width of the available waterway, that is, the space between the shallow waters along the two shores, the fairway is occasionally reduced to only 7 miles in width. There is a strong current. In a word, even in times of peace not even a single ship, leave alone a fleet, would risk, except in case of pressing necessity, passing through in foggy or thick weather, in which the coast-line (by day) or the lights (at night) would be obscured. To this must be added the fact that on the north shore (Yezo) the Japanese military port of Mororan was situated, whilst the naval base of Aomori lies on the southern shore (Nippon). To choose this route would simply have meant committing suicide.

The Straits of Korea, to the westward of Tsu-shima, if not really a strait, was something of the kind, for along a distance of 40 miles the mainland and the islands of the South Korean Archipelago near by approached the island of Tsu-shima within 25 miles. So far as I recollect the "strategists" did not consider this route either.

There remain two routes—the Straits of Korea, east of Tsu-shima, and the Straits of La Perouse.

The one as well as the other possesses the general feature (to describe them graphically) of two funnels joined at their narrow ends, and opening both ways. The shortest distance between Capes Krilon (Sagalien) and Soya (Yezo) is 22 miles, but to the south-east of Krilon lies, at a distance of 11 miles, the very dangerous shoal Kamen Opasnosti, which hardly shows above the surface of the water, and rises up sheer out of a great depth, so that its neighbourhood cannot be detected by the lead—a very serious factor in a fog, and which reduces the width of the strait almost by one-half. As regards the eastern arm of the Straits of Korea, its narrowest part—between the southern extremity of Tsu-shima and the islands of Ikishima—measures 25 miles, showing no shoal water anywhere. The passage is quite clear close up to either shore.

Moreover, the eastern funnel of the Straits of La Perouse does not open into the ocean, but towards the Sea of Okotsk; it is, so to speak, based on the chain of the Kurile Islands, which one has to pass when coming from the ocean before reaching the straits itself. Those who have navigated the waters of the Far East know full well from personal experience, and those who have not can see from the notes in the sailing directions, what it is like near the Kuriles in spring; this is the empire of fogs, which are, as sailors say, *"as white as milk."*

Our *"armada,"* which only managed with difficulty to maintain something in the shape of a formation even in clear weather and under the most favourable navigational conditions, was to pass the Kuriles in a thick fog, go through badly marked channels between the islands, safely get into the funnel of La Pérouse, avoid Kamen Opasnosti, and then, on reaching the open sea, to endeavour to get to Vladivostok![5] I beg leave to point out that I am now discussing the question purely from the navigator's point of view, in which I leave out of count any considerations regarding possible interference by the Japanese.

The passage through the Straits of Korea presented no such difficulties. Its funnel opens out into the Yellow Sea, quite free and up to the full breadth; in the same way at the north-eastern end it rapidly opens from 25 to 75 miles (the scene of the battle) into the Sea of Japan. Here there is ample room for manoeuvring.[6] The current could be calculated with certainty. Navigation was free from danger. The thicker the fog, the worse the weather, the better for us. Here, in this wide expanse, these were our best allies. Up in the north they were our enemies. And God alone knows which was more terrible as an enemy, they or the Japanese.

Thus spoke the old navigators, who had grown grey in the pursuit of their calling. I now come to the tactical points.

Sudden appearance.—Where was this easiest of accomplishment? To steam round Japan and through the Straits of La Pérouse, even with the exceptionally large supply of coal the ships already had on board, was impossible. We should therefore have had to coal somewhere on the way. Where? At sea?— The Pacific in the latitudes of Japan is not to be compared with the tropical regions, where the weather can be predicted all the year round by the *Almanac*. Here we might have had to wait for weeks without getting weather suitable for coaling at sea. The "fresh water strategists" could, of course, leave such trifles out of count, but we, the seamen, had to take it into consideration.

---

5. To show how far from simple this route was, the fate of our prize, the steamer *Oldhamia*, can best be cited, as she was sent to Vladivostok that way. She was commanded by an experienced merchant seaman, T——, who had selected his assistants. She did reach the straits, but piled up on the rocks off Urup Island, and had to be burnt to avoid falling into the hands of the Japanese.

6. It is sad to have to mention it, but nearly two years after the Battle of Tsu-shima I had to listen, at a meeting of an honoured society, to a respected lecturer comparing this battle with the Battle of Salamis, honestly persuaded that our fleet had also to pass through narrows in which the ships were only able "to steam one behind the other," whilst the opponents had full opportunity for manoeuvring. My dear compatriots, how is it that you are so struck with blindness that it does not even occur to you to consult a chart and to measure the distances yourself with a pair of compasses? Is it laziness? Have you forgotten all you ever learnt, or are you so accustomed to blindly believe everything that is printed with the permission of the "superior authority"?

If one cannot coal at sea one must make for the coast, enter some bay, or seek shelter behind some headland.—Where? On what coast?—Naturally, the Japanese, since no other enters into our calculations. But then how about the "sudden appearance"? Our cards were then fully exposed on the table, our route would be absolutely known, and after we had overcome all navigational difficulties, had got safely past all obstacles, had escaped with the help of God from all the traps which had been laid for us in the straits—when we had then reached the open sea again, then we should be met by—the Japanese Fleet in its full strength, full of confidence, bold, and "spoiling for the fray"!

If, on the other hand, we were to coal for the last time off the northern end of Formosa (where the weather still sticks to the Almanac), and if we were then to efface our traces as far as possible, we could appear in the Straits of Korea in three days. With a certain amount of luck the principle of the "sudden appearance" could here be realised, and indeed with greater likelihood than *via* the Straits of La Pérouse, where there were not one but many "ifs." (See note following).

★★★★★★

Note:—Up to a certain degree this supposition was realised. It can be gathered from the official Japanese accounts that on May 25 and 26 every trace of our squadron had been lost by the Japanese. During the night of 26-27, Togo, who with the main body was somewhere near Fusan (probably Masampo), knew absolutely nothing of our whereabouts, and was expecting information, both from the north as well as from the south. Only at 4.25 a.m. on May 27 the Japanese armed merchant cruiser *Shinano Maru*, which had been steaming about at haphazard in the fog, came across one of our hospital ships, which were following the squadron. After she had made her out (which was not difficult, thanks to her appearance as settled by the Hague Conference— white funnels, white hull, with a complete green band and a large red cross), she concluded quite correctly that the latter was following the squadron, and on steaming ahead she soon discovered our main body, which she at once reported.

How is this to be explained? Are we to take it to have been the result of a carefully prepared scheme of look-out ships? By no means.

115

The fog reduced the radius of vision to 2 miles, and along the 100 miles across the Straits of Korea the Japanese only had sixteen look-outs. If the *Shinano Maru* had passed the same spot ten minutes later she would have seen nothing. No; here again, like always in this unhappy war, one must admit with deep bitterness that God was not with us.

★★★★★★

The keeping together the entire force at the decisive moment. When we had effaced our traces (in which we actually succeeded), and had steered straight from the ocean for the centre of the wide funnel of the Straits of Korea, we had every cause to hope that we should be able to enter it up to our full strength, without previous losses from shoals, mines strewed in our path, or torpedo attacks. By using the Straits of La Perouse, with the preceding passage through the Kuriles, such hope would, at the best, have been very slight.

Let us, however, assume (this view is especially favoured by our "strategists," who love to prophesy after the event) that in our passage through the Straits of La Perouse we had been especially favoured by the Heavenly Hosts, and had had the opportunity for coaling at sea undisturbed; that on passing through the Kuriles an invisible hand had lifted the veil of fog at the right moment, and for the length of time necessary for us, and then had let it drop again so as to hide our further progress, etc. Even then they would eventually have discovered us in the centre of the fairway between Cape Krilon and Soya! For here it is not the case of a needle in a bundle of hay, but of an entire fleet.

Even assuming that though they had discovered us, they had not had time to do us any damage.[7]—The distance from La Perouse to Vladivostok is 515 miles, exactly the same as from Vladivostok to Masampo, where, according to our latest information, Togo was at that time (as a matter of fact he was there). Assuming that all had gone well so far, and that he received there, where he was expecting us from the south, a short telegram: "The Russian fleet to its full numbers is passing between Cape Krilon and Soya." He weighs without special haste, and proceeds north at a speed half as much again as ours, for the purpose of cutting us off. The result would have been the same decisive fight for the command of the sea, without which we were not able to

---

7. As it afterwards turned out, the Japanese had stationed a special squadron under Rear-Admiral Nakao to watch and protect the northern straits. It would therefore have been hardly possible to have got through with impunity, that is, without losses.

reach Vladivostok.

Now, wherein lies the advantage of the route through the Straits of La Pérouse which has been so readily championed after the event?—In the most favourable case, after all the numerous "ifs "had been successfully settled, the result was the same as in the choice of the nearest, and from a navigating point of view most suitable route, *via* the Straits of Korea—the decisive battle with the Japanese Fleet.

The moral element.—Quite apart from the ill effect which the sudden transition from a stay of six months in the tropics to the cold, foggy atmosphere of the Sea of Okotsk, where icebergs are met with even at the end of June, might have on the weakened physical strength of the crews, the general mood in the squadron, its spirit, played an essential part in the choice of route; that *moral* to which every commander is bound to attach so much value.

I have repeatedly pointed out the causes which reduced the crews of the ships to a condition which was not far removed from complete demoralisation. I will not repeat these, but merely state that if the fleet still existed as a corporate body, this was exclusively thanks to its trust and belief in its chief and his indomitable energy. Yet it seemed to me (though I may have been mistaken) that even this tie was beginning to loosen. It was beyond their strength. When even amongst the officers, voices were heard from time to time which expressed the thought: "If only the Japanese would come and sink us! "one may well guess what went on in the depths of the masses, in the souls of these twelve thousand men, physically and morally exhausted from over-exertion!

The discontent of which murmurs reached one on all sides, which manifested itself in hideous and wild excesses—was it not the instinctive expression of the feeling which could not express itself in words: "that things can't go on like this," that there was just enough spirit left for a battle, none for any further waiting?

I could not help remembering those sad moments during my Port Arthur time when, from the midst of this uninstructed mass, which has not grasped what the conduct of war means, which does not judge with the head but with the heart, there arose suddenly these unintelligible words; when that strange suspicion was uttered aloud, which up to then had only been whispered about in dark and secluded corners: "Treason! The authorities at home have betrayed us"

Here, perhaps, it would be expressed differently. Here, perhaps, they might say: "Where are you leading us to? Again not to battle? How much longer is this to last? When will this end? Do you want to wear us out completely?"

This it was that we had to reckon with.

The decision was made. The route by the Straits of Korea was chosen.

In the (somewhat faint) hope of drawing the enemy's attention away from that spot, perhaps to cause a division of his forces, it was decided to send the *Kuban* and *Terek* ahead to the east coast of Japan, there to carry on cruiser war on the lines of communication leading to Tokio from the east (from America) and from the south (from Hong Kong). Their appearance in these waters could, provided they had instantly shown the greatest activity, easily cause it to be assumed that the boldness of their attitude was only to be explained by the vicinity of the fleet, which was evidently going round Japan and making for the Straits of La Pérouse.

Unhappily, these cruisers (I am unable to judge why) did not manifest their presence on the coast of Japan in any way. The Japanese had not even a suspicion that they were anywhere in that neighbourhood.

A not inconsiderable difficulty was caused by the anxious warnings received from the Naval General Staff: we were not to be a burden upon the poorly equipped and armed port of Vladivostok, and not to count on supplies by the Siberian railway. On one side the most elementary of tactical maxims bade us go into battle as little hampered as possible, and, as a matter of course, not to take any fleet auxiliaries with us which would interfere with our free movements. On the other side, we were bound to take into account these amiable communications. To send these vessels on, simply to break the blockade into Vladivostok, meant letting them deliberately fall into the hands of the Japanese, who were watching every approach to that port. To take the whole of these impedimenta with us, to be convoyed and protected by the fleet itself, was incompatible with every tactical maxim.

To send these ships into some neutral port, with a view to covering their ultimate arrival by a diversion, in the event of our getting through to Vladivostok ourselves ?— That might not have been a bad solution. But let us take the case of, say, a not complete defeat, or even only of considerable losses and damages, in consequence of which the fleet would have been prevented for some time from making such a diversion, what would then have been our situation? How could we have tided over this period, seeing that we were "not to be a burden upon the port, and not to count on the railway?" A compromise had therefore to be arrived at.

The admiral decided as follows:—The warships were to take on board as much in the way of stores of all kinds as the space provided for their reception on board would hold.[8] The auxiliary steamers *Anadyr*, *Irtysh*, and *Korea* (the largest and best, having a speed of 14 knots) were to embark the largest possible amounts of such articles as were most wanted: mines, material for repairing the armament, spare parts of machinery, etc.[9] The repair ship *Xenia* was to hand over to the *Kamtchatka* everything that the engineer captain and the constructor on the staff considered useful, including lathes and mechanics' work-benches. On the other hand, so as to gain space, the former was to hand over to the latter everything that was not absolutely indispensable; the best workmen of the *Xenia* were, if they wished it, to be transferred to the *Kamtchatka*; the latter was to discharge her worst workmen and such as were not prepared to proceed to the theatre of war; six auxiliaries were to be sent to Saigon, seven auxiliaries and the repair ship *Xenia* to Shanghai.

The three above-named, specially selected vessels and the *Kamtchatka* were to follow the fleet and share its fate in the attempt to reach Vladivostok. Besides this it was decided to take with us the ocean tugs and pumping vessels *Russ* and *Svir*, for the assistance of ships damaged in action or by mines, as well as the hospital ships, *Orel* and *Kostroma*. The vessels sent off to Saigon and Shanghai were, immediately on arrival there, to fill up with coal and stores, with the assistance of certain local agents, and be prepared to sail for a rendezvous which they knew of, the instant a prearranged telegram reached them.

At that time we had not definitely ceased having to reckon with international law. It never occurred to us that our supply ships, ordinary steamers flying the merchant flag, could possibly be interned in a neutral port, under the influence of England, that hospital ships could possibly become prizes, be taken to a hostile port and deprived

---

8. These spaces (holds, store-rooms, etc.) on board a man-of-war are arranged so that they can stow the principal articles in the way of stores of all kinds for a period of four months; but as there is always a certain amount of space over, it is possible to stow larger quantities, sufficient to last up to six or even eight months.

9. Besides this, these three vessels (Which were of very large displacement) carried in the aggregate over 15,000 tons of coal, that is, an amount sufficient to fill up the bunkers of the fleet once.

of every possibility of fulfilling their special and only duty—to render aid to the sick and drowning.

On May 14 we sailed. So as not to weary the reader with a detailed description of the formation of the fleet, I will state briefly that the cruising formations (by day and by night) were of the same general character as the ones employed on the voyage to the coast of Annam.

The auxiliaries which had come with Admiral Nebogatoff joined our vessels of the class; they replaced the four which had been sent to Saigon. The *Monomak* joined the cruiser division under Admiral Enquist, and the four battleships were placed in rear of the battle squadron; they were formed there in line abreast. This was not done without a special reason: steaming in line abreast gives the best practice in station-keeping.

My diary will now give, briefly, as is usual when at sea, but accurately, the events in their chronological sequence.

I venture to confine myself altogether for these days to my diary, though it only contains the most necessary remarks, which are, I fear, so disconnected as to be, in part, not easily intelligible.

CHAPTER 7

"The Reckoning"

Today, May 14, is Sunday, and Russian Mayday. One would think that these are the most favourable auspices for starting on a journey. At 6 a.m. the ships commenced to leave the bay. About 8.30 we took up cruising formation, then the auxiliaries received the signal: "Take destroyers in tow." Jonquières was present in the *Guichen* in a somewhat demonstrative manner.

Now he was able to report with a clear conscience that we were off at last. An amiable gentleman! One could not help feeling that his good wishes were sincere. (They had been transmitted by wireless.) What should we answer him?—"*Adieu, mon Amiral*" or "*Au plaisir de vous revoir?*"

By eleven o'clock we had shaped our long course and were going 9 knots. May fortune favour us!

The spirits in the fleet are not so bad. They will just keep up till the fight begins. Jokes are even made. It is said that the next admiral who comes out with the "Third Squadron "will fly his flag in the *Slava*,[1] but that he would not reap any glory.[2] Either he would reach us, if God so willed it, or he would find in our stead an empty space, and then he would not be able to accomplish anything. Not bad! Something like the Dying Gladiator's *Morituri te salutant*. Lieutenant S—— is more gloomy than the night. He croaks. Pointing at the chart (and our track on it), he says: "*Via dolorosa*." After mass and the prayer for a safe passage we emptied a glass of "Mumm's extra dry" in honour of the start.

Lieutenant S—— spoke out again: "Feasting at the time of the

---

1. A battleship then nearing completion.—Trans.
2. "*Slava*" means "glory."—Trans.

121

plague." I remonstrated with him, even good-naturedly scolded him. Why was he wallowing in his grief? We knew that well enough ourselves. Now we must hold out; it was not in our power to choose anything else. More than once one could not die. . . .

May 15.—So far all is going well. Late in the evening, as I was wandering through the ship, I looked into the wardroom. I found W—— (the chief engineer) sitting with K—— and G—— (naval reserve sub-lieutenants) drinking beer and eating sandwiches.

"What is the meaning of this?"

"Don't you understand? A navigator, too, like you! There is a difference of seven hours in longitude. Now just at this hour every German in St Petersburg is eating his dinner at the 'Caterinenhof.'" They laugh. Capital fellows! The devil take all presentiments!

Weather calm. Warm. Met three steamers, crossed the trade route (normal track) from Singapore to Hong Kong.

May 16.—As regards night cruising we have hit it off well. It will be full moon in two days' time. The night is as bright as the day. Searchlights are quite unnecessary now. So long as we are not free to move about as we like (we are convoying the auxiliaries), torpedo attacks at night are our greatest danger. Defects make their appearance on board some of the ships. We are now three days out, and the following have already had breakdowns: *Tamboff* twice, *Orel* (battleship), *Navarin* and *Sissoi* each once. They did not last long, but it always means a delay, and the worst of it is one does not feel quite certain that these defects have now been put to rights properly. How shall we fare in action? The scouts are ahead, they have spread. We try to push them further out whilst keeping touch by wireless. But it won't work. It is hopeless! Whose fault is it? The inexperience of our torpedo officers or the Slaby-Arco system, which the Technical Committee accepted? The devil take the lot! . . .

May 17.—In the morning a fresh breakdown on board the *Navarin*. We had to ease down for five hours. The scouts are reduced to mere look-outs within signal distance. This is now accepted as the rule. At half-past five in the evening the *Orel* sheers out of the line; her steering engine had gone wrong. It is especially hot and close to-day. The sun is in the zenith, and a death-like silence reigns everywhere.

May 18.—The night passed quietly. At daybreak we stopped engines and commenced coaling. In the "Third (Nebogatoff's) Division "it is badly done; they are not accustomed to it. However, they are not much in need of it. By 3 p.m. the business is finished. *Tamboff* and *Mercurya* are detached to Saigon, and we express to them by signal our special thanks for the "admirable assistance rendered to the squadron." At 8 o'clock we were once more formed up. Suddenly—a fresh delay.

On account of the *Tamboff's* departure, the destroyer she had been towing is turned over to the *Livonia*. The latter messed about with her for an hour and a half before she was ready to go ahead. We now moved off, and exactly two hours later the hawser parted and the old story began once more. The *Livonia* was at last relieved of the job she was not equal to, and the destroyer was turned over to the *Svir*. It is terrible. The whole of this time we were crawling along at 3 knots. At 8 p.m. we sighted a steamer astern. We sent the *Oleg* to overhaul her. She was English; the captain said his cargo was petroleum; that he had no papers; that he was bound for Nagasaki. We made him keep company and put off the inspection and decision to the morning.

May 19, 2 a.m.—The *Apraxin's* machinery has developed defects. She reported by signal that the repairs would take twenty-four hours and that until then she could not make more than 6 knots. Not bad for a beginning! Cursed be our "strategists" and the "reinforcements" sent out by them! The steamer *Oldhamia* appears highly suspicious. K——— (naval reserve sub lieutenant), an experienced merchant seaman, declares the steamer's coal-bunkers are nearly empty; the coal on board would just last to Nagasaki; all the same, the steamer was down to her "Plimsol-mark."[3] Petroleum in tins or casks is a bulky but light load. He has sailed with such a cargo. They had then filled up, not only all the holds, but all empty spaces, even carried a deckload; the ballast tanks had been filled with water (to ensure her stability); they had taken on board more than the normal stowage of coal, and still the plimsol-mark had been several feet out of the water.

On board the *Oldhamia* they had little coal left; the cargo was confined to the ordinary holds, the upper deck was clear. What, then, produced this deep draught? It was evident that down below, underneath the petroleum tins, there was something heavy. The captain declared

---

3. A special mark painted on the outside of the hull, which is placed according to certain rules by Lloyds, and which indicates when the ship is fully laden. When this mark disappears below water the ship is overladen to a dangerous extent, and no company will insure her.

he had no papers.

On questioning the crew it turned out that, with the exception of two men who were in the captain's confidence, the whole lot had only been shipped the day before sailing, had, therefore, not been on board when the cargo was being stowed, and could not give any definite information as to the contents of the holds. The captain and his two mates, the engineers as well as the two men who had been present when the holds were stowed, did not, or rather would not give any explanation.

On the other hand, one of the seamen (a German) informed us that he had gathered from a conversation between two of those in the secret, which he had chanced to overhear, that the forehold contained shell, the main-hold guns.

The admiral decided to seize the steamer and to send her to Vladivostok, where the nature of the cargo could be ascertained. As she had not enough coal on board to steam that distance, the *Livonia* was ordered to supply the *Oldhamia* with 600 tons. We sent a working party with several officers to the steamer. We lay stopped the whole forenoon. At 10 a.m. we stopped another steamer. She was Norwegian. She was empty, bound south. We let her go.

We made use of the stoppage to distribute amongst the ships copies of General Order No. 240, of May 19, dealing with the night cruising formation while passing the Japanese islands, and with the measures of precaution to be taken against mines, which might have been strewn in our path. (The measures to be taken against masked night attacks, as to the possibility of which we had received information from our agents, had already been laid down in General Order No. 216 of May 3.) At 11.30 a.m. we proceeded. The *Livonia* is towing the *Oldhamia* and coaling her at the same time. Whilst this is going on, a special working party is endeavouring to search through the fore and after holds.

This work is much impeded by the fact that the cases are badly stowed (intentionally or in consequence of hurried loading). It was necessary to make regular shafts, the sides of which had to be secured, and yet the unloading progressed very slowly from want of practice in this kind of work. A further suspicious circumstance: a cargo which is stowed so carelessly takes up still more space—whence, therefore, the draught up to the mark?

May 20, 5 a.m.—How strong is the force of habit, the love of that element with which one is bound up, in the service of which one has spent the best part of one's life. Last night it came on to blow from the east. Towards midnight the *Livonia* and *Oldhamia* had to cast off. During the night the sea got up. Scuttles had to be closed. The spray is already coming over. We are rolling. But what a sunrise! I hurry on deck to get fresh air, and feel disinclined to go below again. It is thus that I love the ocean.

There is a certain amount of sea, a grand, refreshing sea breeze is blowing. One takes it in in deep breaths. We are just passing Batan and Sabtan (islands between Formosa and the Philippines). Thank God! We seem to have left that awful stuffy belt of calms behind us. I greet thee, boundless ocean!

May 21.—Nothing of any consequence happened yesterday; or during the night either. This morning the working parties returned from the *Oldhamia*. It had not been found possible to search the holds right down. Never mind—it will all be cleared up at Vladivostok. She is going through the Straits of La Pérouse by herself. T—— (a naval reserve sub-lieutenant) of the *Suvoroff* is placed in command. He was permitted to select his mates. The crew is provided by several of the ships. The skipper, the engineer, and their mates had to be removed out of her, as they were inclined to be troublesome.

Attempts had been made to damage the machinery, even to sink the steamer. Where were they to be taken to? On board one of the men-of-war? The admiral had a sudden access of tender feeling: why should one bring neutrals under fire, even if they did deal in contraband of war? He had them sent to the only neutral territory in the neighbourhood—the hospital ship, *Orel*, under the protection of the Red Cross.

From there we received the astonished signal: "Five healthy Englishmen have come on board. What are we to do with them?" The admiral's reply was somewhat in the sense of: Look after their health until the next port.—At 2 p.m. first the *Zemtchug*, then the *Ossliabia*, and eventually the *Svetlana* sighted a balloon. The latter even reported its bearing and altitude. The *Oleg* and *Zemtchug* were detached in that direction, but without any result. From us (flagship) the balloon was also seen, by many people in fact. I did not see it. Flag-Lieutenant N—— pretended that it was not a spherical balloon, but a large kite or aroplane, which had broken loose. It was at a great height and travelling south. If it carried any passengers I don't envy them.

Towards evening the sky became overcast. There was thunder and it came on to rain.

May 22.—The night was hazy, but cool. One notices that we have left the tropics. At 8 a.m. we altered course to N. 20° W.; this takes us between Miyako and Liu-Kiu.

Overcast, foggy, some sea running, wind N.N.E. We meant to coal today, but it was not possible, on account of the weather.

Yesterday the *Kuban*, and today the *Terek*, parted company, to cruise off the east coast of Japan. God grant that they may attract as much attention as possible! The wind is backing to N.W. We are carrying out evolutions, so as to work up the "Third Division." They have had no practice whatever.

Only one formation ever succeeds: the formation of "huddled-up-mass." A sad sight! Towards noon the weather improved somewhat. Perhaps it will be of use to us now. It prevented our coaling, but on the other hand it prevented us from sighting the islands between which we passed; that means, we have not been seen from there. Our whereabouts is up to now a riddle. God grant that we may be able to coal tomorrow, when we shall be quite out of sight of the islands, and at the same time in an utterly unfrequented region, not crossed by any regular steamer tracks!

Towards evening it fell calm.

May 23.—The night passed quietly. At 5.30 a.m. we stopped engines and started coaling. It is calm, but the look of the weather is suspicious. There is an appearance of rain. By visual and wireless signal the ships were informed that this will probably be the last time of coaling. We were to do our very best to have still the normal stowage in our bunker on the morning of May 26.[4]

Bad news of Fölkersam: his mind is wandering, temperature 95° F., pulse 60. I asked the fleet surgeon what this meant, translated into ordinary language. He mumbled something about "the end," waved me aside and passed on. The captain of the *Ossliabia* received secret orders not to strike the flag when Fölkersam had died. The nerves of all were so sensitive. The death of an admiral on the eve of battle! How would this be taken? Perhaps without any special emotion, but perhaps they would take it as an ill omen, suddenly break down and loose heart.

We made use of the time devoted to coaling to issue the last Gen-

---

4. How impudently those lied who pretended that the ships had been overloaded with coal during the battle!

eral Order. It began with the words: "Ready for action any hour. . ."[5]

May 24.—The weather is decidedly getting worse. All the better! We had no more breakdowns, and no more delays. That is excellent! The spirits are good. They have all pulled themselves together, and appear to be full of confidence.

May 25.—Over night the rainy weather has set in determinedly. The sky is uniformly grey. There are frequent light showers. A fresh breeze is blowing. Before sending off the collier transports we wanted to fill up the destroyers' bunkers for the last time, for there will hardly be any opportunity to do so between here and Vladivostok. It did not succeed owing to the state of the weather. But what is to be done? If nothing special happens, what they have on board ought to suffice. All the same, something in reserve never does any harm.

When 90 miles off Shanghai (estimated distance) we despatched the auxiliaries to that port. The *Dniepr* and *Rion* go with them. These latter are to convoy the defenceless ships as far as the Yangtse, and are then to carry out cruiser operations on the southern trade routes leading to the ports of Western Japan and the Yellow Sea.

Touching signals were exchanged at the parting. Our range of vision is reduced by the rain to 2 to 3 miles, so that from the southern point of Formosa up to now no one has seen us.[6] That is not so bad. Let us hope that it will continue like this. S—— is wandering up and down the bridge, blacker than the night. I take him by the arm. . . .

"Well, don't you see we have come so far, and . . ."

"And?"

"And we shall get further yet."

"We are going, we are going. . . . How did you put it then? I don't recollect. . . . Oh, yes.—*To our reckoning.*"[7]

---

5. General Order No. 243 of May 23 :—Who can tell whether all would yet have been lost if the captains of the *Byedovy* and Bystry had faithfully carried out their task as laid in this order—to take the admiral and his staff to another undamaged ship the instant the *Suvoroff* might have to haul out of the line of battle? The last wound, and the one which caused him the greatest suffering, the admiral received about forty minutes after the *Suvoroff* had been deprived of the power of leading the squadron.

6. It was so in fact.

7. The days of May 25, 26, and 27 have been fully described in the chapter following (*The Battle of Tsu-shima*).

Preface to Chapter 8

The paucity of war experience since the introduction of the steam-driven armoured ship invests the battle of Tsu-shima with supreme importance. Between Trafalgar and the 27th May 1905, there had been only two fleet actions on a large scale—those of Lissa and of the Yalu—and the first was fought before the wooden vessel had disappeared and the rifled gun had become universal. The various minor engagements which occurred during this long period were either destitute of teaching, or failed to provide an adequate basis for conclusions capable of serving as guides to a rational system of tactics or to a scientific shipbuilding policy.

It has, therefore, followed, in this country especially, that the evolution of the warship has been frequently capricious, indicating the absence of any clear principles, and entailing an immense total expenditure upon vessels unsuited to our national requirements, but happily not forced to demonstrate their inutility,

In all wars, whether by sea or land, some few general lessons stand out unmistakably; but the difficulty of arriving at a just estimate of the relative significance of the causes which have led to victory or to defeat is always extreme. Genius, which may be defined as an unerring sense of proportion, is necessarily rare, and the person with an *idée fixe* in favour of some particular method or weapon will generally discover, in every conflict, evidence in support of his faith. This tendency will be most marked when national experience of war is lacking, and we are, therefore, compelled to draw our inspirations from fighting carried on by other peoples.

In the long series of wars which culminated in the Nelson era, broad principles had been evolved and had been grasped by the leaders of naval thought. More than ninety years have elapsed since the British Navy was called upon to fight a great fleet action, and meanwhile technical progress of all kinds, advancing by giant strides, has opened out new possibilities tending to bewilder the imagination and to invite mistakes and impolicy.

Even when, as now, valuable war experience is available, there is always a risk of false deductions. Conditions differ so greatly that generalisations based upon special episodes may be misleading and even dangerous. Thus the American Navy and our own have unquestionably suffered from shallow reasoning derived from the peculiar operations of the Civil War. Similarly, the action off Lissa led to a cult of the ram which has left a deep impress upon shipbuilding, while a few isolated successes obtained by torpedoes, in exceptional circumstances, have given rise to exaggerated claims on behalf of this weapon which can only end in disappointment.

Instances could be multiplied, and the obvious moral is the vital necessity for the most careful study by the clearest available brains before translating any so-called lesson of war into national policy. In a single year a navy of the magnitude of our own may be committed to many millions of expenditure, the result of which will affect its fighting efficiency for nearly a quarter of a century. The vital need for caution and for profound study of all such experience as is forthcoming is, therefore, evident.

The Battle of Tsu-shima is by far the greatest and the most important naval event since Trafalgar, and the navy which is able to draw the most accurate conclusions, technical as well as tactical, from its experiences and to apply them in terms of policy and of training will secure marked advantage in the future.

At the Battle of the Yalu the Japanese and Chinese fleets were numerically equal—twelve ships—but the former had only three vessels (all under 3000 tons) carrying side armour, and eight were protected cruisers.[1] The Chinese, on the other hand, had five vessels with side armour, including two battleships, and six protected cruisers. 1 In heavy armament the Chinese had a great superiority, the Japanese having the

GUNS.	JAPAN.	CHINA.
12-inch and over . . .	3	8
Over 8-inch and under 12-inch	8	17
Intermediate	27	15
Q.F. 6-inch and 4.7 inch. .	67	2

1. These cruisers had no armour protection for their guns.

129

advantage in quick-firing guns, as shown below:

At Tsu-shima the classification of armoured ships engaged was as follows:

CLASS.	JAPAN.	RUSSIA.
Battleships	4	8
Coast-defence Armour-clad .	...	3
Armoured Cruisers . .	8	3
TOTAL, . .	12	14

The respective armaments were:

GUNS.	12-IN.	10-IN.	9-IN.	8-IN.	Q.F. 6-IN.	Q.F. 4.7 IN.
Japan ,	16	1	...	30	160	...
Russia .	26	15	4	8	102	30

In heavy guns (9-inch and over) the Russians had the large preponderance of 28, the proportion being 45 to 17. In the smaller types, 4.7-inch to 8-inch, on the other hand, the Japanese superiority was 50, and in the 6-inch Q.F. type alone it was 58. A fair inference seems to he that the Japanese secondary armaments played the most important part in the first and practically decisive period of the battle.

In both actions the Japanese had the highest average speed—about 2 knots at the Battle of the Yalu and much more at Tsu-shima, where the three Russian coast-defence ships, the older battleships, and the three armoured cruisers were poor steamers. Excluding, on the Russian side, the *Sissoy-Veliki, Navarin,* and *Nicolay I,* the difference of average battleship speed was only 0.6 knots; but the condition of the Russian vessels was such that they could not approach their theoretical maximum.

These were the antecedent technical conditions of a great battle which, in the startling decisiveness of its results, and in the fact that the victors lost no ship, challenges comparison with that of the Nile. The tangled chain of causation now requires to be unravelled by the coolest heads at our disposal, excluding all previous bias, and seeking only to apportion the true relative values of the various factors involved with the single object of securing the sound direction of future naval policy.

What part did superior speed play in carrying destruction to the Russian fleet? What guns established the initial superiority of fire and wrought the havoc, moral and material, which ensured victory? What purpose did armour serve, and how did its distribution conform to the needs of the battle? It is upon the answers to such questions as these that our naval policy must depend.

Underlying the experience of the Battle of Tsu-shima there are undoubtedly principles of general application. It is for us to ascertain those principles, and to apply them as a test to all ship designs and tactical theories.

The merit of this little work is that it records the impressions of a naval officer who apparently had no official duties to absorb his attention. Captain Semenoff had also the advantage of being present on board the *Cesarevitch* at the action of the 10th August 1904, when it was vital to the Japanese to take no great risks. He significantly notes the difference of conditions. At Tsu-shima, Admiral Togo was determined to force a decisive action, Moreover, the Japanese had, meanwhile, improved their fuses. Thus, in the later action:

> Shells seemed to be pouring upon us incessantly. . . . It seemed as if these were mines, not shells. . . . They burst as soon as they touched anything. . . . No 1 It was different to the 10th August

Incidentally the author notes the "portmanteaus" (Japanese 12-inch shell) "curving awkwardly head over heels through the air and falling anyhow on the water." This shows that some of the Japanese 12-inch guns—numbering only sixteen—were so much worn as to be unable to give adequate rotation to their projectiles, which consequently could only have hit the Russian ships by accident.

The *Suvuroff*, where Captain Semenoff's experiences were gained, was a ship of 13,500 tons, with a continuous armour belt 12 feet broad, tapering in length at the water-line from 8 inches to 6 inches, and vertically from 6 inches to 4 inches above. Her heavy armament consisted of four 12-inch guns in 10-inch turrets, standing upon 10-inch barbettes built up from the armoured deck. The secondary armament of twelve 6-inch guns was mounted in 6-inch turrets standing upon 6-inch barbettes, all built up from the upper deck. Below the

6-inch barbettes were armoured ammunition hoists carried down to the belt level. A main armoured deck (3 to 2 inches) at the water-line level extended all over the ship.

Such was the *Suvoroff*, which was driven out of the line in less than forty minutes, and after being reduced to the hopeless state described by Captain Semenoff, was gratuitously torpedoed by the Japanese. Being the flag-ship of the commander-in-chief she was doubtless singled out as a target; but, of her three sister-ships, the *Alexander III.* was sunk by gun fire about five hours after the beginning of the action; the *Borodino* also sank in five hours, apparently as the result of the explosion of a magazine; and the *Orel* surrendered on the 28th with main turrets not seriously injured and thick armour not penetrated.

The general impression conveyed by Captain Semenoff, and confirmed from other sources, is that the Russian ships were overwhelmed by the volume of the Japanese fire, and that frequency of hitting rather than weight of shells should be the main object If this conclusion is correct, the principle which guided the British Navy in the days of Nelson—to close to effective range and then deliver the most rapid fire possible—has been strikingly reaffirmed. Effective ranges have increased; but this principle remains unchanged and is probably unchangeable.

The trouble which arose from the outbreak of fire on board the *Suvoroff* and from the wreckage of the bridges and spar-deck, the men killed in the conning tower, the penetration of the armoured deck near the bow, the downdraught of smoke, the estimate of range ("a little more than 20 cables") at a critical moment—all these points, which present themselves in the narrative, claim attention and careful comparison with other accounts.

Captain Semenoff s impressions of the manoeuvring of the fleets may well be somewhat vague; but it is worth collating with other observations. Lastly, the graphic touches of the author show with painful distinctness the terrible strain imposed upon human endurance. Few who read his account of the heroic signalmen "standing silently and outwardly calm," unwilling to go below the armoured deck, wishing only for orders, and feeling "themselves indispensable to the fight," will be inclined to accept the recent theory that partly trained and half-disciplined men are fit to find a place on board ship in modern naval war.

Upon a correct understanding of the lessons of Tsu-shima the expenditure of minions of public money and the efficiency of the navy in the near future must mainly depend. If this simple narrative can, in however small a degree, help us to attain such an understanding, its publication will be abundantly justified.

G. S. Clarke.

London, 10th November 1906.

To the Everlasting Memory
Of the Heroes Who
Perished!

Translator's Note to Chapter 8

The following account of the Battle of Tsu-shima, fought on 27th May 1905, is a translation of the narrative of Captain Vladimir Semenoff, a Russian naval officer who was on board the flag-ship (*Knyax Suvuroff*) during the engagement. It is of more than usual interest, as the writer had previously served in the *Cesarevitch* at Port Arthur, and had taken part in the disastrous sally from that port on 10th August 1904.

At the great battle of which he now relates his experiences, he was present in an unofficial capacity, which gave unlimited opportunity for observation. Moreover, the fact of his being able to make a series of notes at the time (till too seriously wounded) puts an additional stamp of reality on to his already most graphic account

It should be remembered that the Russian Baltic fleet—Russia's final and supreme appeal to the God of Battles—left Cronstadt for the Far East on 11th September 1904, and during all the long months till the following May was slowly making its way, *via* the Cape of Good Hope, to Japanese waters. The difficulties encountered during that prolonged voyage were enormous. The nerves of officers and men, who constantly apprehended attempts to destroy the fleet, were in a continual state of tension: news of the outside world and especially of events in the Far East was practically unobtainable: and yet officers and men, despite the additional disadvantage of having to take their ships into action after these many months at sea, fearlessly entered into an engagement which they knew meant death, and fought their ships with a self-devotion and courage which has earned for them the admiration of the world.

Admiral Togo—flying his flag on the *Mikasa*—awaited the enemy in Japanese waters. His fleet, which, since the fall of Port Arthur on 2nd January 1905, had been relieved of its blockading duties, had spent the intervening months in repairing damage and bringing itself up to the highest state of preparation in expectation of the coming of the Baltic fleet.

To a nation like ourselves, whose first line of defence is the navy, I venture to think that these pages will give food for thought, as, besides enabling the reader to see the paralysing and awful effect of high explosives thrown on board a modern battleship in action, they supply us with a picture of what a losing engagement means to those who lose.

When first I took up the original volume I read it merely with a view to extracting information *re* fire effect, gun power, weather conditions, formations, and other factors complementary to the result of the battle. But the narrative appeared so realistic that the thought occurred to me to place the following translation before the public,

The speed maintained by the opposing fleets during the battle is shown in the diagram attached. Dates have been expressed according to the English calendar (which is thirteen days in advance of the Russian)—otherwise the writer's own words and colloquial style have, as far as possible, been faithfully adhered to, to the detriment of literary style in translating.

It may be mentioned that this narrative comes as a supplement to the very interesting account by Politovsky of the voyage of the Baltic fleet to the Far East—recently translated by Major Godfrey and published by John Murray under the title *From Libau to Tsushima*.

Politovsky went down in the *Suvoroff*, and his story ends with the arrival of the fleet at Shanghai on 23rd May, the date on which he posted his last letter to Russia, The following narrative commences on 25th May, as the fleet swung out of Shanghai to meet its destiny.

A. B. L.

7th November 1906

CHAPTER 8

Leaving Shanghai

A fresh breeze mournfully droned through the wire rigging and angrily dispersed the ragged, low-lying clouds. The troubled waters of the Yellow Sea splashed against the side of the battleship, while a thin, cold, blinding rain fell, and the raw air penetrated to one's very bones. But a group of officers still stood on the after-bridge, watching the silhouettes of the transports slowly disappearing in the rain haze.

On their masts and yard-arms signals were being flown, the last messages and final requests of those who had been our fellow-travellers on the long tedious voyage.

Why is it that at sea a friendly greeting of this kind, expressed merely by a combination of flags, touches one's heart so deeply, and speaks to it even more than salutes, cheers, or music? Why is it that until the signal has been actually hauled down every one looks at it, silently and intently, as if real words, instead of motley coloured pieces of cloth, were fluttering in the breeze, and becoming wet with rain? Why is it that on the signal being hauled down everyone turns away, quietly moving off to his duty, as if the last quiet handshake had been given, and "goodbye" had been said forever?

Well!—how about the weather?" said someone—to break the silence.

"Grand," answered another with a smile, "If we get this all the way to Vladivostok, then thank the Lord! why, a general battle will be impossible."

Once more a signal was made to the fleet, and, having cast off the majority[1] of our transports at Shanghai, we take up our fresh and *last* "order of march."

1. All, except the naval transports carrying war stores, were left at Shanghai.—A.B.L.

Ahead, in wedge formation, was the scout division consisting of three ships—the *Svietlana, Almaz,* and *Ural:*, next came the fleet in two columns. The starboard column consisted of the 1st and 2nd armoured squadrons, *i.e.* eight ships the *Suvoroff, Alexander, Borodino, Orel,*[2] *Sissoy, Navarin, Nakhimoff.* On the port side were the 3rd armoured and cruiser squadrons, *i.e.* eight ships the *Nicolay, Senyavin, Apraxin, Ushakoff,* and the cruisers, *Oleg, Aurora, Donskoy,* and *Monomakh.* On either beam, and parallel with the leading ships, were the *Zemtchug* and *Izumrud,* each accompanied by two torpedo boats, acting as scouts for the port and starboard columns. In rear of, and between, the wakes of these columns steamed a line of transports which we *were obliged* to take to Vladivostok[3]—the *Anadir, Irtish, Korea, Kamchatka*—and with them the repair and steam-tugs, *Svir* and *Russ,* ready to render assistance in case of need. With the cruiser squadron were five torpedo-boats, whose duty it was to co-operate with the former in protecting the transports during the battle. Astern of all came the hospital ships, *Orel* and *Kostroma.*

This disposition of the fleet would make it possible, if the enemy appeared unexpectedly, for the various squadrons to take order of battle quickly and without any complicated manoeuvres (*i.e.* without attracting attention). The scout division was to turn from whichever side the enemy appeared and to join the cruisers, which were to convoy the transports out of action, and protect them from the enemy's cruisers. The 1st and 2nd armoured squadrons were to increase speed, and, having inclined to port *together,*[4] were to take station in front of the 3rd armoured squadron and proceed on their former course.

---

2. Evidently the *Oslyabya* was omitted by a printer's error. She should come in as the fifth ship, *i.e.* after the *Orel,* and leading the 2nd armoured squadron.—A.B.L.

3. Cruel irony! We were attempting to force our way through to our *base,* and had been ordered to take with us, if possible, everything in the way of materials and supplies that we might require, so as not to overtax it. The railway was only able with difficulty to supply the army, and we were under no circumstances to count upon its help.

4. "Together" has a literal meaning: the ships all change direction simultaneously to the same side and at the same angle. By doing this they take up a new formation, parallel to their former line, and to starboard or to port of it, moving ahead or not according to the size of the angle of turning. Shortly after changing direction the order is again given to turn "together" at the same angle, but to the opposite side, and the ships thus find themselves once more in single column line ahead, but at some distance to starboard or to port of their original course.

"Together" is the direct opposite to "in succession," when each ship changes direction as she comes to the spot in which the leading ship has turned—*i.e.* follows her.

The result would be that the three squadrons would then be in single column line ahead, and the centre of our fleet would consist of twelve armoured ships. The *Zemtchug* and *Izumrud* were to manoeuvre according to circumstances and, taking advantage of their speed, together with the torpedo-boats assigned to them, were to take station ahead, astern, or abeam of the armoured ships. They were to be on the further side of the fleet from the enemy, out of the range of his shells; their duty being to prevent the enemy's torpedo boats from getting round the fleet

Above was the plan of battle, worked out beforehand and known to every officer in the fleet The various details as to formations dependent on the direction in which the enemy appeared, the instructions for fire control, the manner in which assistance was to be rendered to injured ships, the transfer of the admiral's flag from one ship to another, the handing over of the command, etc., etc., were laid down in special orders issued by the commander-in-chief, but these details would scarcely be of interest to readers unacquainted with naval matters.

The day (25th May) passed quietly. Towards evening it was reported that an accident had happened to the *Senyavin's* engines, and all that night we steamed slowly. In the ward-room of the *Suvoroff* the officers grumbled and swore at the "old tubs," [5] as they nicknamed Nebogatoff's ships, but, although natural, it was hardly fair, for we ourselves were little better. The prolonged voyage had been a long mournful indictment of our boilers and machinery, while our martyrs of engineers had literally had to "get oil out of flints," and to effect repairs although with no material at hand with which to make them.

That night, the first cold one after six months in the tropics, we slept splendidly, but, of course, by watches, *i.e.* half the night one half of the officers and crew were at the guns, and the other half the remainder.

On 26th May the clouds began to break and the sun shone fitfully, but although a fairly fresh south westerly breeze had sprung up, a thick mist still lay upon the water.

Being anxious to avail himself of every moment of daylight while passing the Japanese coast, where we would most probably be attacked by torpedoes, the Admiral arranged for the fleet to be in the centre of its passage through the straits of Tsu-shima at noon on the 27th May. According to our calculations this would give us about four hours to

5. "*Samotopy*" literally "self-sinkers."—A.B.L.

spare, which we employed in practising manoeuvres for the last time.

Once again, and for the *last* time, we were forcibly reminded of the old truism that a "fleet" is created by long years of practice at sea in time of peace (cruising, not remaining in port), and, that a collection of ships of various types hastily collected, which have only learned to sail together on the way to the scene of operations, is no fleet, but a chance concourse of vessels.

Taking up order of battle was moderately performed, but it was spoilt by the 3rd squadron, and who can blame its admiral or captains? When near Madagascar, and during our wanderings off the coast of Annam, our ships to a certain extent had been able to learn their work, and to get to know one another. They had, in fact, been able to "rehearse." But as the 3rd squadron, which joined the fleet barely a fortnight ago, [6] had only arrived in time to finish the voyage with us and take part in the battle, there was no time for it to receive instruction.

Admiral Togo, on the other hand, had commanded his squadron continuously for eight years without hauling down his flag. Five of the vice-admirals and seven of the rear-admirals taking part in the Tsu-shima battle, in command of squadrons, ships, or as junior flag officers, were his old comrades and pupils, having been educated under his command. As for us, we could only regret our unpreparedness, and in the coming fight there was nothing for us to do but to make the most of what we had.

Rozhdestvensky thought (and facts later fully justified the opinion) that in the decisive battle Togo would be at the head of his twelve best armoured ships. Against them our admiral was also to lead twelve similar ships (which he handled magnificently), and in the duel between them it was thought the centre of gravity of the fight would certainly lie. The difference between our main force and that of the Japanese was very material. The oldest of Togo's twelve ships the *Fuji*, was two years younger than the *Sissoy*, which, among our twelve best, came sixth in seniority! Their speed was one-and-a-half times as great as ours, but their chief superiority lay in their new shells, of which we had no inkling.

What with manoeuvres, etc., the 26th May passed almost imperceptibly.

I do not know the feeling on board the other ships, but in the

6. Admiral Nebogatoff, with the 3rd squadron, joined the main fleet on 9th May.— A.B.L.

Suvoroff we were cheerful and eager for the fray. Anxious, of course, we were, but not so over-anxious as to worry. The officers went their rounds, and looked after their men more than usual; explained details, talked, and found fault with those immediately under them more than was their wont. Some, the thought suddenly occurring to them, put their keepsakes and the letters which they had just written into the treasure chest for safety.

"He evidently means to leave us!" said Lieutenant Vladimirsky, the senior gunnery officer, pointing to a sailor who was busy rummaging in a bag.

"What! made your preparations for going already?"

"I?" said he in amazement; and with a grin—"Yes—I am quite ready!"

"Look here!" said Lieutenant Bogdanoff, the senior torpedo officer, who was a veteran of the former war and had been wounded at the capture of the Taku forts—"Tomorrow—or rather tonight you'll please go to the office and get your accounts made up!"

This humour had no effect

"And haven't *you* a presentiment? *You've* been under fire before," asked a young sub-lieutenant, coming up, with his hand in his pocket, in which was evidently a letter destined for the treasure chest.

Bogdanoff got annoyed. "What do you mean by a presentiment? I'm not your fortune-teller! I tell you what! If Japanese guns begin talking to us tomorrow you will feel something soon enough,—but you won't feel anything before then!"[7]

Some more officers approached. Times without number we had hotly discussed the question,—would we meet the whole of the Japanese fleet at Tsu-shima, or only part of it?

Optimists asserted that Togo would be misled, and would patrol to the North to look out for us, as the *Terek* and *Kuban* had on the 22nd gone round the eastern shores of Japan endeavouring to attract as much attention there as possible. [8]

Pessimists declared that Togo was as well able as we were to understand the conditions, and would know that a single coaling was not sufficient to enable us to steam all round Japan; we should have to coal again. And where? We were no longer in the tropics; the weather here

---

7. A play upon the words. The Russian translation of "presentiment" is "feeling before."—A.B.L.

8. Fate had not been kind to us. The *Terek* and *Kuban* met no one all the time that they were there) and no one knew of their presence in those waters.

was anything but reliable, which meant we could not count upon coaling at sea. Take shelter in some bay?—but there were telegraph stations, and, of course, intelligence posts, everywhere. Togo would learn of it in good time, so what would he gain by hastening northward? Even if we succeeded in coaling at sea and slipped unnoticed into one of the Straits, we couldn't conceal our movements there, thanks to their narrowness. And the— submarine and floating mines, sown along our course, and attacks by torpedo boats, which would be easy even in broad daylight!

It was impossible to pass unnoticed through these Straits even in a fog or in bad weather; how then could a fleet accompanied by transports hope to escape observation? Even if the Almighty did bring us through all this, what was beyond?—the meeting with the Japanese fleet which from Tsu-shima could always come out across our course while our fleet would have already been harassed in the Straits by torpedo-boats as well as every conceivable type of mine.

"Gentlemen—Gentlemen! let me speak!" exclaimed the first lieutenant and senior navigating officer, Zotoff, who was always fond of discussions and liked making his voice heard.

"It is quite clear that the best course for us is up the eastern side of the gulf of *Korea*. My chief reason for saying so is because here it is wide and deep, while there is room for us to manoeuvre, and it can be navigated without danger in any weather. In fact, the worse the weather the better for us. All this has been talked over till nothing more remains to be said, and considered till nothing is left to consider; even disciples of Voltaire themselves would admit this. Presumably Togo is no greater fool than we, and knows this. I assume that he also knows how to use a pair of compasses and is acquainted with the four rules of arithmetic!

"This being so he can easily calculate that, if we steam round Japan, deciding in the face of our knowledge to brave the mines before meeting him, it would still be possible for him to intercept us on the road to Vladivostok, if, at the same time as we come out of the ocean into the Straits, he starts from . . . Attention, gentlemen! . . . from the northernmost point of Tsu-shima. There is no doubt that arrangements have been made to organise a defence of the Straits by mines. The naval ports of Aomori and Mororan are on either side. If anyone doesn't know it he ought to be ashamed of himself. Togo may tell off some of his smaller mining vessels to go there, but he, with his main force (I would even go so far as to say with the whole of his fleet)—

where will he be? No, I will put another question: Where ought he to be? Why! nowhere else but off the northern point of Tsu-shima, He can gain nothing by loitering about at sea, so he will be lying in some bay."

"In Mazampo, for instance?" asked Sub-Lieutenant Ball, the junior navigating officer.

"Mazampo—if you like—but let me finish. It is childish to hope that the Japanese main fleet will be out of the way. I think we have reached the culminating point of our adventures. Tomorrow the decision must be made: either vertically"—and, putting his hand above his head, he energetically waved it downwards in front of him—"or"—quietly moving his arm out to the right, and dropping it slowly downwards in a circular direction—"a longer route, but to the west all the same."

"How? Why? Why to the west?" broke in the bystanders.

"Because though the end may not come at once," shouted Zotoff, "the result will be the same! It's absurd to think of steaming victoriously into Vladivostok, or of getting command of the seal The only possible chance is a dash through! and having dashed through, after two, three, or at the most four sallies, we shall have burnt all our supplies of coal, and have shed our blossoms before we have bloomed! We shall have to prepare for a siege, take our guns on shore, teach the crew to use bayonets—"

"*A bas! A bas! Conspuez le prophête!*" interrupted some. "Hear! Hear! Strongly[9] said!" shouted others. "What about Austria's Parliament!"

"Let him finish," growled Bogdanoff in his bass voice. Zotoff, availing himself of a quiet moment continued:—

"Having postponed a discussion of questions of the distant future—a discussion which makes those who take part in it so excited, I will venture to say a few words concerning what is immediately at hand. I foresee three possibilities. Firstly:—If we have already been discovered, or are discovered in the course of the day, we shall certainly be subjected at night to a series of torpedo attacks, and in the morning shall have to fight the Japanese fleet, which will be unpleasant. Secondly:—If we are not discovered till tomorrow we shall be able to commence the fight at full strength, without casualties, which will be better. Lastly, and thirdly:—If the mist thickens and dirty weather comes on, thanks to the width of the Straits, we may either slip through, or be discovered too late, when there will be only

9. *Verbatim* in the context.—A.B.L.

the open sea between us and Vladivostok.—This would be excellent. On these three chances those who wish may start the totalisator! For myself, preparing for the worst, and foreseeing a broken night, I suggest that we all take advantage of every spare hour to sleep."

His words had the desired effect

CHAPTER 9

Doings in the "Suvaroff"

Fate had apparently been kind to us, as up to the present we had not been discovered. The sending of telegrams in the fleet was forbidden, so we were able to intercept Japanese messages, and our torpedo officers made every effort to fix the direction from which they emanated. On the morning of 26th May and later on the same day, a conversation between two installations had begun, or perhaps more correctly speaking it was the reports of one ahead of and nearer to us to which the other, more distant and on the port side, was replying. The messages were not in cipher, and although our telegraphists were unaccustomed to the strange alphabet, and notwithstanding the gaps in the sentences by the time we received them, it was still possible to pick out separate words, and even sentences. "Last night" . . . "nothing" . . . "eleven lights . . . but not in line" . . . "bright light . . . the same star . . ." etc.

In all probability this was a powerful coast station on the Goto Islands, reporting to some one a long way off what had been seen in the Straits.

Towards evening we took in a conversation between other installations, which at night had increased to seven. The messages were in cipher, but by their brevity and uniformity and by the fact that they commenced and ceased at fixed times, we were able to calculate with tolerable accuracy that these were not reports, but merely messages exchanged between the scouts. It was clear that we had not been discovered.

At sunset the fleet closed up, and in expectation of torpedo attacks half the officers and crew were detailed for duty at the guns, the remainder sleeping by their posts, without undressing, ready to jump up on the first sound of the alarm.

144

The night came on dark The mist seemed to grow denser, and through it but few stars could be seen. On the dark deck there prevailed a strained stillness, broken at times only by the sighs of the sleepers, the steps of an officer, or by an order given in an undertone, Near the guns the motionless figures of their crews seemed like dead, but all were wide awake, gazing keenly into the darkness. Was not that the dark shadow of a torpedo-boat? They listened attentively. Surely the throb of her engines and the noise of steam must betray an invisible foe?

Stepping carefully, so as not to disturb the sleepers, I went round the bridges and decks, and then proceeded to the engine-room. For a moment the bright light blinded me. Here, life and movement was visible on all sides. Men were nimbly running up and down the ladders; there was a tinkling of bells and buzzing of voices. Orders were being transmitted loudly, but, on looking more intently, the tension and anxiety—that same peculiar frame of mind so noticeable on deck— could also be observed. And then it suddenly occurred to me that all this—the tall, somewhat bent figure of the admiral on the side of the bridge, the wrinkled face of the man at the wheel stooping over the compass, the guns' crews chilled to the bone at their posts, these men talking loudly and running about, the giant connecting-rods whose steel glittered dimly in the dark, and the mighty hissing of steam in the cylinders—was one and the same thing.

I suddenly remembered the old sea legend of the ship's spirit dwelling in every rivet, nail, and screw, which at the fated moment takes possession of the whole ship with her crew, and turns both crew and surroundings into one indivisible supernatural being. Of a sudden it seemed that this spirit was looking right into my heart, which beat with unusual rapidity, and for a moment it seemed as if I had become this being to whom the name *Suvoroff*—so sacred to all of us—was no more than a mere rivet!

It was a flash of madness, which quickly passed, leaving behind it only a sensation akin to daring and grim determination.

Alongside of me, the chief engineer, Captain Bernander, my old shipmate and friend, was angrily explaining something to his assistant. I did not hear what he said, nor could I understand why he was so excited when everything had been finally settled. Whether for better or for worse it was impossible to alter things now.

"All in good time, my dear fellow," said I, taking his arm. "Let us go and drink some tea—my throat is parched."

Turning his kind grey eyes on me in astonishment, and without replying, he allowed me to lead him away.

We went up to the ward-room, which at this hour was usually crowded and noisy. It was empty. Two or three officers, after being relieved, as well as some from the nearest light gun batteries, were sound asleep on the sofas, awaiting the alarm, or for their turn to go on watch. The messman, however, who was always ready for any emergency, brought us tea. Again on all sides this dreadful, painful stillness.

"The chief thing is, not to be in too great a hurry.—One straight shot is better than two bad ones.—Remember that we have not a single spare shell, and, till we reach Vladivostok, none are to be got," came in a somewhat inaudible voice from behind the closed door of the stern cabin. Evidently a sub-lieutenant, Fomin by name, was holding forth.

"Preaching!" angrily said Bernander, helping himself to some hot tea,

I saw that he was very annoyed about something and wished to unburden himself.

"Well! tell me all about it! What is the matter?"

"It is all this cursed German coal," he said, and lowering his voice and looking round—"You know, of course, that we had a fire in the bunkers?"

"Yes! I know; but surely, thank goodness, they put it out? Do you mean there's another?"

"No! Not quite! Listen! There's a vast difference between rapid-burning and slow-burning coal Much more is consumed. Compared to good coal, 20 to 30 *per cent*—"

"Shut up!" I interrupted. "Why, what's up with you? Are you afraid you'll run out? Up till now, surely, you have been burning our surplus! You ought to have in hand the full normal quantity."

"Full or not, we shall have less than 1000 tons by morning."

"But it's 600 miles to Vladivostok! Where do you want to go? "

"Have you forgotten the *Cesarevitch?* On 10th August, when her funnels were shot away, she burnt 480 tons in the twenty four hours! Well—we are burning more!"

"Pooh! your nerves are unstrung," I exclaimed. "All your bunkers haven't caught fire!"

"You don't understand!" angrily exclaimed Bernander, and, quickly finishing his tea, he seized his cap and went out,

I remained in the ward-room, settled myself down in an easy-chair, and, making myself comfortable, dozed. I heard indistinctly the watch being relieved at midnight. Some of the officers coming off duty came in to get some tea, and in low voices abused the infernal rawness of the night air. Others stretched themselves on sofas, sighing with relief at being so comfortable, and said: "We'll sleep till four! it's a holiday at home!"

I also went to sleep.

About 3 a.m. I awoke, and again went round the ship and up on deck. The scene was just the same as in the evening, but it was lighter. In the last quarter the moon had risen well up, and against the mist, dimly whitened by its silver rays, the ship's funnels, masts, and rigging were sharply outlined. The breeze, freshening, blew cold, making me pull the cape of my coat more over my head.

Going on to the fore-bridge, I found the admiral sleeping in a chair. The commander, wearing soft slippers, was pacing rapidly but quietly up and down the bridge.

"What are you doing wandering about?" he asked me.

"Oh, just having a look round. Gone to sleep?" and I nodded towards the admiral.

"Only just. I persuaded him to. Why shouldn't he? We can take it that the night has passed all right. Up to the present we haven't been discovered. They are still calling each other up, and now, even though they do find us, it's late. It will be daybreak in a couple of hours. Even if their torpedo-boats are near us, they won't be able to collect Besides, how can they find us in weather like this? Look! you can't even see the rear of the fleet! It's 200,000 to 1 against anyone running into us accidentally! But I don't like the breeze. It's freshening. Let's hope it won't break up the mist. If it does tomorrow will mean the end of the *Suvoroff*. But it's suddenly coming on thicker," he said eagerly. "Why, we have been going for twenty-four hours without being seen. If it is the same tomorrow, we'll give them the slip! They are on the move, and keep calling each other up, and they haven't yet come on us! They'll have to wait for our second coming, out of Vladivostok! That'll be a different tale. My! what a stew they must be in! What fun!" and putting his handkerchief in his mouth so as not to disturb the admiral, he laughed so heartily, and seemed so free from care, that I envied him,

It should be stated that V. V. Ignatzius, in the first place, was one of those who was firmly convinced that the success of our voyage—this desperate adventure—depended solely on the extent of co-operation of Saint Nicolas "The Casual" and other heavenly powers, and, in the second place, bearing in mind the Japanese custom of concentrating their fire on the flag-ship, he believed that both he and his ship were doomed to destruction in the first decisive engagement. But, in spite of this, he never for a moment lost his invariably buoyant and cheery manner. He joked, chaffed, and eagerly threw himself into all the little details of daily life on board, while now (I really believe) he was, inwardly, much amused, picturing to himself the anger and disappointment of the Japanese in the event of our actually slipping past them.

But the Japanese "got the 200,000th chance," and more.

At dawn on 27th May, about 5 a.m., the auxiliary cruiser *Sinano Maru* almost ran into our hospital ships, and it was due to this that the whole fleet was discovered. We were unable to see what had happened, but by the changed character of the messages it became at once apparent that our presence was known. The scouts no longer merely called each other up, and we now took in reports, which were being transmitted further and further to the north. [1]

Messages came in from both sides, so the admiral recalled the *Almaz, Svietlana* and *Ural*, in order to protect our helpless rear (transports) from sudden attack.

About 6 a.m. the *Ural* came up at full speed, reporting by semaphore that astern of the fleet four ships, which it was impossible to recognise in the mist, were crossing from starboard to port.

At 6.45 a.m. a vessel appeared on the starboard beam, which, as her course brought her nearer to us, was soon recognised as the *Idzumi*. About 8 a.m., despite the mist, we were able to take her distance as 10,000 yards. The alarm sounding, the after turret threateningly raised her 12-inch guns, but the *Idzumi*, guessing her danger, commenced rapidly to beat a retreat.

We might, of course, have detached a good cruiser to drive her off, but alas! there were in the fleet only two ships answering to this description the *Oleg* and the *Aurora*, also possibly the scout *Svietlana*; of the remainder, the *Donskoy* and *Monomakh* were respectable veterans, slow, though passably armed, The *Ural* and *Almaz* were swift, but had only toy guns. Besides, each moment we were expecting to meet our formidable opponent, when every gun and shell would be of value. If the issue of the battle were to be decided by a duel between our three

---

1. According to Japanese reports, Togo, who was stationed with his main body somewhere off Fusan, was at this time in complete ignorance of our whereabouts and was waiting for news from both north and south.

armoured squadrons and the twelve best Japanese ships, the whole of the rest of the enemy's fleet would fall to the lot of our cruiser squadron. A struggle for which we must indeed reserve our strength! Rozhdestvensky decided accordingly to ignore the *Idzumi's* daring sally, and sent no one in pursuit of her.

Shortly after 8 a.m., on the port bow, the *Chin-Yen, Matsushima, Itsukushima*, and *Hashidate* appeared out of the mist, steaming on an almost parallel course. Ahead of them was a small, light cruiser, apparently the *Akitsushu*, which hurriedly drew off to the north as soon as we were able to see her well (and equally she us), and the whole squadron began slowly to increase their distance and gradually to disappear from sight

At about 10 a.m. the light cruisers *Chitose, Kasagi, Niitaka*, and *Otawa*, also appeared on the port beam, and it became evident to all of us that the decisive moment could not now be long postponed.

At a signal from the flag-ship, the 1st and 2nd armoured squadrons steamed ahead, and, turning "together," 2 points[2] to port, began to take position ahead of the 3rd squadron. The transports were ordered to keep more to starboard and astern of the fleet, while the cruisers were to cover them on the port side. To starboard of the transports was the *Monomakh*, detailed to protect them from the *Idzumi* and suchlike vessels.

At 11.20 a.m., when the distance of the Japanese light cruisers was 10,000 yards, the *Orel* fired an accidental shot (which she immediately reported by semaphore). Unable with smokeless powder to tell by which of the leading ships it had been fired, the fleet took it as a signal from the *Suvoroff*, and opened fire. Of the whole fleet the fire of the 3rd squadron was the heaviest.

The Japanese cruisers turned to port and, firing also, rapidly drew off. The flag-ship then signalled, "*Ammunition not to be wasted*," and when the firing ceased, "Ships' companies to have dinner at once."

At midday, finding ourselves on a line with the southernmost point of Tsushima, we shaped course N.23°E. for Vladivostok.

The officers also had breakfast now, in turn, and as quickly as possible. Today there was to have been as usual a big breakfast in the wardroom, with the admiral and his captain and staff as guests: but on this occasion it naturally could not take place as the admiral and captain were unable to leave the bridge, and the staff only dashed down to the admiral's table to eat a few mouthfuls.

---

2. A point = 11¼°

Having gone down to my cabin to fill my cigarette-case before the fight, I happened to look in at the ward-room at the psychological minute. Although the dishes were being handed anyhow and whatever came nearest was taken, champagne sparkled in the glasses, and every one was standing up, silently listening to the toast proposed by the senior officer, A. P. Makedonsky.

On this, the great anniversary of the sacred Coronation of their Highnesses, may God help us to serve with honour our beloved Country! To the health of the Emperor! the Empress!—To Russia!

The ward-room resounded with cheers, and their last echoes had scarcely died away ere the alarm sounded on deck. Everyone rushed to their stations, to find that some Japanese light cruisers had again appeared on our port bow, but this time they were accompanied by torpedo-boats, which evidently intended to cross our bows. Suspecting that their plan was to lay floating mines (as they had done on 10th August), the admiral ordered the 1st squadron to turn to starboard, so as to drive off the enemy by threatening him with the fire of our five best battleships.

With this intention the ships of the 1st squadron turned "in succession" 8 points (90°) to starboard, and should afterwards have turned "together" 8 points to port. The first half of the manoeuvre was most successfully performed, but the signal for the second was evidently misunderstood, as the *Alexander* followed the *Suvoroff*, while the *Borodino* and *Orel*, which had already commenced to turn correctly "together," imagining then that they were mistaken, turned back and followed the *Alexander*. Consequently the 1st squadron found itself in single column line ahead, parallel to the 2nd and 3rd squadrons, but somewhat ahead of them.

This unsuccessful manoeuvre, however, had a most important result The enemy's cruisers and torpedo boats, afraid of being caught between the fire of both columns, abandoned their intention of crossing our course, and hurriedly drew off to port. These cruisers probably also reported to Togo that we were steaming in two columns, and he (being then out of sight and far ahead of us on the starboard bow) decided to cross over to our port side, so as to throw himself with all his strength upon our port and weakest column.

As soon as the Japanese drew off, the 1st squadron at once increased speed, inclining to port so as again to take station ahead of the

2nd squadron.

At 1.20 p.m., when the 1st had got ahead of the 2nd and 3rd squadrons and was steering on its former course, the flag-ship signalled:

The 2nd squadron, maintaining its formation, will take station astern of the 1st.

And now, far ahead of us in the distance, could be dimly seen approaching through the mist the Japanese main force. Their ships were crossing our bows from starboard to port, following on an almost south-west course. The *Mikasa*, as soon as she crossed our bows, at once altered course to the southward, followed by the *Shikishima*, *Fuji*, *Asahi*, *Kasuga*, and *Nisshin*.

Meanwhile, though the flag-ship was already being worked from the conning tower, Rozhdestvensky was still standing with his staff on the upper fore-bridge.

I frankly confess that I did not agree with his opinion as to Togo leading all his twelve armoured ships in column; on 10th August he ordered six of them to work independently, instead of joining his squadron. I was inclined to think that Kamimura would operate independently and, when my six old Port Arthur acquaintances hove in sight, I said triumphantly:

"There they are, sir—*all six*—just as on 10th August."

But Rozhdestvensky, without turning, shook his head.

"No, there are more—they are all there," and he went down into the conning tower.

"To your stations, gentlemen," said the flag-captain quickly, as he followed the admiral

And there, sure enough, following after the first six ships, and slowly appearing out of the mist, came the *Idzumo*, *Yakumo*, *Asama*, *Adzuma*, *Tokiwa*, and *Iwate*.

CHAPTER 10

Russians Open Fire

"Now the fun will begin," thought I to myself, going up to the after-bridge, which seemed to be the most convenient place for carrying out my duty of seeing and noting down everything, as from there I could see both the enemy and our own fleet Lieutenant Reydkin, commanding the after starboard 6-inch turret, was also there, having dashed up to see what was going on, as the fight was apparently to commence to port, and his turret would not be in action.

We stood side by side, exchanging now and again abrupt remarks, not understanding why the Japanese intended crossing to our port side, when our weak spot—the transports and cruisers covering them—was astern, and to starboard of us. Perhaps, having commenced the fight while steering on the opposite course, and having taken advantage of their superior speed, they calculated on rounding us from the stern, in order to fall at the same time on our transports and weak rear! If so, a raking fire would present no difficulties.

"Hullo! Look! What *are* they up to?" said Reydkin, and his voice betrayed both delight and amazement

I looked and looked, and, not believing my eyes, could not put down my glasses. The Japanese ships had suddenly commenced to turn "in succession" to port, reversing their course!

If the reader recollects what has been said previously on the subject of turns, he will easily understand that this manoeuvre made it necessary for all the enemy's ships to pass in succession over the point on which the leading ship had turned; this point was, so to speak, stationary on the water, making it easy for us to range and aim. Besides—even with a speed of 15 knots, the manoeuvre must take about fifteen minutes to complete, and all this time the vessels, which had already turned, would mask the fire of those which were still coming up.

"*How* rash!" said Reydkin, who could not keep quiet. "Why, in a minute we'll be able to roll up the leading ships!"

"Please God, we may!" thought I.

It was plain to me that Togo, seeing something which he had not expected, had suddenly changed his mind. The manoeuvre was undoubtedly risky, but, on the other hand, if he found it necessary to steer on the opposite course, there was no other way of doing it He might have ordered the fleet to turn "together," but this would have made the cruiser *Iwate* the leading ship in action, which he evidently did not wish. Togo accordingly decided to turn "in succession," in order that he should lead the fleet in person, and not leave success at the commencement of the action to depend upon the presence of mind and enterprise of the junior flag-officer. (The *Iwate* flew Rear-Admiral Simamura's flag.)

My heart beat furiously, as it had never done before during the six months at Port Arthur. If we succeeded! God grant it! Even though we didn't sink one of them, if we could only put one out of action! The first success—was it possible?

Meanwhile Rozhdestvensky hastened to avail himself of this favourable opportunity.

At 1.49 p.m., when the manoeuvre had been performed by the *Mikasa* and *Shikishima* (two only out of the twelve), the *Suvoroff* fired the first shot at a range of 6,400 yards, and the guns of the whole fleet thundered forth. I watched closely through my glasses. The shots which went over and those which fell short were all close, but the most interesting, *i.e.* the hits, as in the fight of 10th August, could not be seen. Our shells on bursting emitted scarcely any smoke, and the fuses were adjusted to burst inside after penetrating the target. A hit could only be detected when something fell—and nothing fell! In a couple of minutes, when the *Fuji* and *Asahi* had turned also and were following the first ships, the enemy began to reply.

The first shells flew over us. At this range some of the long ones turned a complete somersault, and could clearly be seen with the naked eye curving like so many sticks thrown in the air. They flew over us, making a sort of wail, different to the ordinary roar.

"Are those the portmanteaus?" [1] asked Reydkin, smiling.

"Yes. Those are they."

---

1. At Port Arthur the long Japanese shells of big calibre guns were nicknamed ("*chemodani*") "portmanteaus." Indeed, what else could you call a shell, a foot in diameter and more than 4 feet long, filled with explosive?

But what struck me most was that these "portmanteaus," curving awkwardly head over heels through the air and falling anyhow on the water, exploded the moment they touched its surface. This had never happened before.

After them came others short of us—nearer and nearer. Splinters whistled through the air, jingled against the side and superstructure. Then, quite close and abreast the foremost funnel, rose a gigantic pillar of smoke, water and flame. I saw stretchers being carried along the fore-bridge, and I leaned over the rail.

"Prince Tsereteli!" [2] shouted Reydkin from below, in reply to my silent question, as he went towards his turret.

The next shell struck the side by the centre 6-inch turret, and there was a tremendous noise behind and below me on the port quarter. Smoke and tongues of fire leapt out of the officers' gangway; a shell having fallen into the captain's cabin, and having penetrated the deck, had burst in the officers' quarters, setting them on fire.

And here I was able to observe, and not for the first time, the stupor which seems to come over men, who have never been in action before, when the first shells begin to fall. A stupor which turns easily and instantaneously, at the most insignificant external shock, into either uncontrollable panic which cannot be allayed, or into unusually high spirits, depending on the man's character.

The men at the fire mains and hoses stood as if mesmerised, gazing at the smoke and flames, not understanding, apparently, what was happening. I went down to them from the bridge, and with the most commonplace words, such as "Wake up! Turn the water on!"—got them to pull themselves together and bravely to fight the fire.

I was taking out my watch and pocketbook to make a note of the first fire, when something suddenly struck me in the waist, and something large and soft, though heavy, hit me in the back, lifting me up and hurling me on to the deck. When I again got up, my note-book and watch were in my hands as before. My watch was going; but the second hand was slightly bent, and the glass had disappeared. Stupefied by the blow, and not myself, I began carefully to hunt for it on the deck, and found it unbroken. Picking it up, I fitted it in to my watch—and, only then realising that I had been occupied with something of no importance, I looked round.

I had probably been unconscious for some time, as the fire had been extinguished, and, save for two or three dead bodies on which

2. A flag-sub-lieutenant.

154

water was pouring from the torn hoses, no one was to be seen. Whatever had struck me had come from the direction of the deck house aft, which was hidden from me by a mantlet of hammocks. I looked in the direction where the flag-officers, with a party of poop signalmen, should have been. The shell had passed through the deck house, bursting inside. Of the ten or twelve signalmen, some seemed to be standing by the starboard 6-inch turret, others seemed to be lying in a huddled group. Inside was a pile of something, and on the top lay an officer's telescope.

"Is this all that is left?" I wondered, but I was wrong, as by some miracle Novosiltseff and Kozakevitch were only wounded and, helped by Maximoff, had gone to the dressing station, while I was lying on the deck occupied with mending my watch.

"Hullo! a scene that you are accustomed to? Like the 10th August?" said the irrepressible Reydkin, peeping out of his turret.

"Just the same!" I replied in a confident tone. But it was hardly so: indeed, it would have been more correct to say—"Not in the least like."

On 10th August, in a fight lasting some hours, the *Cesarevitch* was struck by only nineteen large shells, and I, in all seriousness, had intended in the present engagement to note the times and the places where we were hit, as well as the damage done. But how could I make detailed notes when it seemed impossible even to count the number of projectiles striking us? I had not only never witnessed such a fire before, but I had never imagined anything like it Shells seemed to be pouring upon us incessantly, one after another. [3]

After six months with the Port Arthur squadron I had grown indifferent to most things. Shimose and melinite were to a certain extent old acquaintances, but this was something new. It seemed as if these were mines, not shells, which were striking the ship's side and falling on the deck. They burst as soon as they touched anything—the moment they encountered the least impediment in their flight. Handrails, funnel guys, topping lifts of the boats' derricks, were quite sufficient to cause a thoroughly efficient burst The steel plates and superstructure on the upper deck were torn to pieces, and the splinters caused many casualties. Iron ladders were crumpled up into rings, and guns were

---

3. Japanese officers said that after Port Arthur had capitulated, while waiting for the Baltic fleet, they worked up to their high state of preparation as follows:—At target practice every gun captain fired five live shells out of his gun. New guns were afterwards substituted for those worn out

literally hurled from their mountings.

Such havoc would never be caused by the simple impact of a shell, still less by that of its splinters. It could only be caused by the force of the explosion. The Japanese had apparently succeeded in realising what the Americans had endeavoured to attain in inventing their "Vesuvium."

In addition to this, there was the unusual high temperature and liquid flame of the explosion, which seemed to spread over everything. I actually watched a steel plate catch fire from a burst. Of course, the steel did not burn, but the paint on it did Such almost non combustible materials as hammocks, and rows of boxes, drenched with water, flared up in a moment. At times it was impossible to see anything with glasses, owing to everything being so distorted with the quivering, heated air. No! It was different to the 10th August! (See note following).

★★★★★★

Note:—According to thoroughly trustworthy reports, the Japanese in the Battle of Tsu-shima were the first to employ a new kind of explosive in their shells, the secret of which they bought during the war from its inventor, a colonel in one of the South American Republics. It was said that these shells could only be used in guns of large calibre in the armoured squadrons, and that is how those of our ships engaged with Admiral Kataoka's squadron did not suffer the same amount of damage, or have so many fires, as the ships engaged with the battleships and armoured cruisers. Very convincing proofs of this were the cases of the *Svietlana* and *Donskoy*. On 28th May the former was subjected to the fire of two light cruisers, and the latter to the fire of five. In the first place, both were able to hold out for a considerable time, and in the second (and this is most important), they did not catch fire, although on both ships—the *Donskoy*, which was one of the older type, arid the *Svietlana*, which was like a yacht—there was considerably more combustible material than on the newer type of battleship.

For a great many years in naval gunnery two distinct ideas have prevailed one is to inflict on the enemy, although not necessarily much (in quantity), severe and heavy damage—*i.e.* to stop movement—to penetrate under the water line—to get a burst in the hull below the water line—briefly, to put the ship at once out of action. The other is to pour upon him the greatest volume of fire in the shortest time—though it be above water and the actual damage caused by each individual shot be immaterial—in the hope of paralysing the ship, trusting that if this were done it would not be difficult to destroy her completely—that she would, in fact, sink by herself.

With modern guns, in order to secure the first of the above ideas, solid armour-penetrating projectiles must be employed— *i.e.* thick-coated shells (whose internal capacity and bursting charge is consequently diminished), and percussion fuses with retarded action, bursting the shell inside the target. To secure the second idea shells need only be sufficiently solid to ensure their not bursting at the moment of being fixed. The thickness of their walls may be reduced to the minimum, and their internal capacity and bursting charge increased to the utmost limits. The percussion fuses should be sensitive enough to detonate at the slightest touch.

The first of the above views prevails chiefly in France, the second in England. In the late war we held the first, and the Japanese the second.

★★★★★★

I hurriedly went to the admiral in the conning tower. Why? At the time I did not attempt to think, but now feel sure that I merely wished to see him, and by seeing him to confirm my impressions. Was it all imagination? Was it all a nightmare? Had I become jumpy?

Running along the fore-bridge I almost fell, slipping in a pool of blood (the chief signalman—*Kandaooroff*—had just been killed there). I went into the conning tower, and found the admiral and captain both bending down, looking out through the chink between the armour and the roof.

"Sir," said the captain, energetically gesticulating as was his wont, "we must shorten the distance. They're all being killed—they are on fire!"

"Wait a bit. Aren't we all being killed also?" replied the admiral.

Close to the wheel, and on either side of it, lay two bodies in officers' tunics—face downwards.

"The officer at the wheel, and Berseneff!"[4] was shouted in my ear by a sub-lieutenant—Shishkin—whose arm I had touched, pointing to the bodies. "Berseneff first—in the head—quite dead."

---

4. A colonel of the marine artillery—flag gunnery officer.

157

The range-finder was worked Vladimirsky shouted his orders in a clear voice, and the electricians quickly turned the handles of the indicator, transmitting the range to the turrets and light gun batteries.

"We're all right," thought I to myself, going out of the conning tower, but the next moment the thought flashed across me: "They can't see what is going on on board." Leaving the tower, I looked out intently on all sides from the fore-bridge. Were not my recent thoughts, which I had not dared to put into words, realised?

No!

The enemy had finished turning. His twelve ships were in perfect order at close intervals, steaming parallel to us, but gradually forging ahead. No disorder was noticeable. It seemed to me that with my Zeiss glasses (the distance was a little more than 4,000 yards), I could even distinguish the mantlets of hammocks on the bridges, and groups of men. But with us? I looked round.

What havoc!—Burning bridges, smouldering debris on the decks,—piles of dead bodies. Signalling and judging distance stations, gun-directing positions, all were destroyed. And astern of us the *Alexander* and *Borodino* were also enveloped in smoke. No! it was very different to the 10th August

The enemy, steaming ahead, commenced quickly to incline to starboard, endeavouring to cross our T. We also bore to starboard, and again we had him almost on our beam.

It was now 2.5 p.m.

A man came up to report what had taken place in the after 12-inch turret. I went to look. Part of the shield over the port gun had been torn off and bent upwards, but the turret was still turning and keeping up a hot fire.

The officer commanding the fire parties had had both his legs blown off and was carried below. Men fell faster and faster. Reinforcements were required everywhere to replace casualties, even at the turrets into which splinters could only penetrate through the narrow gun ports. The dead were, of course, left to lie where they had fallen, but yet there were not enough men to look after the wounded. There are no spare men on board a warship, and a reserve does not exist. Each man is detailed for some particular duty, and told off to his post in action. The only source which we could tap was the crews of the 47 millimetre, and machine, guns, who from the commencement of the fight had been ordered to remain below the armoured deck so as not to be unnecessarily exposed. Having nothing to do now, as all their guns, which were in exposed positions on the bridges, had been utterly destroyed, we made use of them, but they were a mere drop in the ocean.

As for the fires, even if we had had the men, we were without the means with which to fight them. Over and over again the hoses in use were changed for new ones, but these also were soon torn to ribbons, and the supply became exhausted. Without hoses how could we pump water on to the bridges and spar-deck where the flames raged? On the spar-deck, in particular, where eleven wooden boats were piled up, the fire was taking a firm hold. Up till now, this "store of wood" had only caught fire in places, as the water which had been poured into the boats prior to the commencement of the action was still in them, though it was fast trickling out of the numerous cracks momentarily being made by the splinters.

We, of course, did everything possible: tried to plug the holes, and brought up water in buckets. [5] I am not certain if the scuppers had been closed on purpose, or had merely become blocked, but practically none of the water we used for the fire ran overboard, and it lay, instead, on the upper deck. This was fortunate, as, in the first place, the deck itself did not catch fire, and, in the second, we threw into it the smouldering debris falling from above—merely separating the burning pieces and turning them over.

Seeing Flag-Sub-Lieutenant Demchinsky standing by the ladder of the fore-bridge, with a party of forecastle signalmen near the starboard forward 6-inch turret, I went up to him. Golovnin, another sub-lieutenant, who was in charge of the turret, gave us some cold tea to drink, which he had stored in bottles. It seems a trifle, but it cheered us up.

Demchinsky told me that the first shell striking the ship had fallen right into the temporary dressing station, rigged up by the doctor in what seemed the most sheltered spot on the upper battery (between the centre 6-inch turrets by the ship's *ikon*). He said that it had caused a number of casualties; that the doctor somehow escaped, but the ship's chaplain had been dangerously wounded. I went there to have a look at the place.

The ship's *ikon* or, more properly speaking, *ikons* as there were several of them, all farewell gifts to the ship, were untouched. The glass

---

5. By the admiral's order the iron oil drums, instead of being thrown, away, had been converted into buckets, and these home-made contrivances were placed about the decks.

of the big *ikon* case had not even been broken, and in front of it, on hanging candlesticks, candles were peacefully burning. There wasn't a soul to be seen. Between the wrecked tables, stools, broken bottles, and different hospital appliances were some dead bodies, and a mass of something, which, with difficulty, I guessed to be the remains of what had once been men.

I had not had time properly to take in this scene of destruction when Demchinsky came down the ladder, supporting Flag-Lieutenant Sverbeyeff, who could scarcely stand

He was gasping for breath, and asked for water. Ladling some out of a bucket into a mess kettle, I gave him some, and, as he was unable to use his arms, we had to help him. He drank greedily, jerking out a few words—"It's a trifle tell the flag-captain—I'll come immediately—I am suffocated with these cursed gases—I'll get my breath in a minute." He inhaled the air with a great effort through his blue lips, and something seemed to rattle in his throat and chest, though not, of course, the poisonous gases. On the right side of his back his coat was torn in a great rent, and his wound was bleeding badly. Demchinsky told off a couple of men to take him down to the hospital, and we again went on deck

I crossed over to the port side, between the forward 12-inch and 6-inch turrets, to have a look at the enemy's fleet It was all there, just the same—no fires—no heeling over—no fallen bridges, as if it had been at drill instead of fighting, and as if our guns, which had been thundering incessantly for the last half-hour, had been firing—not shells, but the devil alone knows what! (See note following).

★★★★★★

Note:—In the Battle of Tsu-shima the Japanese losses were:—

Killed	113
Dangerously wounded	139
Severely wounded	243
Slightly wounded	42

These figures are sufficiently eloquent, even allowing for the reports of Japanese officers to be somewhat partial Almost half of the casualties (252 out of 537) were killed and dangerously wounded, the other half were severely and slightly wounded less than 8 *per cent*. The total number was insignificant. Our shells evidently either never burst, or burst badly, *i.e.* in a few large pieces. The Japanese bursting charge was seven times stronger than ours, and consisted not of pyroxylene, but of shimose (and perhaps of something still more powerful). Shimose, higher than pyroxylene. In fact, one might say that a Japanese shell bursting well did as much damage as twelve of ours bursting equally well. And this ours rarely succeeded in doing!

★★★★★★

Feeling almost in despair, I put down my glasses and went aft.

"The last of the halyards are burned," said Demchinsky to me. "I think I shall take my men somewhere under cover." Of course, I fully agreed. What was the use of the signalmen remaining under fire when nothing was left for them to signal with!

It was now 2.20 p.m.

Making my way aft through the debris, I met Reydkin hurrying to the forecastle. "We can't fire from the port quarter," he said excitedly; "everything is on fire there, and the men are suffocated with heat and smoke."

"Well! come on, let's get someone to put the fire out."

"I'll do that, but you report to the admiral. Perhaps he will give us some orders."

"What orders can he give?"

"He may alter the course. I don't know!"

"What! leave the line? Is it likely?"

"Well I anyway, you tell him."

In order to quiet him, I promised to report at once, and we separated, going our ways. As I anticipated, the admiral only shrugged his shoulders on hearing my report and said, "They *must* put the fire out. No help can be sent from here."

Instead of two dead bodies, five or six were now lying in the conning tower. The man at the wheel having been incapacitated, Vladimirsky had taken his place. His face was covered with blood, but his moustache was smartly twisted upwards, and he wore the same self-confident look as he had in the wardroom when discussing "the future of gunnery."

Leaving the tower, I intended going to Reydkin to tell him the admiral's reply and to assist in extinguishing the fire, but instead I remained on the bridge looking at the Japanese fleet

161

CHAPTER 11

Spirit of the Men

After steering on their new course for a quarter of an hour, the enemy had again forged a considerable distance ahead, and now the *Mikasa*, at the head of the column, gradually inclined to starboard to cross our T. I waited for us to incline to starboard also, but the admiral held on to the old course for some time longer. I guessed that by doing this he hoped to lessen the distance as much as possible, which would naturally have assisted us, since, with our wrecked range-finders and gun-directing positions, our guns were only serviceable at close quarters. However, to allow the enemy to cross our T and to subject ourselves to a raking fire was not to be thought of counting the moments anxiously I watched and waited. The *Mikasa* came closer and closer to our course. Our 6-inch starboard turret was already preparing to fire, when—we sharply inclined to starboard. Breathing freely again, I looked around.

Demchinsky had not yet gone below with his men but was hard at work, apparently moving the cartridge boxes of the 47-millimetre guns off the deck into the turret, so that there should be less risk of their exploding in the fire and causing greater damage. I went to ask him what he was doing, but before I was able to say anything the captain appeared at the top of the ladder just behind me. His head was covered with blood and, staggering convulsively, he clutched at the hand-rail. At that moment a shell burst quite close to us and, losing his balance from the sudden explosion, he fell, head foremost, down the ladder. Luckily we saw it and were able to catch him.

"It's nothing—only a trifle," he said in his ordinary quick way of speaking. He tried to force a smile and, jumping up, endeavoured to go on. But as to go on to the hospital meant another three ladders, we put him, in spite of his protests, on a stretcher.

A man reported that the after turret had been blown up[6] and almost simultaneously there resounded above us a rumbling noise accompanied by the sharp clank of falling iron. Something large and heavy fell with a crash; the ship's boats on the spar-deck were smashed to bits; burning debris fell all round us and we were enveloped in an impenetrable smoke. At the time we did not know what had happened, but afterwards we learned that it was the foremost funnel which had fallen.

The terrified signalmen, losing their presence of mind, huddled together right under the falling spar-deck, and carried us with them in their rush. It took some time before we could compel them to stop and listen to reason.

It was now 2.30 p.m.

When the smoke had somewhat cleared I tried to go to the poop to see what had happened to the after turret, but along the upper deck no communication between bow and stern was possible.

I attempted to pass through the upper battery, whence to the poop the nearest way was through the admiral's cabin, but here the staff officers' quarters were burning furiously. Turning back, I met Flag Lieutenant Kruijanoffsky on the ladder hurrying downwards.

"Where are you going to?"

"Into the steering compartment; the rudder is disabled," he shouted to me in passing,

"That is all that is wanting," thought I to myself, rushing up on deck.

Quickly going on to the fore-bridge I could not at first get my bearings, because, not far to starboard, our fleet was steaming past, bearing on an opposite course. The *Navarin*,—which ought to have been astern—was now coming up to us, going at full speed and cutting through a big breaker. She especially impressed herself on my memory. It was evident that, owing to our steering-gear being out of order, we had turned nearly 16 points.

The line of our fleet was very irregular and the intervals varied, especially in the 3rd squadron. I could not see the leading ships; they were to windward of us and hidden by the smoke of the fires. The enemy was also in the same direction. Taking my bearings by the sun and wind, I should say that our fleet was steering approximately S.E.,

---

6. The ships nearest to us reported afterwards that the armoured shield on our after turret had been blown right up above the bridges, and then was seen to fall crumpled up on to the poop. What had actually happened was not known.

and the enemy stood to the N.E. of us.

In the event of the flag-ship falling out of the line during the battle, the torpedo-boats *Biedovy* and *Buistry* were immediately to come to her assistance in order to take off the admiral and staff and put them on board an uninjured ship. But, however much I looked on either side, no torpedo-boats were to be seen. Could we signal? But with what? All means of signalling had long since been destroyed.

Meanwhile, though we were unable to see the enemy on account of the smoke, they had a good view of us, and concentrated their fire on the battered battleship in the hope of sinking us. Shells simply poured upon us—a veritable whirlwind of fire and iron. Lying almost stationary in the water, and slowly working her engines so as to get on the proper course and follow the fleet, the *Suvoroff* offered her battered sides in turn to the enemy, firing wildly from those of her guns which were still serviceable, and, alas ! they were few in number. The following is what Japanese eyewitnesses wrote about us: (See note following quotations).

On leaving the line the flag-ship, though burning badly, still steamed after the fleet, but under the fire we brought to bear upon her, she rapidly lost her foremast and both funnels, besides being completely enveloped in flames and smoke. She was so battered that scarcely anyone would have taken her for a ship, and yet, even in this pitiful condition, like the flag-ship which she was, she never ceased to fire as much as possible with such of her guns as were serviceable.

I will quote another extract from a report on the operations of Admiral Kamimura's squadron:

The *Suvoroff*, subjected to the fire of both our squadrons, left the line. Her upper part was riddled with holes, and she was entirely enveloped in smoke. Her masts had fallen and her funnels came down one after the other. She was unable to steer, and her fires increased in density every moment But, even outside the fighting line, she still continued firing, so that our bravest sailors credited her with making a plucky resistance.

★★★★★★

Note:—In order to establish a connection between the facts which I personally saw and noted down, and in order to be able to explain the Japanese movements, I shall have recourse to sources which can hardly be suspected of partiality towards us. I refer to two Japanese official publications which are both entitled *Nippon-Kai Tai-Kai-Sen* (*The Great Battle in the Sea of Japan*). The books are illustrated by a number of photographs and plans taken at different moments of the fight, and contain the reports of various ships and detachments. A few quite immaterial differences in description of detail by various witnesses have not been removed, as they only give the stamp of truth to the publication.

I must request my readers to excuse the heavy, and at times incoherent language introduced by me in these quotations. The reason for this is my wish to keep as near as possible to the original, and, in the construction of its sentences, Japanese is totally different to any European language.

★★★★★★

And now to return to my personal observations and impressions.

Amidst the rumbling fire of our own guns, the bursting of the enemy's shells, and the roaring of the flames, I was, of course, unable to think about the direction to which we were turning—whether to or from the wind, but I soon found out When the battleship, turning on her course, lay stern on to the wind, the smoke from the flames of the burning spar-deck leapt right up to the fore-bridge where I was standing. While occupied in looking for the torpedo-boats, I had probably not noticed the danger creeping towards me, and only realised it on finding myself enveloped in an impenetrable smoke. Burning air parched my face and hands, while a caustic smell of burning almost blinded me. Breathing was impossible. I felt I must save myself, but to do so I had to go through the flames, for there was no other way on to the poop. For a moment the thought flashed across me to jump from the bridge on to the forward 12-inch turret, but to remember where I was, to choose places to which and whence to jump, was impossible. How did I get out of this hell? Perhaps some of the crew who had seen me on the bridge dragged me out! How I arrived on the upper battery on a well-known spot near the ship's *ikon*, I can't remember, and I can't imagine!

Having recovered my breath, drunk some water and rubbed my eyes, I looked about It seemed quite pleasant here. The large *ikon* case was still unbroken, and with the exception of the first shell which had destroyed the temporary dressing station, the quiet of this little corner had apparently been undisturbed. Among some of the crew who were standing by I recognised a few of Demchinsky's signalmen, and, in reply to my enquiries as to his whereabouts, they told me that having been wounded he had made his way to the hospital

They were standing silently and outwardly were calm, but from the way in which they looked at me I noticed that they were all possessed by some undefined feeling of fear, as well as of expectation and hope. They appeared to believe, or to wish to believe that I was still able to issue the necessary order which would save them, and so they waited. But what order could I give? I might advise them to go below—to take cover under the armoured deck and await their fate, but this they could have done of their own accord. They wanted a different order, for they still felt themselves indispensable to the fight, if it were to be continued. These "tempered" men were just the men we wanted.

And to me, indeed, it seemed useless as well as cruel to shatter their belief—to stamp out the last spark of hope—to tell them the hard truth—to say, in fact, that it was of no use our fighting, and that all was over. No! I couldn't! On the contrary, I was filled with a desire to mislead them—to feed that flame of hope. Rather let them die in the happy consciousness of victory, life, and glory, coming perhaps in a few moments.

As already said, the place where the church was usually rigged[7]— and which the doctor had (so unluckily) selected for his temporary dressing station—had been fairly fortunate, but now, abaft the centre 6 -inch turrets, the fire had commenced to make its way. Proceeding thither, we set to work dragging away the burning extinguishing it, or throwing it overboard through the huge holes in the ship's side. Finding an undamaged water main and a piece of a hose (without a nozzle), we worked quietly and in earnest. We extinguished some burning furniture, but alongside it, behind the thin, red-hot, steel partition separating us from the officers' quarters, another fire burst forth, whose roar could at times be heard even amidst the noise of the battle. Occasionally a man fell wounded, and either lay where he was, or got up and walked or crawled to the ladder leading below. No attention was paid to him—What mattered it? one more, one less!

How long we were thus employed—five, ten, or fifteen minutes—I do not know, but suddenly the thought occurred to me, "The conning tower—what is happening there?"

---

7. In a ship there is no proper church compartment. The church is only rigged when a service is to be held.

I went up quickly, fatigue and depression at once vanishing. My mind was as clear as possible, and I saw at once that, as the smoke was pouring through the great rents on the port side, the starboard must be the windward side. I proceeded thither. Creeping with difficulty on to the upper deck through the torn hatchway, I scarcely recognised the place where a short time since we had stood with Demchinsky. Movement was literally impossible. Astern, the spar-deck had fallen down and was burning in a bright flame on the deck; in front of me was a heap of debris. The ladders to the bridge had gone and the starboard end of the bridge had been destroyed; even the gangway under the bridge on the other side was blocked.

I was obliged to go below again and come up on the port side. Here, matters were rather better, as, although fallen and burning, the pieces of the spar-deck were not scattered about in such confusion as on the other side. The 6-inch turret appeared to be still uninjured, and was keeping up a hot fire; the ladder to the bridge was whole, but blocked with burning hammocks, which I at once set five or six men, who were following me, to throw into the water standing on the deck Suddenly a shell whistled past us, quite close. Everything seemed to start up, and splinters rained upon us. "That must be in the 6-inch turret," thought I to myself, half closing my eyes, and holding my breath so as not to swallow the gas. Sure enough, as the smoke cleared away, only one helpless-looking gun stuck defiantly out of the turret, while out of the armoured door of the latter came its commander, Lieutenant Danchich.

"Mine's done for too; the muzzle of one has been carried away, and the elevating gear of the other is smashed." Going to the door I looked in. Of the gun's crew two lay huddled up in a curious manner, while one sat motionless, staring with wide-open eyes, holding his wounded side with both hands. A gun captain, with a worried, business-like look, was extinguishing some burning cloths.

"What are you doing here?"

"I want to go to the conning tower."

"Why? There's no one there."

"No one! What do you mean?"

"It's a fact. Bogdanoff has just passed through; he said it was all smashed to pieces—had caught fire, and they'd abandoned it. He went out just as the bridge fell in—right on to me—I wasn't touched—lucky!"

"Where's the admiral?"

At this moment there was another explosion quite close to me, and something from behind hit me in the right leg. It was not hard, and I felt no pain. I turned round to look, but none of my men were to be seen. Were they killed, or had they gone below?

"Haven't we any stretchers?" I heard Danchich ask anxiously.

"For whom?" I said

"Why! for you. You're bleeding."

Looking down I saw that my right leg was standing in a pool of blood, but the leg itself felt sound enough.

It was 3 p.m.

"Can you manage to go? Stop—I'll tell off some one to go with you," said Danchich, making what seemed to me an unnecessary fuss.

I was annoyed, and angrily said: "Who wants to be accompanied?" and bravely started to go down the ladder, not realising what had happened. When a small splinter had wounded me in the waist at the beginning of the fight, it had hurt me; but this time I felt nothing.

Later, in the hospital, when carried there on a stretcher, I understood why it is that during a fight one hears neither groans nor shouts. All that comes afterwards. Apparently our feelings have strict limits for receiving external impressions, being even deeply impressed by an absurd sentence, A thing can be so painful that you feel nothing, so terrible that you fear nothing.

Having passed through the upper and lower batteries, I descended to the mess deck (under the armoured one), to the hospital, but I involuntarily went back to the ladder.

The mess deck was full of wounded, [8] They were standing, sitting, lying—some on mattresses put ready beforehand—some on hastily spread tarpaulins—some on stretchers—some just anyhow. Here it was that they first began to feel the dreadful noise of deep sighs and half-stifled groans was audible in the close, damp air, which smelt of something sour and disgustingly sickly. The electric light seemed scarcely able to penetrate this stench. Ahead somewhere, in white coats stained with red splotches, busy figures were moving about, and towards them all these piles of flesh, clothes, and bones turned, and in their agony dragged themselves, expecting something from them. It seemed as if a cry, motionless, voiceless, but intelligible, a cry which reached to one's very soul, a request for help, for a miracle, for relief from suffering—though at the price of a speedy death—rose up on all sides.

I did not stop to wait my turn, and, not wishing to put myself

8. There were probably more here than in the whole of the Japanese fleet.

before others, quickly went up the ladder to the lower battery, where I met the flag-captain, who had his head bandaged. (He had been wounded in the back of the neck by three splinters.)

On enquiry I learned that at the same time as the steering gear had been injured and the flag-ship had left her place, the admiral and Vladimirsky were wounded in the head in the conning tower. The latter had gone below to get his wounds dressed, and had been succeeded in command by Bogdanoff, the third lieutenant. The admiral's orders were to steer after the fleet

The fore-bridge was struck by numerous projectiles. Splinters of shells, which penetrated in large quantities under the mushroom-shaped roof of the conning tower, had destroyed all the instruments in it, and had broken the compass, but luckily the telegraph to one engine and the voice-tube to the other were still working. The bridge had caught fire, and the hammocks—with which we had proposed to protect ourselves from splinters—as well as the small chart house behind the conning tower, were also burning. The heat became unbearable, and what was worse—the thick smoke prevented our seeing, which, without a compass, made it impossible to keep on in any particular direction. The only thing left for us to do was to steer from the lower fighting position and abandon the conning tower for some place whence one could see. At this time there were in the conning tower the admiral, the flag-captain, and the flag navigating officer—all three wounded; Lieutenant Bogdanoff, Sub-Lieutenant Shishkin and one sailor apparently uninjured. Bogdanoff was the first to come out of the tower on the port side of the bridge, and, pluckily pushing aside the burning hammocks, he dashed forward, disappearing into the flames, which were leaping upward.

Following after him, the flag-captain turned to the starboard side of the bridge, but here everything was destroyed; the ladder was gone and there was no road. Only one way remained—below, into the lower fighting position. With difficulty dragging aside the dead bodies which were lying on the deck, they raised the hatch over the armoured tube, and through it let themselves down into the lower fighting position. Rozhdestvensky, although wounded in the head, back and right leg (besides several small splinter wounds), bore himself most cheerfully. From the lower fighting position the flag-captain proceeded to the hospital, while the admiral—leaving here Colonel Filipinoffsky (the flag navigating officer), who was slightly wounded, with orders that, in the absence of other instructions, he was to steer on the old course—

went off to look for a place from which he could watch the fight

The upper deck being a mass of burning wreckage, he was unable to pass beyond where the ship's *ikon* hung in the upper battery. From here he tried to get through to the centre 6-inch turret on the port side, but was unable to, so proceeded to the starboard turret. It was here that he received the wound which caused him so much pain. (A splinter struck his left leg, severing the main nerve and paralysing the ball of the foot) He was carried into the turret and seated on a box, but he still had sufficient strength at once to ask why the turret was not firing, and to order Kruijanoffsky, who then came up, to find the gun captains, fall in the crews, and open fire. The turret, however, had been damaged and would not turn. Kruijanoffsky, who had just returned from the disabled steering gear, reported that the rudder had been repaired, but that all three communicators with it were cut. Also there were no means of conveying orders from the lower fighting position to the steering gear, as voice-tubes did not exist, the electric indicators were injured, and the telephone refused to work. It became necessary to steer from the lower fighting position, which meant to turn round in circles rather than to go ahead.

The events which I am relating in chronological order, and in the form of a connected narrative were, of course, not recorded in this manner by me, but were told me at different times and by different people. To attempt, however, to give in detail these half-finished sentences, interrupted suddenly by the burst of a shell dose by—the jerked-out remarks thrown at one in passing—the separate words accompanied by gestures, more eloquent far than any words—would be impossible and useless. At that moment, when everyone's nerves were highly strung, an exclamation or wave of the hand took the place of many words, fully and clearly interpreting the thought which it was desired to express. Put on paper they would be unintelligible.

Time was measured by seconds; and there was no occasion for words.

There was no actual fire in the lower battery as yet; it was coming from above. But through the hatches, torn funnel casings, and shot holes in the middle deck, burning debris was felling below, and here and there small fires burst forth. The men, however, set to work, most pluckily rigging up cover for the wireless fighting station with sacks of coal. The trolleys with the 12-pounder cartridges which had been collected here (as the ammunition supply rails had been damaged) were in danger of catching fire, so several had to be thrown overboard.

However, despite the difficulties in extinguishing the fire, it was at length got under.

Besides spreading in the natural course it was assisted, of course, by the enemy's projectiles, which continued to rain upon us. The losses among the crew still continued to be heavy, and I myself was wounded in the left elbow, as well as being struck by two small splinters in the side;

CHAPTER 12

Defeat Inevitable

I remembered that in the event of the flag-ship leaving the line, the torpedo-boats, *Biedovy* and *Buistry*, were to come to her in order to transfer the admiral and his staff to another and uninjured ship. In such circumstances, in order to avoid confusion, until the flag had been transferred or until a signal had been made as to the handing over of the command, the fleet was to be led by the ship following the one which had fallen out of the line. I do not presume to be able to say whether our other ships could see that no torpedo-boats had come up to the *Suvoroff!* Whether they could all see that no signal was possible from the battered, burning battleship, minus funnels and masts! Whether it ought in consequence to have been taken for granted that the command naturally devolved on the next ship according to seniority! and whether she should in some way or another have shown that she had taken over command! In any case the *Alexander* (more correctly, her captain, Bukvostoff) carried out the orders and did her duty. After the flag-ship had fallen out of the line, receiving no fresh instructions, she took the lead and continued the fight.

From the time when I saw the *Alexander* passing close to us on a south-easterly course, she steamed for twenty minutes, gradually inclining to the south in order to prevent the enemy from getting ahead and crossing her T. At the same time the Japanese, elated by their first success, again endeavoured to realise their main idea of a concentrated attack on the leading ship, and so wrapped up were they in this objective that they went ahead too fast, leaving nothing to prevent the *Alexander* passing astern in a north-easterly direction.

She immediately took advantage of this and turned sharp to the north, calculating with luck to fall in force upon their rear and subject them to a raking fire. The Japanese in their reports fix the time of this movement differently; some at 2.40 p.m., others at 2.50 p.m. (the moment of the sinking of the *Oslyabya*, which under the concentrated fire of six of Admiral Kamimura's armoured cruisers had left the line even before the *Suvoroff*). According to my own calculations, the latter time was the more likely to be correct If the enemy's fleet had turned "in succession," as it had done at the commencement of the battle, this manoeuvre of the *Alexander*'s might have been successful, but, realising the gravity of the moment, Togo, on this occasion, gave the order to turn 16 points to port "together." The manoeuvre was not altogether successful. The 1st squadron (*Mikasa, Shikishima, Fuji, Asahi, Kasuga,* and *Nisshin*) performed it correctly, but Kamimura, with his cruisers—probably not having made out the signal and expecting the order to turn "in succession" on to the former course—quickly passed our fleet as well as his own battleships (which were on the opposite course), and masked their fire. He then had plenty of room to turn (he turned "in succession") and, after overtaking the battleships, to form single column line ahead.

For a moment confusion prevailed, for which the Japanese might have paid dearly, but owing to its condition our fleet was unable to reap the advantage. Making full use of their speed, the Japanese not only succeeded in righting their distances, but attained their object, *i.e.* came out across the *Alexander*'s course, forcing her to the south.

Through the starboard portholes of our batteries we were now able plainly to see the *Alexander*, which was almost on our beam and steering straight towards us—the remainder following her. The distance rapidly diminished, and with our glasses we could clearly see her battered sides, broken bridges, burning cabins and spar-deck, but her funnels and masts were still standing. After her came the *Borodino*, burning furiously. The enemy had already succeeded in forging ahead, and we now lay between the fleets. Our ships approached from starboard, *i.e.* the port side of the *Suvoroff*, and we came under a hot fire. Our forward 12-inch turret (the only one that was now serviceable) took an active part in the fight, and no attention was paid to falling shells.

I was wounded in the left leg, but only looked down with regret at my torn boot! We all waited, holding our breath, watching the Japanese fire, which was apparently concentrated on the *Alexander*. At times she seemed completely enveloped in flames and brown smoke, while round her the sea literally boiled, throwing up great pillars of water. Nearer and nearer she came, till the distance was scarcely 2,000 yards. Then—one after another, we saw a whole series of shells strike her fore-bridge and port 6-inch turret, and turning sharply to starboard she steamed away, having almost reversed her course, while after her went the *Borodino*, *Orel*, and others. The turn was hastily made, being neither "in succession" nor "all together," [1] and the line ahead formation was not maintained. A deafening clamour resounded in our batteries.

"They've given it up. They are going off. They couldn't do it," I heard on all sides.

These simple folk had, of course, imagined that our fleet was returning to the flag-ship in order to rescue her. Their disenchantment was distressing to witness, but still more was it distressing to realise the true significance of what had happened.

How pitiless is memory!—A scene never to be forgotten came clearly and distinctly before my eyes—just such another scene—the same awful picture. After Prince Utomsky's signal on the 10th August our battleships had steamed north-west in the same disorder and just as hurriedly.

"They couldn't do it!"

And the awful, fatal word, which I had not even dared to think, rang in my brain, and seemed to be written in letters of fire on the smoke, on the battered sides, and even on the pale, confused faces of the crew.

Bogdanoff was standing beside me. I caught his eye, and we understood one another. He commenced to talk of it, but suddenly stopping, looked round, and said in an unnaturally calm voice: "We seem to be heeling over to port"

"Yes—some 8 degrees," I answered, and, pulling out my watch and notebook, jotted down:

> 3.25 p.m. a heavy list to port, and a bad fire in the upper battery."

I often afterwards thought: why is it that we hide things from one another and from ourselves? Why did not Bogdanoff express his thoughts aloud? and why was it that I did not dare to write even in my own notebook the cheerless word "*Defeat*"? Perhaps within us there still existed some dim hope of a miracle, of some kind of surprise which would change everything? I do not know.

---

1. Whether this turn was intentional or accidental, owing to the damage done to her steering communicators, will forever remain a secret.

After the *Alexander* had turned, the enemy's ships also turned 16 points "together," and this time the manoeuvre was successfully performed—so successfully, in fact, that it seemed as if they were merely at drill and not in action.

Steering on an opposite course, they passed under our bows, and from the *Suvoroff* it seemed as if we could almost cut into their column. We inclined to starboard after our fleet. (This was, of course, only imagination, for, not being able to steer by surrounding objects but only by compass in the lower fighting position, we were in reality not moving ahead, but were only turning to starboard and to port; remaining almost in the same place.) In passing close to us, the enemy did not miss his opportunity of concentrating his fire on the obstinate ship which refused to sink, and it was, apparently, now that our last turret, the forward 12-inch, was destroyed. According to Japanese reports their torpedo-boats came up at the same time as their fleet and attacked us unsuccessfully, but I did not see them.

A shell entered the gun port of the fourth (from the bows) 12-pounder gun of the lower battery on the port side, and it was a lucky shot, for in addition to carrying away the gun it penetrated the armoured deck. The water poured into the damaged port, and being unable to run back on account of the list to port, fell through this hole into the mess deck, which was most dangerous.

Bogdanoff was the first to call attention to it, and we at once started to make some kind of an obstacle out of coal sacks, and anything else that was handy, so as to cover the hole and stop the water getting in. I say "we," because the few hands left in the battery could not be brought to obey orders. They huddled in corners in a sort of stupor, and we had almost to drag them out by force, and were obliged to work ourselves to set them an example. We were joined by Flag Torpedo Officer Lieutenant Leontieff and Demchinsky, but the latter could only encourage us with words, as both his wrists were bandaged.

At 3.40 p.m. a cheer broke out in the battery, which was taken up all over the vessel, but we were unable to ascertain what had caused it or whence it had originated. Rumour had at that one of the enemy's ships had been seen to sink; some even said two—not one. Whatever may have been the truth, this cheering had the effect of quickly changing the feeling on board, and the depression from which we had been suffering, both on account of the fire which we had seen poured into the *Alexander,* and because of the departure of the fleet, vanished Men who had been skulking in corners, deaf to the commands and even requests of their officers, now came running to us asking: "Where could they be of use, and what at?" They even joked and laughed: "Hullo! that's only a 6-inch! No more 'portmanteaus' now!"

Sure enough, since the enemy's main body had steamed off, we had only been subjected to the fire of Admiral Dewa's light cruisers, which, in comparison to what we had been under before, was almost imperceptible.

Commander V. V, Ignatzius had remained below after the second wound in his head had been dressed, and, unable to restrain himself at such a moment, paying no heed to the doctors, he ran up the ladder into the battery, shouting: "Follow me, lads! To the fire—to the fire I we have only got to get it under!"

Various non-combatants in the mess deck (belonging to the hospital), and men who were slightly wounded and had gone down to get their wounds dressed, doubled after him, A chance shot struck the hatchway, and when the smoke cleared away neither ladder, nor commander, nor men with him, were in existence!

But even this bloody episode did not damp the men's ardour. It was only one in a hundred others.

In the lower battery where, owing to insufficiency of hands, fires momentarily became more numerous, men came, and work went merrily. Of the ship's officers, besides Bogdanoff, there came Lieutenant Vuiruboff, junior torpedo officer, a robust-looking youth, who, in an unbuttoned coat, rushed about everywhere giving the lead, while his shout of "Tackle it! Stick to it!" resounding amongst smoke and flames, gave strength to the workers. Zotoff came for a short time; he was wounded in the left side and arm. Prince Tsereteli looked out from the mess deck, asking how things were going. Kozakevitch was carried past, wounded a second time, and now dangerously. My servant, Matrosoff, appeared and almost dragged me by force to the dressing station. I got rid of him with difficulty, telling him to go at once to my cabin and get me some cigarettes.

"Very good, sir!" he said, going off as he was bid, and we did not meet again.

"To the guns! Torpedo boats astern! To the guns!" was shouted on deck.

It was easy to say, "To the guns!" but of the twelve 12-pounder guns in the lower battery only one, on the starboard side, was now serviceable, and there was no chance of using it The torpedo-boats carefully came up from astern (according to the Japanese, this was about 4.20 p.m.), but in the light gun battery aft (behind the wardroom) there was still one uninjured 12 pounder. Maximoff, a volunteer, on whom the command of the battery had devolved after the officers had fallen, opened a hot fire, and the torpedo-boats, seeing that this strange look-ing, battered vessel could still show her teeth, steamed off to wait for a more favourable opportunity.

This event suggested to me the idea of noting the means we had with which to protect ourselves against torpedo attack, or, more prop-erly, to what degree of helplessness we had arrived. There were in the lower battery about fifty men of the crew—all of various ratings. Among them, however, were two gun captains. Of the guns, only one was really serviceable, though the gun captains proposed to "repair" another by substituting for its injured parts pieces from the other ten which were quite unserviceable. There was also Maximoff's gun in the stern light gun battery.

Having finished my inspection of the lower battery I went through the upper to the forward light gun battery (not one of the turrets was fit for action), and I was struck with the picture it presented, il-lustrating, more clearly than I had yet seen, the action of the enemy's projectiles.

There were no fires; everything that could ignite had already been burned. The four 12-pounder guns had been torn off their mountings, and in vain I looked on them for marks of direct hits. None could be seen. The havoc had clearly been caused by the force of the explosion, and not by the impact of the shell How was this? Neither mines nor pyroxylene were stored in the battery, so the enemy's shells must have exploded with the force of mines.

To my readers, walking about the crippled wreck of a ship like this and inspecting the damage done may appear strange, but it must be remembered that a peculiar, even extraordinary condition of affairs prevailed on board. "So fearful as not to be in the least terrible." To everyone it was perfectly clear that all was over. Neither past or future existed. We lived only in the actual moment, and were possessed with an overpowering desire to do something, no matter what.

Having again gone down to the lower battery, I was proceeding to the stern light gun battery, which I wished to inspect, when I met Kursel.

Verner von Kursel, a Courlandian by birth, and a general favourite with every one in the *Suvoroff*'s ward-room, had been in the merchant service almost since his cradle, and could speak every language in Europe, though he was equally bad at all of them. When they chaffed him about this in the ward-room he used to say quite seriously: "I think that I'm better at German than any other!" [2] He had seen and been through so much that he never lost his presence of mind, and nothing prevented him meeting his friends with a pleasant smile.

And so now, nodding his head to me in the distance, he cheerily asked:

"Well! How are you passing the time?"

"Badly," I answered,

"Oh! that's it, is it? They don't seem able to hit me yet, but I see that you have been wounded."

"I was."

"Where are you off to?"

"To have a look at the light guns in the stern and get some cigarettes from my cabin; I have smoked all I had."

"To your cabin?" and Kursel grinned. "I have just come from there, I'll go with you."

Indeed, he seemed likely to be a useful companion, as he knew the most sheltered way.

Having got as far as the officers' quarters, I stopped in amazement. Where my cabin and the two adjoining ones had been was an enormous hole! Kursel laughed heartily, thoroughly enjoying his joke, but growing angry I waved my hand and quickly retraced my steps. Kursel overtook me in the battery and offered me a cigar.

The fires in the lower battery had all been got under and, encouraged by this success, we determined to try our luck in the upper battery. Two firemen produced some new half-made hoses; one end of them we fastened to the water-main with wire, and the other we tied to the nozzle. Then, armed with these and using damp sacks to protect us from the flames, we leaned out through the church hatch whence, having succeeded after some little time in putting the fire out which had been burning in the dressing station we were able to go into the upper battery. All hands worked splendidly, and we soon had extinguished the fire in the part assigned to the church. Then another fire started abaft the centre 6-inch turrets—the place which had been selected, on account of its being protected, for putting the cartridge boxes of the 47-millimetre guns taken down from the bridges. Their removal had been well ordered, for no sooner had we set about extin-

2. Courland is one of the Baltic Provinces where German, is spoken.—A.B.L.

guishing the fire which was now raging near them than they began to explode. Several of the men fell killed and wounded, and great confusion at once ensued.

"It's nothing—it will cease in a moment," said Kursel.

But explosions became more and more frequent. The new hoses were destroyed, one after the other, and then, suddenly, quite dose, there was a loud crash, accompanied with the ring of tearing iron. This was not a 6-inch shell, but the "portmanteaus" again. The men became seized with panic, and, listening to nothing and nobody, rushed below.

When we went down into the lower battery, bitterly disappointed at our want of luck just when things seemed beginning to go so well, something (it must have been a splinter of some kind) struck me in the side and I staggered.

"Wounded again?" enquired Kursel, taking his cigar out of his mouth and leaning tenderly over me,

I looked at him and thought: "Ah! if only the whole fleet were composed of men as cool as you are!"

CHAPTER 13

End of the "Suvoroff"

Meanwhile, having turned abruptly away from the *Suvoroff*, our fleet had steamed off, gradually inclining to starboard so as not to give the Japanese a chance of crossing its T, which they evidently were trying to do. The consequence was that both belligerents moved on the arcs of two concentric circles. Ours on the smaller—the Japanese on the larger.

About 4 p.m. it seemed as if fortune for the last time was endeavouring to smile upon us. In the midst of the thick smoke which was pouring from the damaged funnels, from the guns which were in action, and from the fires on board, and which mingled with the mist still lying on the water, the enemy's main force seemed to separate from and lose sight of ours. Japanese reports, of which I have availed myself, comment very briefly and somewhat obscurely on this event. Nothing is clear save that Togo, believing our fleet was somehow breaking through to the north, went thither in search of it. Kamimura being of a different opinion proceeded with his cruisers in a south and south-westerly direction. At least, the above will alone explain the glowing panegyrics which I find in the reports entitled *The Prowess of Admiral Kamimura*. If it had not been for this "prowess," possibly the fight would have ended on 27th May, and our fleet would have had time to close up and recover.

Steering on a south and afterwards south-westerly course, Kamimura heard a heavy cannonade proceeding to the west He accordingly hastened there to find Admiral Kataoka attacking (till now with little success) our cruisers and transports. Kamimura, commencing to take an active part in the fight, then came upon our main body, which, having almost described a circle with a 5-mile diameter, was returning to the spot where the *Alexander* had made her abrupt turn, and round which the *Suvoroff* was so helplessly wandering.

It was about 5 p.m.

I was standing with Kursel in the lower battery smoking and talking of subjects, not in any way connected with the fight, when suddenly we seemed to be in the midst of the fleet, which, devoid of all formation, was moving northwards. Some ships passed to starboard—some to port—the *Borodino*—Captain Serebryanikoff—leading. The *Alexander*, badly battered and with a heavy list—lying so low that the water almost came into the portholes of the lower battery—was still fighting, firing with such of her guns as were serviceable. I did not see her, but was told that the whole of her bows, from the stem to the 12-inch turret, were torn open.

Having closed up to the main body, the cruisers and transports steamed astern and somewhat to port—attacked by detachments of Admiral Kataoko's squadron. (In addition to Kataoko himself, Admirals Dewa, Uriu, and Togo junior were also there.) Kamimura remained farther to starboard, *i.e.* to the east—also heading for the north.

"Portmanteaus" were still raining on us. Word had been received from the engine-room that the men were being suffocated and rapidly falling out, as the ventilators were bringing down smoke instead of air; soon there would be no men left to work the engines! Meanwhile, the electric light grew dim, and it was reported from the dynamo engines that steam was scarce.

"Torpedo-boats ahead!"

We rushed to our only gun (the other had been found to be past repair), but it turned out to be the *Buiny*, which happened to be passing us, and was on her own initiative coining alongside the crippled battleship to enquire if she could be of any assistance.

Kruijanoffsky was ordered by the flag-captain, who was standing on the embrasure, to semaphore to her (with his arms) to "take off the admiral."

I was watching the *Buiny's* movements from the battery, when suddenly the admiral's messenger, Peter Poochkoff, hastened towards me.

"Please come to the turret, sir! a torpedo-boat has come alongside, but the admiral won't leave."

I ought to mention here that Rozhdestvensky had not been to the dressing station, and none of us knew how badly he was wounded because, to all enquiries when he was hit, he angrily replied that it was only a trifle. He still remained sitting on the box in the turret, where he had been placed.

At times he would look up to ask how the battle was progressing, and then would again sit silently, with his eyes on the ground. Considering, however, the state the ship was in, what else could he do? His conduct seemed most natural, and it never occurred to us that these questions were merely momentary flashes of energy—short snatches of consciousness.

On the arrival of the torpedo-boat being reported, he pulled himself together, and gave the order to "Collect the staff," (see note following), with perfect clearness, but afterwards, he only frowned, and would listen to nothing.

★★★★★★

Note:—Of all the wounded members of the staff, who were below, under the armoured deck, it was only possible to "collect" two Filipinoffsky and Leontieff. The former was in the lower fighting position, which was hermetically separated from the mess deck, and received a current of fresh air through the armoured tube of the conning tower. (All the same he had to sit by candle light, as the lamps had gone out.) The latter was at the exit hatch. The mess deck was in darkness (the electric light had gone out) and was full of suffocating smoke. Hurrying along to find the staff, we called them by name; but received no answers. The silence of the dead reigned in that smoky darkness, and it is probable that all who were in the closed compartments under the armoured deck, where the ventilators took smoke instead of air, gradually becoming suffocated, lost consciousness and died. The engines had ceased to work. The electric light had given out for want of steam; and no one came up from below. Of the 900 men composing the complement of the *Suvoroff*, it would not be far wrong to say that, at this time there remained alive only those few who were gathered together in he lower battery and on the windward embrasure.

★★★★★★

Assisted by Kursel I crept through the open half-port of the lower battery, out on to the starboard embrasure in front of the centre 6-inch turret I was in need of help, as my right leg had become very painful, and I could only limp on the heel of my left.

The boatswain and some sailors were at work on the embrasure, sweeping overboard the burning debris which had fallen from the spar-deck above. Lying off our starboard bow, and some three or four cables distant, was the *Kamchatka*. Kamimura's cruisers were pouring as heavy a fire into her as into us, but she was an easier victim.

The *Buiny* kept close alongside, dancing up and down, Her Captain, Kolomeytseff, shouting through his speaking trumpet, asked: "Have you a boat in which to take off the admiral? We haven't!" To this the flag-captain and Kruijanoffsky made some reply. I looked at the turret Its armoured door was damaged and refused to open properly, so that it was very doubtful if anything as big as a man could get through. The admiral was sitting huddled up, with his eyes on the ground; his head was bandaged in a bloodstained towel.

"Sir, the torpedo-boat is alongside! we must go." I said.

Call Filipinoffsky," he replied, without moving.

Rozhdestvensky evidently intended to lead the fleet after hoisting his flag on another ship, and therefore wanted to have with him the flag navigating officer, who was responsible for the dead-reckoning and safety of manoeuvres.

"He will be here in a minute; they have gone for him." The admiral merely shook his head.

I have not laid stress on the fact that before transferring him to another ship it was necessary to try and arrange some means of getting him there.

Kursel, with the boatswain and two or three sailors, had got hold of some half-burned hammocks and rope from the upper battery, and with these had begun to lash together something in the shape of a raft on which to lower the admiral into the water and put him on board the torpedo boat It was risky, but nothing else was to hand.

The raft was ready. Filipinoffsky appeared, and I hurried to the turret.

"Come out, sir! Filipinoffsky is here."

Rozhdestvensky gazed at us, shaking his head, and not uttering a syllable.

"I don't want to. No."

We were at a loss how to proceed.

"What are you staring at?" suddenly said Kursel. "Carry him; can't you see he is badly wounded?"

It seemed as if it was only for these words and the impulse they supplied for which we were waiting. There was a hum of voices and much bustling about Some forcing their way into the turret, took hold of the admiral by his arms and raised him up, but no sooner had he put his left leg to the ground than he groaned and completely lost consciousness. It was the best thing that could have happened.

"Bring him along! Bring him along! Splendid! Easy now! the devil! Take him along the side! Get to the side, can't you? Stop—something's cracking! What? his coat is being torn! Carry him along!" were the anxious shouts one heard on all sides. Having taken off the admiral's coat, they dragged him with the greatest difficulty through the narrow opening of the jammed door out on to the after embrasure, and were just proceeding to fasten him to the raft, when Kolomeytseff did, what a man does only once in his life, and then when inspired. My readers who are landsmen will not realise all the danger of what we were to attempt, but sailors will easily understand the risk. Kolomeytseff brought his vessel alongside and to windward of the mutilated battleship, out of whose battered gun ports stuck her crippled guns, and from whose side projected the broken booms of her torpedo-nets.[2] Dancing up and down on the waves the torpedo-boat at one moment rose till her deck was almost on a level with the embrasure, then rapidly sank away below; next moment she was carried away, and then again was seen struggling towards us, being momentarily in danger of staving in her thin side against one of the many projections from this motionless mass.

The admiral was carried hurriedly from the after to the bow embrasure, along the narrow gangway between the turrets and the battered side of the upper battery. From here, off the backs of the men who were standing by the open half-port, holding on to the side, he was lowered down, almost thrown, on board the torpedo-boat, at a moment when she rose on a wave and swung towards us. [3]

"Hurrah! the admiral is on board!" shouted Kursel, waving his cap.

"Hurrah!" cheered everyone.

How I, with my wounded legs, boarded her, I don't remember. I can only recollect that, lying on the hot engine-room hatch between the funnels, I gazed at the *Suvoroff*, unable to take my eyes off her. It was one of those moments which are indelibly impressed upon the mind.

Our position alongside the *Suvoroff* was extremely dangerous, as, besides the risk of being crushed, we might, at any moment, have been sunk by a shell, for the Japanese still poured in a hot fire upon both the

---

2. It was impossible to come up on the leeward side, because of the smoke and flames.

3. He was transferred to the *Biedovy* on the morning of 28th May.—A.B.L.

flag-ship and the *Kamchatka*. Several of the *Buiny's* crew had already been killed and wounded with splinters, and a lucky shot might at any moment send us to the bottom.

"Push off quickly!" shouted Kursel from the embrasure.

"Push off—push off don't waste a moment—don't drown the admiral!" bawled Bogdanoff, leaning over the side and shaking his fist at our captain.

"Push off—push off!" repeated the crew, looking out of the battery ports and waving their caps.

Choosing a moment when she was clear of the side, Kolomeytseff gave the order "Pull speed astern."

Farewell shouts reached us from the *Suvoroff*. I say from the "*Suvoroff*" but who would have recognised the, till recently, formidable battleship in this crippled mass, which was now enveloped in smoke and flames?

Her mainmast was cut in half. Her foremast and both funnels had been completely carried away, while her high bridges and galleries had been rent in pieces, and instead of them shapeless piles of distorted iron were heaped upon the deck. She had a heavy list to port, and, in consequence of it, we could see the hull under the water line on her starboard side reddening the surface of the water, while great tongues of fire were leaping out of numerous rents.

We rapidly steamed away, followed by a brisk fire from those of the enemy's ships which had noticed our movements.

It was 5.30 p.m.

As I have previously remarked, up to the last moment in the *Suvoroff* we none of us were aware of the nature of the admiral's wounds, and, therefore, the immediate question on board the *Buiny* was, which ship was he to board in order to continue in command of the fleet? When, however, the surgeon, Peter Kudinoff, came to render first aid, we at once learned of how the matter lay, for Kudinoff declared that his life was in danger; that he was suffering from fracture of the skull—a portion of it having entered his brain—and that any jolt might have fatal results. Taking into consideration the condition of the weather—a fresh breeze and a fairly heavy swell—he said it would be impossible to transfer him to another ship. Moreover, he was unable to stand, and his general condition, loss of power and memory, wandering, and short flashes of consciousness, rendered him incapable of any action.

From the *Buiny's* engine-room hatch, on which I had chanced to take up my position on going aboard, I proceeded to the bridge, but found that I was not able to stand here because of the rolling, and could only lie. However, while lying down, I was so in the way of those on duty that the commander advised me in as nice a way as possible to go elsewhere—to the hospital.

We were now overtaking the fleet, and the flag-captain decided that before making any signal, we must in spite of above consult the admiral, and this was entrusted to me. Picking my way astern with great difficulty, I went down the ladder and looked into the captain's cabin. The surgeon had finished dressing the admiral's wounds, and the latter was lying motionless in a hammock with half-closed eyes. But he was still conscious.

On my asking him if he felt strong enough to continue in command, and what ship he wished to board, he turned towards me with an effort, and for a while seemed trying to remember something.

"No—where am I? You can see—command—Nebogatoff," he muttered indistinctly, and then, with a sudden burst of energy, added, "Keep on Vladivostok—course N.23°E.," and again relapsed into a stupor.

Having sent his reply to the flag-captain (I don't remember by whom, but I think it was by Leontieff) I intended to remain in the ward-room, but there was no room. All the cabins and even the upper deck were full of men, as, before coming to the *Suvoroff*, the *Buiny* had picked up over 200 men at the spot where the *Oslyabya* sank. Amongst them were wounded sailors who had been swimming about in the salt water, and others who, when taken up, had been half drowned. The latter, contracted with cramp, and racked with tormenting coughs and pains in their chests, seemed with their bluish faces to be in a worse plight than the most badly wounded.

Passing on to the upper deck I seated myself on a box by the ladder to the officers' quarters.

Signals were fluttering from our mast and orders were being given by semaphore to the torpedo-boats, *Bezuprechny* and *Biedovy*, which were now close up to us. [4] We had already caught up the fleet and were steaming, together with the transports, which were covered, ahead and to starboard, by our cruisers. Still further to starboard, and some 30

---

4. The *Bezuprechny* was ordered to go to the *Nicolay* and to give (by semaphore) the late commander's instructions to the new, *i.e.* Nebogatoff. The *Biedovy* was sent to the *Suvoroff* to take off the remainder of her complement, but the flag-ship could not be found.

cables off, was our main force. The *Borodino* was leading, and after her came the *Orel*; but the *Alexander* was nowhere to be seen. [5] In the distance, still further off, could dimly be made out in the dusk, which was now rapidly creeping on, the silhouettes of the Japanese ships— steaming parallel to us. The flashes of their guns twinkled incessantly along the line, but the stubborn fight was not yet at an end!

Alongside of me I recognised an officer of the *Oslyabya*, and asked him what had actually caused his ship to sink?

Waving his arm in a helpless sort of way, and in a voice full of disgust, he jerked out:

"How? it's not very pleasant to remember. Absolutely no luck, that's what sunk her. Nothing but bad luck! They shot straight enough— but it wasn't shooting. It wasn't skill either. It was luck—infernal luck! Three shells, one after the other, almost in the same identical spot— Imagine it! All of them in the same place! All on the water line under the forward turret! Not a hole—but a regular gateway! Three of them penetrated her together. She almost heeled over at once—then settled under the water. A tremendous rush of water and the partitions were naturally useless."

"The devil himself couldn't have done anything!" he hysterically exclaimed, and, covering his face with his hands, went on deck.

About 7 p.m. the enemy's torpedo-boats appeared across the course on which our main force was steering, but rapidly drew off as our cruisers opened fire on them.

"Perhaps they've laid mines!" I thought to myself, and turned on my box, trying to make myself more easy.

"The *Borodino*! Look! the *Borodino*!" was shouted on all sides.

I raised myself, as quickly as possible on my arm, but where the *Borodino* had been nothing was visible save a patch of white foam!

It was 7.10 p.m.

The enemy's fleet having turned sharply to starboard, bore off to the east, and in its place was a group of torpedo-boats, which now surrounded us in a semicircle from the north, east, and west. Preparing to receive their attacks from astern, our cruisers, and we after them, gradually inclined to port, and then bore almost direct to the west straight towards the red sky. (There was no compass near me.)

At 7.40 p.m. I still was able to see our battleships, steaming astern of us devoid of formation, and defending themselves from the ap-

---

5. She had gone down about 5,30 p.m.

proaching torpedo-boats by firing. *This was my last note.*

Feeling weak from loss of blood and from the inflammation of my wounds, which were dirty and had not been bandaged, I began to shiver. My head swam, and I went below to get help.

And what of the *Suvoroff*? This is how a Japanese report describes her last moments:

> In the dusk, when out cruisers were driving the enemy northwards, they came upon the *Suvoroff* alone, at some distance from the fight, heeling over badly and enveloped in flames and smoke. The division (Captain-Lieutenant Fudzimoto) of torpedo boats, which was with our cruisers, was at once sent to attack her. Although much burned and still on fire—although she had been subjected to so many attacks, having been fired at by all the fleet (in the full sense of the word)—although she had only one serviceable gun—she still opened fibre, showing her determination to defend herself to the last moment of her existence—so long, in fact, as she remained above water. At length, about 7 p.m., after our torpedo-boats had twice attacked her, she went to the bottom.

To the Everlasting Memory of the Heroes Who Perished!

COMPOSITION OF THE OPPOSING FLEETS.

RUSSIAN.	JAPANESE.
1st Armoured Squadron.	**1st Squadron.**
Knyaz Suvoroff. (*Flag.*)	*Mikasa.* (*Flag.*)
Imperator Alexander.	*Shikishima.*
Borodino.	*Fuji.*
Orel.	*Asahi.*
	Kasuga.
	Nisshin.
2nd Armoured Squadron.	**2nd Squadron.**
Oslyabya.	*Idzumo.*
Sissoy Veliki.	*Yakumo.*
Navarin.	*Asama.*
Admiral Nakhimoff.	*Adzuma.*
	Tokiwa.
	Iwate.
3rd Armoured Squadron.	
Imperator Nicolay.	
Admiral Senyavin.	
Admiral Apraxin.	
Admiral Ushakoff.	

CRUISERS.

<table>
<tr><td>RUSSIAN.</td><td>JAPANESE.</td></tr>
</table>

RUSSIAN.	JAPANESE.
Cruiser Squadron.	**3rd Squadron.**
Oleg.	**1st Division.**
Aurora.	*Itsukushima.*
Dmitri Donskoy.	*Matsushima.*
Vladimir Monomakh.	*Hasidate.*
	Chin Yen.
	2nd Division.
	Suma.
	Chiyoda.
	Idzumi.
	Akitsushu.
	3rd Division.
	Kasagi.
	Chitose.
	Otawa.
	Niitaka.
	4th Division.
	Naniwa.
	Takachiho.
Scout Division.	*Tsushima.*
Svietlana.	*Akashi.*

AUXILIARY CRUISERS.

Almax.	16 Cruisers.
Ural.	

CRUISERS DETAILED FOR CO-OPERA-
TION WITH TORPEDO-BOATS.

RUSSIAN.	JAPANESE.
Zemtchug.	*Toyohashi.*
Izumrud.	*Maya.*
	Takao.
	Chihaya.
	Tatsuta.
	Uji.
	Yaeyama.
	Chokai.
	Yamato.
	Tsukushi.

DESTROYERS AND TORPEDO-BOATS.

9 Destroyers.	25 Destroyers.
	12 Torpedo-Boats, 1st Class.
	55 ,, 2nd Class.
	19 ,, 3rd Class.

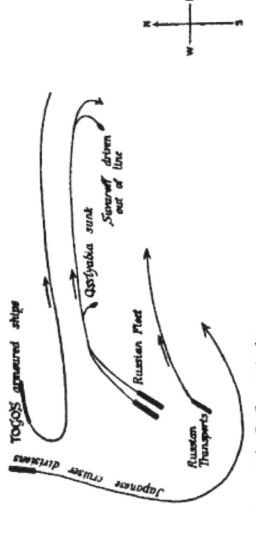

First phase of the Battle 2 to 3 pm.

TOGOS armoured ships

Japanese cruiser divisions

Russian Fleet

Russian Transports

Osslyabia sunk

Sverieff driven out of line

N W E S

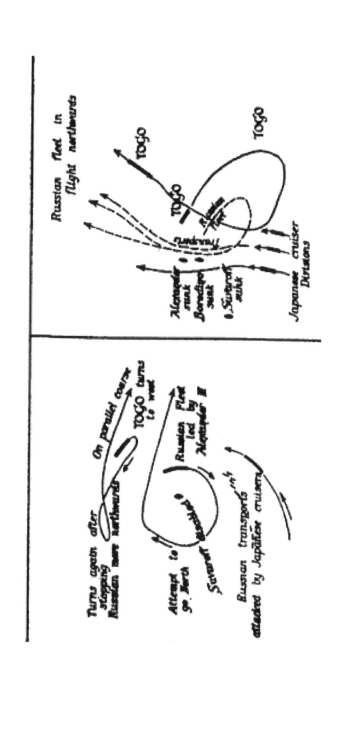

Russian fleet in flight northwards

TOGO

TOGO

TOGO

Alexander sunk
Borodino sunk
O. Suvaroff sunk

Transports

Japanese cruiser Divisions

On parallel course

Turns again after stopping Russian more northwards

TOGO turns to west

Russian Fleet led by Nebogatoff II

Attempt to go North

Suvaroff disabled

Russian transports attacked by Japanese cruisers

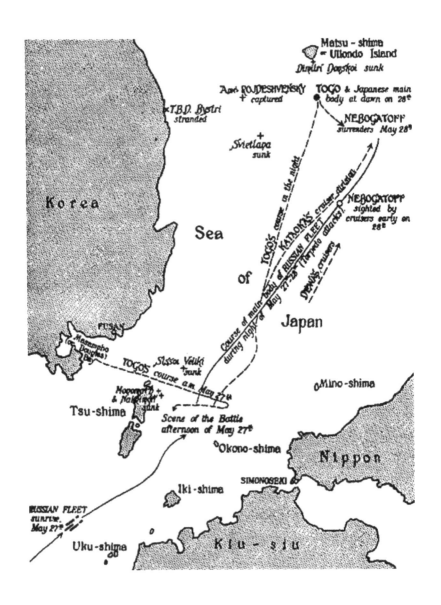

Matsu - shima
or Ullondo Island
Dimitri Donskoi sunk

Adml ROJDESHVENSKY
+ captured

TOGO & Japanese main
body at dawn on 28ᵗʰ

NEBOGATOFF
surrenders May 28ᵗʰ

Svietlapa
+ sunk

NEBOGATOFF
sighted by
cruisers early on
28ᵗʰ

Korea

Sea

of

Japan

KAMORA'S cruiser division

Course of main body of RUSSIAN FLEET
during night of May 27-28 (Torpedo attacks)

DEWA'S cruisers

TOGO'S course in the night

TBD. Byestri
stranded

FUSAN

Masampho
(or Douglas)
Bay

TOGO'S course a.m. May 27ᵗʰ

Sissoi Veliki
+ sunk

Nopomar +
& Nakimoff
+ sunk

Tsu-shima

Scene of the Battle
afternoon of May 27ᵗʰ

Okono-shima

Mino-shima

Nippon

SIMONOSEKI

Iki-shima

RUSSIAN FLEET
sunrise
May 27ᵗʰ

Uku-shima

Kiu - siu

CHAPTER 14

The Surrender

The last entry in my note-book, on the fateful day of May 14, 1905, is timed at 7.40 p.m., lying on the deck of the torpedo-boat *Buoyni*. I still saw our ironclads, steaming astern, scattered pell-mell, but keeping at bay with their fire the greedy, baiting pack of the enemy's torpedo-boats.

Through loss of blood and the violent inflammation which was setting in in my still undressed and dirt-begrimed wounds, I now experienced a sense of utter feebleness, shivering, nausea, and, above all, a tormenting thirst.

My diary, which had hitherto been kept by me uninterruptedly from day to day, and sometimes even from hour to hour, came here to an abrupt termination. And it was only a week after, on May 22, that I could muster strength enough to handle a pencil and scrawl, with unsteady hand, the few straggling words:

> Tvassaki [1] also found something extraneous . . . (in the wound.) Clipped. . . . The devil! dragging me about from place to place on stretchers. Rotten. They say the wound was awfully dirty. [2] All round the seat of the wound a cruel contusion. The whole muscle battered out of all shape and torn aslant; frightfully painful, although all but lifeless. Dimensions (of the main wound): 130 millimetres long and from 25 to 37 millimetres deep. Oki lays hopes on strong constitution—says, 'very strong blood.'

---

1. The Japanese surgeon, into whose ward I was transferred from that of Doctor Oki, who rendered me the first aid.

2. No wonder—nine hours without any kind of a makeshift dressing even, at first in the smoke of the flames and under spouts of dirty salt water, and after this, sprawling about on the deck, no less dirty, of the torpedo-boat!

On the same day, during a temporary rally, I scribbled a few more abbreviated notes, illegible and utterly meaningless to a stranger, but very eloquent when speaking to my memory.

Guided by these lights, I shall try to record more or less systematically, what befell me during the intervening blank space in my diary.

After having made my last entry (on the *Buoyni*), I felt myself to be at the end of my tether, and (how, I don't remember) got down to the ward-room of the torpedo-boat. Here the assistant surgeon, Peter Coudinoff, found me (according to his evidence) sitting by the table in a large pool of blood. He said the time was about midnight. Strange to say, as far as I can remember, the heavy wound on the right leg, which was the cause of so much . . . trouble to me subsequently, at that time was practically painless. If there was any pain at all, it was located beyond the wound, in the knee and the hip, while the whole of the leg obeyed me very badly.

I remember perfectly, though, what a frantic row I kicked up when the assistant surgeon took hold of the left boot and tried to pull it off. The slightest pressure on the fractured big left toe and the two adjoining toes, which were also badly mangled, caused such excruciating sensations, as could only find adequate expression in the rich phraseology of a boatswain. For the boot, with the hole torn in it by the splinter, was filled, not with blood alone, but with salt bilge-water as well; and in this "brine" the wounded toes soaked for well nigh nine hours.

Assistant Coudinoff—(God bless him with health and happiness for many a long year!)—took in the situation at a glance. Whereupon he cautiously cut the boot and sock in two, and thus removed them easily. And then he went through his business so tenderly, in so painstaking a manner! In order that I should not remain barefooted, he managed to rummage out a slipper from somewhere, cut lout the whole of its forward part in such a way that only a narrow strip spanned the instep; and this improvised sandal he bandaged fast to the sole of my foot.

What a dear old soul, and how deeply grateful I felt (and always shall feel) to him!

Now, however, with regard to further accommodation, his task proved much more troublesome: all the spare mattresses even were occupied, let alone bunks and wall-sofas.

"Oh, you . . ." grumbled Coudinoff reprovingly, paying no heed whatever to my staff-officer's shoulder-straps, "what was all your foolhardiness for? If you had come to me sooner, I'd have found room for you!"

"Well, well, don't get so fierce about it,"

I answered meekly; "we must shift as best we can."

Of course it never occurred for a single moment to Coudinoff, any more than to me, to pull a mattress from under some of the sailors on the torpedo-boat—even those only slightly wounded.

However, he managed to get hold of somebody's oilskins. True, that even twice folded these oilskins had not much resemblance to a mattress, but still it was not the bare iron deck! And Coudinoff's own flannel shirt, rolled into a lump, for my head to recline upon, was almost a cushion!

On May 22 I wrote in my diary, referring to that night:

Had to stretch myself on the deck (iron) with oilskins for bedding. . . . Beastly cold, uncomfortable; . . . heavy seas. . . . Bandage shifted off. Coudinoff came, put it right again; fetched a tarpaulin cover. . . .

By the way, the meaning of the last sentence has ever been a puzzle to me; was it that Coudinoff contrived to procure, in addition to the oilskins, both a tarpaulin and a blanket for a cover, or just a tarpaulin only, to serve as bedding and cover at once. However, this is immaterial.

All the night through I shivered violently with fever. Glimpses of surrounding reality were all intermingled with delirious visions . . .; for instance, I recollect quite plainly, as if it had happened just now, how the commander of the torpedo-boat appeared in the wardroom, summoned a council-of-war, and asked for everybody's opinions, down to the juniors. . . .

On the occasion of the subsequent trial (regarding the surrender of the torpedo-boat *Bedovy*), the commander of the *Buoyni* declared, as witness, that he never summoned any war-council of any kind, and never inquired about my opinions, and what's more, could not have inquired, as he never even suspected my presence in the wardroom: he only caught a momentary glimpse of me at the moment of our transhipment from the *Suvoroff*, and immediately forgot all about my very existence, absorbed by manifold and pressing business. . . .

Of the ship's-officers belonging to the *Buoyni*, one at least (midshipman Khrabro-Vassilevski) witnessed that he clearly remembered my presence, as, having descended into the wardroom in the middle of the night from his watch, he trod on somebody's feet, sticking out from under the table, and, endeavouring to smooth over his clumsiness, helped his wounded fellow-officer to a better position, and recognised me in his act.

Towards the morning I dropped off into a fitful slumber. . . . Someone (I don't know who) roused me rather roughly. He was shouting: "Get up! You've got to go over to the *Bedovy*" Somebody helped me to climb up on deck. Steaming not far astern, I recognised the *Dimitri Donskoi*, and, in close proximity to us, two torpedo boats (*Bedovy* and *Grozni*). I inquired: "What's the matter?" But, of course, people were too busy and worried to enter into explanations; so I got the abrupt answer, that "*Buoyni* has got quite 'rickety' and can't make any more headway." There was a heavy swell. Alongside of *Buoyni*, I noticed a cutter from the *Donskoi*; I was led up to the side and told briefly: "Get in, don't keep people waiting," and as I lingered I even heard mumbled swearing. Our torpedo boat was pitching and tossing about, the cutter was dancing along, while the oarsmen were pulling at the oars with all their might, to escape being smashed up against our side, or, worse still, getting their gunwale caught under some projection and capsizing altogether.

"But how am I to get in? It is necessary to jump! And, you see, how can I?"

"What? Talking, are you . . . ?" and, snatching a favourable moment, they lifted me bodily, pushed from behind, and down I jumped into the pinnace, stiffly, awkwardly, falling right on both legs, . . . and forthwith lost my senses from the awful pain. . . . I was brought to again by pain (probably still more excruciating). I found myself stretched on a thwart, with somebody in a sailor's blue jacket sitting right on top of me, and upon my right leg, almost on the very wound, was stretched a big stick, pressing on it. I cannot find words to give any idea how that stick weighed on my leg.

Subsequently it was all explained to me: directly after I had been "heaved off" on to the pinnace, they handed over (almost in the same manner) a stretcher with our unconscious admiral tied fast to it. At this very moment one of the sailors, who was preparing to catch hold of his handle of the stretcher, lost his balance and sat down upon me bodily, and the stretcher's handle fell down with all its weight, pinning down my hapless right leg.

But all these explanatory details were gathered by me very much later; and just then I only saw the back of a blue-jacket sitting right on top of me, and, suddenly seized with fury, I caught hold of the gunwale with one hand, and with the other started pounding his neck with all my might, accompanying my action with the most expressive orders, which I can not recall now, and it would be of no avail anyway, as they could hardly be cited here. [3]

How and when I was dragged up on to the *Bedovy*, I have not the slightest recollection. I can only remember sprawling on its deck, with my head almost touching the mainmast, and in anguished fear tucking up my left foot, which was dressed in the improvised sandal, lest in the general bustle and commotion somebody should stumble across the "cursed toe." I lost all command over my right leg, but then it gave me no pain whatever. The only sensation I experienced there, was that of its sucking-in something warm, and this was not wholly unpleasant (in consequence of what took place during the transhipment, the bandage came off and an abundant haemorrhage set in again).

How long had I lain in this position? Howsoever, the ship was already steaming ahead at full speed on its course, when I attracted the attention of one of the officers. First of all, of course, I asked for something to drink. All the time I had been tormented by a great thirst. Naturally, my request was granted forthwith, and then I was carried downstairs into the wardroom, and here (oh, bliss ineffable) I was snugly installed upon a cosy sofa, a pillow was placed under my head (I think even two!) and a warm, soft blanket spread over me. . . .

The junior surgeon from the *Donskoi*, who remained on the *Bedovy*, was engrossed for a long time still in the task of dressing the Admiral's numerous serious wounds. Although the admiral was tied fast to the stretcher, owing to the transhipment from the *Buoyni* to the pinnace, and then to the *Bedovy*, when he had to submit, *nolens volens*, to being hauled about like a sack of coal, all his bandages (however skilfully they had been adjusted by our benefactor Peter Coudinoff) had shifted from their positions.

At last, enabled to breathe forth freely once more, and having quenched my thirst (and that with no more water, but with tea and lemonade), I "bucked-up" wonderfully, and conceived a bold desire to wash myself; for, catching sight of myself in the looking-glass, I perceived, staring at me wonderingly, a dusky, ferocious face, and upon feeling the top of my head, found no hair on it, but only a species of tightly matted felt, so thoroughly had we all been smoked by the

---

3. In the investigation re the surrender of the torpedo-boat *Bedovy*, it transpired that the man who sat on me was Volunteer Maximoff. He furnished me with all the above details of this episode.

flames, and, I daresay, by the fumes of the *Shimosa* as well.

True it is, my burst of energy did not last very long. I managed to reach the lavatory upon my own legs (although helped along by others), but once installed before the washstand, I could not get along any further. I was helped out by an orderly, who, having propped me up on a bench, fetched a basin and scrubbed and washed me thoroughly "in three waters." After this I felt in heaven. And to crown all this, my new companions vied with each other in proffering me clean underwear and even clothes. I accepted the former gratefully, but the latter I declined gently, but firmly. My tunic, made ragged by splinters of Japanese projectiles, and the tatters of my trousers, drenched in blood, seemed to me an honourable array, which I would not part with for the world.

"Oh, oh! why, you are 'mangled' considerably on the left side!" somebody ejaculated, whilst I was undergoing this change.

And truly, three red patches, hidden from view before by the tunic, shewed up on my white waistcoat—one, the largest, on the waistline, and two smaller ones right under the left shoulder blade. In all probability the splinters were in a red-hot condition when they struck me, which accounted for the pain they caused me; but, on the other hand, without penetrating deeply, they disinfected the wounds they inflicted by, as it were, cauterising them. It was very painful, though, to tear off the shirt, which was glued on to them hard and fast. Just then the doctor made his appearance, having finished with the admiral, and started manipulating me.

During the six months of my Port Arthur campaign, I had had sufficient opportunity to study the facial expressions made by the doctors in the process of examining the wounded (I must say that all these expressions seem to be cast from one mould), and had learned to divine the true meaning of their always encouraging remarks.

In this instance, I perceived at once that the trouble was serious, and that I should have to face unpleasant music. . . .

"Tell me, please, is it (the splinter) in there, or has it gone right through?" I queried, whilst the doctor was pottering away over my right leg. "Seems to me, there is something hard down there. . . ."

"Something hard?" the doctor repeated rather irritably. "Well, if it is there, it will be removed, don't you know. Why, we shall be at Vladivostok tomorrow, at the hospital. There you will be operated on, in accordance with all the rules of the science, and in the meanwhile here, there's but one thing to keep in view—that's cleanliness. . . . And why the devil didn't you get dressed immediately? All this rubbish wouldn't be there now!" he wound up almost angrily. "At least, don't you play the fool of a hero, now that you are off your stumps—just lie here quietly; do you hear?"

What was, in the meanwhile, going on on the torpedo boat? What progress was being made, what decisions were being taken? This did not interest me. The doctor said that tomorrow I would have to go on the operating-table at the hospital of Vladivostok. This was all-important to me. I considered (as, I daresay, I was fully justified in doing) that my business was done,—that, having sustained one very heavy wound, another serious one, three light ones, a number of bruises and two contusions, and having got on a ship which had played the part of a mere spectator in the battle, without firing a single shot, and which not only was free from any damage, but had not a scratch among the crew,—on this ship I was nothing but mere cargo, to be delivered as per instructions. It never occurred to me to demand information from those around me: "How's this and that; and why so, and not otherwise?" This would amount to making a nuisance of one's self. And were I even to interfere with any uncalled-for advice, well. . . . They might not send me "to blazes" openly, having regard to my rank and present condition, but in any case this interference would be met, at best, but condescendingly. . . . "Let him grumble away," they would say, "down there on the sofa. Mustn't excite him."

About noon lunch was served, prepared from tinned provisions. I could eat nothing. With an effort I managed to gulp down a cup of beef-tea with biscuits soaked in it. But I greatly enjoyed two glasses of piping hot tea with brandy and lemonade (doctor's prescription. Perhaps he added something else). At once I felt warm and comfortable, and fell asleep soundly on my sofa, notwithstanding the noise and hubbub of voices which filled the wardroom.

I was awakened by the voice of our flag-captain, who was calling me by name. I seem to recollect plainly (though this, too, may have been my raving fancy), that he stood over me, adjusting the bandage on his head (he had three small splinters in the nape of his head), and saying to me—

"Two smokes sighted—south and east." (This was recorded by me on May 22.)

"Well, what about it? . . . why, full speed ahead, of course!" I replied.

Following the deeply-ingrained habit of the man at the helm, I glanced at the clock—3.15 p.m., and "recorded moment."

"Of course, of course, I thought so too," said the flag-captain, going up on deck again.

I again fell asleep.

Further on my recollections become dim and confused. A good deal of what even now I recall so vividly, as having been lived through by myself, was subsequently refuted by witnesses' statements given under oath.

Thus, for instance, I recorded in my diary on the 22nd—

Dropped off again. Awoke. Clock, 4.15. Speed apparently very moderate. [3] No one about; got anxious; crawled upstairs. Found Illutovitch [4] squatting. Inquired about speed.
Answer: "15."
"How's that? How many boilers going?"
Answer: "2."
"What? Wasn't there steam got up in all of them?"
"No."

It turned out afterwards that I did not awake myself, but was roused by Volunteer Maximoff, and it was not I at all who talked to Illutovitch, but Maximoff related to me his conversation with the engineer, adding that the "smokes" were overtaking us perceptibly. This was why I got anxious and "crawled upstairs." However dull and slowly my brain worked, I could still understand that if we were being given chase by the enemy, then in the emergency of an encounter, we must be in a position to command our extreme speed. . . . Why, a torpedo-boat with only half-steam up is but a mere toy in the enemy's hands. The latter will simply play havoc, or do just whatever he pleases with it. This is as plain as ABC!

Pulling myself up with my hands in some places, crawling on all fours in others, I managed to reach the bridge, but climbing up the vertical ladder was out of the question, of course, so, gripping the lowest step and raising myself on it, I started shouting hoarsely at the top of my voice:—

"Hello, you! Steam! Steam up in all the boilers! Steam! Steam! What are you waiting for? Steam up!"

---

3. An experienced naval officer, placed in the wardroom (aft) of a torpedo-boat, will always define, guided by the vibration of the stern, whether the ship is progressing at slow, medium, or full speed.

4. Chief engineer of the *Buoyni*.

On the wing of the bridge nearest to me, I saw the commander of the torpedo-boat, the flag-captain, and the flag-steersman. This was *not* raving, the incident was witnessed by the signalman Sibireff.

All three were engrossed in a consultation. . . . Then the commander leaned over the handrail of the bridge above me, and cried: "Yes! Yes! at once! Right away!" and forthwith gave his loud command: "Steam up in all the boilers!"

"Aye, aye," the boatswain responded, and passed on the command.

. . . I felt utterly exhausted. The ship was rolling in a heavy sea; my legs felt as if they did not belong to me; with hands giving out and head all in a whirl, it seemed to me that in another moment I should roll down the slanting, slippery iron deck, and topple right overboard.

Well, I heard with my own ears the command: "Steam up in all the boilers!"

And after this: "Let everybody do his duty." So I started crawling back.

Halfway back (this was a trying journey, though the distance was short—only about a hundred feet) a sailor came to my assistance.

Having reached once again my sofa in the wardroom, I flopped down on it, more dead than alive. This excursion to the bridge and back was the last straw. . . .

It transpired afterwards that I was not the only inactive occupant of the wardroom. In one of the bunks, covered by curtains, lay Lieutenant Krijanovski. Having been poisoned by the suffocating gases of the *Shimosa* (though otherwise uninjured), he was tormented all night by attacks of asthma and nausea, and now lay sound asleep.

Of course, at that time I never suspected his presence at all, but now I venture to avail myself of his evidence given at the trial. According to his statement, he had been roused by the doctor, who imparted to him a very alarming piece of intelligence:—"We are being run down, just as if we were standing still. It's a Jap, and no mistake. Our position—rotten, steam up in two boilers only; guns have their coverings on, no torpedoes ready. . . ."

Krijanovski started hurriedly upstairs, caught sight of me, and asked if I would come along; but I replied: "Can't."

All this is a perfect blank in my memory.

I recollect only lying on the sofa (when was this? how much time elapsed?) and listening with bated breath to reports of firing, to the hissing of projectiles, . . . and was conscious of the fact that it was "they" who fired, and that we did not respond.

Then . . . our engines were stopped. Firing ceased.

Whatever was the matter?

And suddenly the thought—clear and sharply outlined—flashed through my mind: "Why, they are surrendering!"

And now I shall be mercilessly candid, not only in regard to my comrades in misfortune, but also towards myself.

At this crucial moment my first thought was not about the honour of St Andrew's flag, [5] not about the honour of my country and her fleet—I only thought about myself.

"Surrender! What about me? And I from the *Diana*! Good job if they shoot me, but what if I am to be hanged, like a thief. . . . [6] No! better do it myself!"

I jumped up from the sofa, snatched down my revolver that was suspended on the hat hook, pulled up the breech spring with a desperate effort. . . . Missed fire. . . . Pulled up again. The confounded cartridge dropped out at last, but at that very moment the ship's surgeon appeared on the scene and gripped my arm angrily. I could not offer any resistance.

"Fate," flitted through my mind; "Come what may . . .!"

We were towed into Sassebo on May 17, in the afternoon, or rather, in the evening. What had I been doing during the two intermediate days? Nothing is recorded about them in my diary. So far as I can remember I was alternately shivering and vainly endeavouring to warm myself, or merging into a feverish heat, then I would sit up on my sofa and enter into passionate controversies with those around me, and be rude and even insulting. . . . I attacked the commander of the *Bedovy*, and expressed my full readiness to give satisfaction in single combat the moment both of us set foot on Russian soil. . . .

---

5. The ensign of the Russian Navy.

6. Readers will remember that, upon being transferred from Port Arthur Captain Semenoff was appointed chief officer of the cruiser *Diana*. This cruiser was sighted and chased by Japanese, and succeeded in running into shelter of the harbour of Saigon—a neutral port. In accordance with international law, this cruiser was dismantled on August 27, 1905, and her officers and crew were eliminated, or "interned," *i.e.*, released-under the pledge that they would not participate again in the war. Captain Semenoff, however, upon his return to St Petersburg, immediately joined Admiral Rojëstvensky's squadron.

CHAPTER 15

The First Impressions

I was being carried on a stretcher, and as it started raining, they covered me up with a blanket, head and all. In the hospital I was at first placed in a separate room, as a serious case.

All round me there was a remarkable animation, but not of the hustle-and-bustle description, not like the busy rush that could be accounted for by the perpetual arrivals almost every minute of fresh transports of the wounded . . . oh, no, not at all! I felt, with an acute sting, that this was a joyful, jubilant animation, and as doctors, and nurses, and hospital attendants in turn approached me, offering me their services, trying to induce me to eat and drink, to cheer me up, I could not help noticing that only by a great effort of will did they succeed in controlling their features from dissolving into radiant smiles.

Yes, that was a day of great rejoicing for the whole of Japan! Everybody was so happy, so brimming over with exultation, that this happiness could not contain itself, and found vent in every trifling utterance, in every gesture and glance. . . . And the source of their exultation was our annihilation.

If but one of them had dared to evince his glee openly in my presence whatever, I think I would be able to clench my teeth in his throat till they would have met there. But all were so affable, so tenderly considerate. . . . And how awfully sickening this was. . . .

They wished to carry me to the operating ward on a stretcher, but, for some reason, I conceived an offence in this intention, and declared that I would go there by myself. A senseless, ridiculous protest (some will say, a silly whim), but I wouldn't (do you understand? I would not) appear helpless and in need of compassion from people whom I hated with all my soul, and upon whom I had sworn revenge, dire and terrible.

An extraordinary excitement seized me (the temperature was above 104° F). Pain I felt none almost; and when I did feel it, it only provoked my wrath. Of course this burst of nervous irritation very soon gave out. Already halfway "thither" I was caught hold of by the arms, and "thence" I was carried all the way.

The situation turned out much more serious even than I imagined.

From the conversation of Dr Oki with his assistant (I have told already, in *Rasplata*, how I mastered the Japanese language and the Chinese grammar for a bet), I gathered that the inflammation of the lymphatic glands had spread, in consequence of the wound being very dirty (and this accounted for the pain in the waist and the knee) and in the wound itself mortification had set in . . . The word "gangrene" (pronounced by the Japanese "*gangoren*") figured very frequently in the doctor's conversation. The consultations resulted in a dilemma: on the one hand, science prescribed immediate amputation of the leg at the hip; but on the other hand, such a decision would be practically equivalent to a sentence of death, as in my state of utter bodily exhaustion, my heart would not have stood the strain of an anaesthetic, and still less, of course, of an operation without one; again, if they chose to await even a partial recovery of strength, the blood poisoning might spread upwards from the hip, and then all operating would be useless.

"Well, then, why haul me about for nothing!" I interrupted their arguing. "Leave me alone! Why, hang it all, what right have you to operate upon me without my consent!"

Doctor Oki murmured angrily, that I, too, had no right to conceal my knowledge of the Japanese language, whereupon they resumed their consultation in subdued tones, and in such a quick jabber, that I could not make head nor tail of it.

They confined themselves for the time being to washing and disinfecting the wounds. Apparently they decided to wait till the morning.

Before bidding me goodbye, the doctor said to me encouragingly in English. "Perhaps all right! Very strong blood."

Why he should have burst out in English, of which tongue his knowledge was very scanty and superficial, I do not know, unless it was in order to avoid further questions.

Upon my return to bed, I was given a cup of something red to drink, slightly astringent and rather bitter to the taste. The assistant surgeon explained to me, that this was *boodaw-su* (wine), but it was the most obviously "doctored" wine I ever drank, for directly afterwards I dropped off into a dead sleep.

On the morning of May 18, upon removing the bandage and feeling the glands in the hip and under the knee, Oki burst into complimentary ejaculations, and then said, in broken Russian, *Poteripite niemunogo,* [1] and fell to work. In the main wound (on the right leg) he cut out a lot of something which he considered superfluous; then he simply cut open the big toe of the left foot, but did not remove the first joint, as I expected he would, and only filed and trimmed the fractured bone, declaring encouragingly: "All right, it doesn't matter if it turns out a trifle shorter; it will still be there, and even a nail will grow on it, though it won't look very attractive."

After this it was mere child's play to extract a decent-sized splinter, which was firmly imbedded in my waist. Two smaller ones, under my left shoulder-blade, which were completely crusted over with scab, he left alone, saying: "Always take plenty of time with these. If they become troublesome, we'll remove them."

They did not deem it safe to administer chloroform after all. The whole operation was carried through with the aid of cocaine, which was injected into the places operated upon, as necessity arose. Three or four injections were made into the big, long wound on the right leg.

What a marvellous remedy, this cocaine! The only pain I experienced at all in the process, was the stinging prick of the injector and afterwards only an itching sensation. When I did let myself go now and then, it was only because I was hauled about like an inanimate object.

Nevertheless, upon the conclusion of the operation, I was for all the world like a fish washed out on the sand; and *à propos* of the cocaine, I suddenly bethought myself of a saying: "*A carp likes to be fried in cream only.*" And so, whilst I was being bandaged up, I burst out laughing, and laughed even more impetuously and without check.

"What is it? What is it?" the doctor started reprovingly. "*Sai-yo na dziki-mono! Ah-ha! Farooko-dess*" [2] and wound up suddenly in Russian: "Captain! a dram of whisky? What do you say?"

"I can't stand it," I replied. "A drop of Cognac, if you could get some."

"*Nobemass! Dziki-mono!*" [3] cried Oki, cheerfully. "*Hayakoo! Hayakoo!*" [4], he added, addressing those beside him.

I was instantly served with a big tumblerful of a stimulant which

---

1. "Hold on; pull yourself together a bit."
2. "Such a brave fellow, too! Oh, oh! it's too bad!"
3. "How fastidious we are! Brave fellow."
4. "Hurry up, hurry up!"

was practically poured down my throat, and which I perceived to be Cognac. I immediately felt warmer and more comfortable, or rather, this nerve-racking feeling of strain, this peculiar sensation, which I could only characterise as "itching all over," abated at once.

"All right, all right! Now then, try and get some sleep! "the nurse in charge of my stretcher was soothingly repeating to me—a dear little creature with a funny sharp-pointed red-cross cap on her head.

And how I longed at that moment to press my lips to this tiny soft hand that was mopping the cold perspiration off my brow so carefully, so tenderly. Where was now all that hatred which was raging in my soul only last night? Now it was absolutely the same to me whatever nationality this young woman belonged to that hovered with soft step around me; and being pitied by her did not seem in the least insulting.

A phrase occurred to me, which was somehow impressed in my memory:

A living soul hath spoken to a living soul.

And I was not in the least angry, when the hospital attendants, while engaged in replacing me in my sickbed from the stretcher, addressed me familiarly: "*Kimo no ftoi! Yass! Yass!*"[5]

The next dressing was carried through in the presence of the chief surgeon, Tadzuki, and his assistant, whose name to my great regret is not recorded in my diary, for I could not pass him without mention. Among the wounded he received the nickname of the "man-ripper," for the tendency he had, whenever the slightest occasion presented itself, to cut a fellow up in pieces, and then sew him together again and adjust everything in finer shape than ever. I must give him full credit for that: this was a surgeon who had received his talent as a heavenly gift at his birth.

To acquire his ability by study would have been impossible. There is not the least doubt that even Oki and Tvassaki, to say nothing about Tadzuki, were greatly superior to him in learning, as they finished their education in European hospitals, while he had never set foot out of Japan; but in emergencies where intuition or inspiration were called upon—when (if I may express myself so) the doctor had to strain his nerves to the utmost to examine the inside of a wound— then it was only he, who was naturally endowed with these qualities, who could do it! And many a time he by a keen stroke of the knife,

---

5. "Strong fellow! Very good, very good!"

without having recourse to any anaesthetic whatever, would solve a problem before which his learned colleagues would stop short in embarrassment.

To start with, the "man-ripper" examined me by means of X-rays, and declared categorically that the bone was merely touched and there were no exfoliations, and then, absorbed in deep thought, he scrutinised the wound steadfastly, . . . and lo! with a few sharp movements of the hand, in which flitted now a knife and now scissors, he dashed off everything that he found superfluous, and this with such lightning speed, that I could hardly catch my breath to give vent to an hundred horsepower oath.

"*Camaw nah! Seemaimasta! Itchi-ban dess!*" [6] he was saying, laughing merrily, and patting me on the shoulder, while his assistants were bandaging up my leg.

"*Naneemo nie!*" [7] I returned, trying to assume the same nonchalant tone.

I recollect vividly how, upon being installed once again in bed, I kept on talking to Volunteer Maximoff, who (bless him) tried to appease me as best he could, listening patiently to my incoherent chatter, in which reminiscences of the Port Arthur siege mingled with those of my former campaigns, plans about future developments of the war, and so on and so on, even dreams about "wiping the slate" and "a sweeping revenge."

This helped me to keep oblivious of the continuous pains in the carved-up right leg . . . pains, now burning, now aching, and *anon* shooting. The other wounds and contusions I did not bother about; they seemed to me to be mere scratches.

Once more they gave me to drink some sour stuff which they called "red wine," and I fell asleep.

Mainly under the soporific influence of this beverage, that was administered to me at the end of the morning and evening dressings, and also at bedtime, the few subsequent days drifted by, as it were, in a mist.

On May 27 I was carried from the separate room which was allotted to me, into the general ward, where all the wounded Russian officers and conductors brought to Sassebo were gathered—twenty-two men in all.

Doctor Tvassaki was charged with the general superintendence of

6. "Right ho. All over. Splendid."
7. "Of course, it's nothing."

this ward. This man earned, not the deepest gratitude only, but the fervent love of all his patients. Here was a man who might appear on the Judgment Day itself with uplifted head, armed with a red-cross band, and firmly conscious that neither the Archangel's sword of fire nor the threshold of hell would check him from helping the sufferers. . . .

On May 22 I felt a little easier, my temperature having abated somewhat. Through the medium of the assistant-surgeon of the ward, I procured a copy-book and a lead pencil from the hospital shop, and filled in the week's blank in my diary in the abrupt, unfinished sentences cited above.

It turned out, however, that I put too great a strain on my strength. I got very much worse. Tvassaki flew into a rage, scolded the assistant furiously, and took my diary away from me.

After this sudden check to my convalescence, I was apparently very bad for several days, as not only was nothing recorded in my diary during that time, but they have remained a perfect blank in my memory ever since. On May 28, however, Dr Tvassaki, yielding presumably to my pressing requests, gave me my copy-book for a moment. I have only scrawled a solitary sentence:—

Stretched out leg for the first time.

This phrase calls for certain explanations. The fact of the matter is, that in addition to the splinter of the enemy's projectile, which tore a considerable amount of flesh out of my right leg, Dr Oki, the "man-ripper," and finally Dr Tvassaki, removed from that wound so much more "superfluous matter," that my leg was almost bared to the bone, and, in common parlance, the flesh had to grow again. And at that everyone of them pounced down on me in turn, crying that I alone was to blame for this—for why did not I get dressed right away!

Anyhow, the only position which I could maintain without suffering unbearably was lying prone on my back, with the right leg doubled up (the knee was propped up by a specially adjusted bracket). Every movement would produce excruciating shooting pains down at the bottom of the wound. And this is why this above-mentioned event was all-important to me then.

"Stretched out leg for the first time," I recorded then, and nothing else, although on that very day we had, all of us, received a delicious remedy, which, in its healing effect, beat all the drugs and even surgical skill all to nothing—a healing balm: that's the true name for it!

I say this again: that nothing is recorded in my diary about that, and therefore I have to fall back considerably on other sources, partly on documents which subsequently came into my hands, and partly on the accounts of comrades.

Sharing, as I do, the unshakable belief that only such notes as have been chronicled directly on the spur of the moment can be considered valuable as historic data, and by no means "reminiscences" of any kind—and particularly those of the wounded—I shall try to be brief.

I remember how an old Japanese hospital attendant came running to my bedside and read to me, gasping and panting in his excitement, an article from a Japanese paper, written in such high-flown style, that he himself could not understand half of what was said in it, but whereof the meaning was clear:—

The Russian *Mikado* thanked his warriors who had shed their blood for their country.

"Tell all your comrades about it, quick! What joy for all of you!" he kept saying.

I don't know whether I have translated correctly the text of the emperor's message addressed to Admiral Rojëstvensky; but in any case, even in my imperfect interpretation, it elicited such great enthusiasm, that all those who were able to move about were soon densely clustered together round my bed; and those who were pinned down to theirs were fuming with angry impatience, and demanding that the "lights" [8] should write down and impart to them this glorious intelligence.

For each one, down in his heart, was gnawed by the one besetting thought:—

True, I was wounded and helpless, but still I am in captivity. Will it be considered and any allowances made? Will it be understood that it has happened through no fault of mine? That we were doomed by fate and not lack of energy or fear of death?

And here—oh, bliss—such a message!

I will cite here the actual text of the message, that sped like lightning throughout all the wards of the hospital, and gave relief even to those whose hours were already numbered, and who had not even strength enough left in them for a jolly good "hurrah," who had but to die with the consciousness of their heroic deed being remembered and appreciated, and they died in happiness and peace of mind. . . .

---

8. So were the slightly wounded patients called in discrimination from "heavies."

Here is what was said in the Japanese paper:

Today, Admiral Rojëstvensky received the following reply from the emperor, in response to his telegram reporting the calamity that had befallen his squadron:—

> I thank you from the bottom of my soul, and all those belonging to the squadron who have honestly fulfilled their duty in the battle, for their self-denying service to their country and to me. It was not willed by the Almighty that Providence should crown your great deed with success, but your undaunted courage will for ever be a source of pride to the Fatherland. I wish you a quick recovery, and may God Almighty give all of you consolation.

Comments on the subject soon followed: that a hero vanquished in an uneven fight is still a hero; that the recklessness of the brave is always apt to elicit more admiration than the discretion of the wise; that there are misfortunes which elevate their sufferers to greater heights; that the blood shed in the cause of one's country is evidently equally appreciated in Russia and Japan; and so on, and so forth. . . .

Yes. That was a glorious day.

Then again an interval of seven days ensued which passed without any entry in the diary. I have a distinct recollection of but one thing, that I was being carried to and from the operating ward twice a day—in the morning and in the evening—and that there invariably was more clipping, and trimming, and cleansing. But what tormented me more than all these excursions, was the ominous thought of the future.

Being, as I was, sufficiently familiar with the ways and customs of the Japanese, I was certain that I would be subjected to an examination, and that they would not be put off with the purely formal excuse, that I had left the *Diana* prior to the ship's official disarmament. Through their agents they were informed, of course, that the order of disarmament was received on August 22 (this telegram, as I have said, was not even in cipher), and knew also full well, that, even officially, the disarmament ensued on August 27, while my departure from Saigon took place on September 2 only, and for that matter could not possibly have taken place sooner, as there was not a single boat sailing for Europe from that port before that date.

So that, in point of fact, I was an officer from a battleship which was disarmed in a neutral port, who, thus released on parole, nevertheless had taken his place again in the fighting line.

In cases of this description, martial justice is notoriously brief and the verdict is clear.

Why, if the English did not hesitate about shooting Sheffers, who was captured hopelessly ill and was brought to the place of execution on a stretcher—what, then, could be expected of the Japanese?

This thought tormented me beyond description. . . . And not exactly the thought of imminent death (one grows accustomed to this idea, when always expecting to face it day and night—any hour—at any odd moment in course of many a long month)—no, it was the method. "To be strangled by the throat, to dangle from a rope, like a common thief. . . . Ough! The horror of it!"

But then I had hopes—I was reminded of an incident of the land campaign. Our men had captured two Japanese spies, who were convicted and summarily sentenced to be hanged; they had sent a petition to Kuropatkin, requesting to be spared this ignominious death, and pleading that, being as they were, officers of the army, they went into that spying business not for their own sakes, but in the interests of their country. The request was granted, and they were afforded the privilege of an honourable death. . . .

But might not such a petition be a humiliation on my part? Why, this would amount to pleading for quarter! And from whom? The *Mikado!* Was this permissible? Ought not I rather to "suffer to the end?"

I even shared my misgivings with several of my comrades, but they dispelled them:—"Why, of course, you can!" And I made up my mind to, if it came to the worst; . . . and if I was to ask at all, well, I would ask, by the way, that . . . it should not be in a convict's garb but in my own old tunic, that had seen so many battles, and without blindfolding, as was done with Sheffers.

My fears were by no means the result of unhinged nerves, or of feverish anxiety. There were facts galore, confirming all the intractability of the Japanese in similar cases. An officer was quoted, who, upon being likewise "interned" at Chefoo, tried to reach Vladivostok on board a passenger boat, but was arrested, and although nothing could of course prove his supposed intention to take a part in the fighting again (he said that he simply wanted to go home by rail, instead of sailing all round the world), was nevertheless sentenced to eight years' hard labour.

I was informed also, that all the wounded officers were interrogated about particulars: What ship is he from? Where was he before? etc.

Nobody came to me, and here the ominous question arose: Why!

Was it because I was being spared the excitement at the instance of the doctors, while I was yet a serious case, or simply because my fate had been already settled?

CHAPTER 16

The Commencement of a Regular Diary

A note, dated June 7, said: "A definite improvement is in progress. Wounds closing up fast."

June 8.—The danger of blood-poisoning is past.

After this an incident followed which I would not record there and then, for fear lest the Japs should read it, but which was deeply imprinted in my memory.

At last I was in my turn subjected to an examination such as all my comrades had long since undergone. Fate had ordained that it should be conducted by a staff officer who was acting in the capacity of assistant to the Japanese naval *attaché* in St Petersburg prior to the outbreak of the war, and who had visited Kronstadt several times "to have a look round everything that was to be seen." He spoke fairly good Russian. At that time I was acting as *aide-de-camp* to the commander-in-chief (Admiral S. O. Makaroff), and in my official capacity I rendered him all possible assistance and hospitality. Thus, two or three times, instead of the customary "meal" at the Naval Assembly, he took his lunch with me, and (as I have reason to believe) did not forget my hospitality.

Needless to say, we recognised each other instantly, and exchanged greetings as old friends, externally at least. Whereupon the following dialogue took place:—

"And so, just before the commencement of the war, you gave up your highly honourable position, and enlisted for active service? "

"Yes, sir, I was appointed chief officer of the *Boyarin*"

"But it is known that the *Boyarin* perished before your arrival, so you were for some time in command of the torpedo-boat *Res-*

hitelny."

"Hang it all, how well posted they are about everything!" I thought.

"That is quite true," I answered.

"And then you were appointed chief officer of the *Angara*. . . . Oh, I understand full well how angry you must have been about that! Was it not so?"

"Naturally," I answered cautiously, feeling the approach of the critical moment.

"And then . . . pardon me, but it is very strange, that from the *Angara* you should have reappeared on the *Suvoroff*! At the capitulation of Port Arthur you were not in the lists of the sick and wounded, who were sent back to Russia on parole. Where were you then? How did you get into the second squadron?"

"Why, is the fellow mocking me?" flitted through my mind. "Doesn't he know that I only spent three weeks on the *Angara*?"

Still, I preserved my composure, and replied coolly: "You will agree, that were you in my place, you would refrain from vouchsafing replies to such questions? Many things are done in warfare. . . . And the war is not over yet, by far. You don't expect me to divulge even the most insignificant of its secrets. . . ."

"Why, no! nothing of the kind!" said the Jap, hurriedly. "I was asking you as a friend, out of sheer curiosity, how it came about that you turned up on the *Suvoroff* from the captured *Angara*. *We can't make this out.*"

He put a sharp emphasis on the last phrase, and forthwith started taking his leave, wishing me quick recovery, and repeating in a hurried manner: "That's all right, you know. That'll be all right, you know."

I was left more nonplussed than ever.

Now I have come to think (perhaps I am mistaken) that the Japanese remembered having partaken of my "bread and salt," and winked, as it were, at his duty, by treating the matter in a purely perfunctory way. He allowed himself to be satisfied with my non-committal reply, without talking to my fellow-officers, some of whom might have betrayed me quite unknowingly, let alone interrogating some of the wounded bluejackets, who would be sure in their naive artlessness to start bragging about their exploits on the *Diana*.

Now I know, of course, exactly what it was that I was indebted to my inquisitor for, and how he could, without incurring any risk of responsibility, dismiss the matter in such a perfunctory way—but then

I was anxiously racking my brains in suspense.

Then I could not have suspected the existence of a purely clerical error of our staff of the Admiralty, thanks to which my old acquaintance found it possible, without breaking his orders, to save from the Japanese court-martial a fellow helplessly prostrate on the sick-bed.

The fact of the matter is, that (owing to an oversight) my appointment to the commission of chief officer of the cruiser *Diana* was not published in the imperial orders to the Naval Department; wherefore in the list of the admirals and officers of the staff (official publication of the Admiralty) revised up to June 1, 1904, I was still named as chief officer of the transport *Angara*, and in the same list, revised up to January 1, 1905, figured already as being "on the staff of the Commander-in-Chief of the Second Squadron of the Pacific Fleet."

It must be said here, in explanation of my bewilderment at the apparent ignorance of my inquisitor, that the Japanese—whose information service was generally conducted in an ideal manner—carefully followed all the movements of the complements of both our army and navy, basing their information on the official documents, without considering for a moment the possibility of any errors or omissions in such data.

The following amusing incident was said to have taken place at the roll-call of the prisoners of Port Arthur.

"Your name?"

"Colonel Yrman!"

"You are mistaken, there is no colonel of this name," says the Japanese officer.

"What do you mean? I am Colonel Yrman!"

"Pardon me, but I must correct you—you are Major-General Yrman. You have been promoted to that rank in one of the latest orders, which probably failed to reach you. I shall be pleased to communicate to you the date and number of the order in question at the earliest possible opportunity. I regret not having them handy now. . . ."

In any case, this accurate and up-to-date information of the Japanese, stood me in good stead, as precluding the necessity of any investigations. In their eyes I was the chief officer of the transport *Angara*, who had contrived to "bolt" somehow from blockaded Port Arthur and join the second squadron.

My inquisitor might have known that there was a Semenoff among the "interned" officers of the *Diana*, but the Semenoffs are about as numerous in Russia as Smiths are in England. And had he asked me: "And prior to *Suvoroff*, were you not the chief officer of the *Diana?*"—I would not have attempted to deny the fact, deeming such an attempt to be both utterly futile and unworthy.

But the examination was conducted in such a manner as to avert this involuntary confession. All this I understand now; but then, as I said, I was in the dark, and therefore torn by suspense.

Everything seemed suspicious to me—the special attention extended to me, the friendly talk of the assistant surgeon, who said that he had taken a part in the siege of Port Arthur, and especially the efforts of the chief surgeon to get me up on crutches as soon as possible, whereas he severely deprecated any "fidgeting "on the part of my comrades. It is very likely, that all this was the effect of nervous tension and worry; that I was not being spied upon any more than my comrades; still, all this could have but a very injurious effect on the progress of my convalescence. A fever broke out again, and in the night of June 13, quite unexpectedly, a copious haemorrhage set in afresh—not only were the bandages soaked right through, but even the sheets were bespattered with blood. And this a month after the infliction of the wounds!

From the diary:—

Today Tvassaki said . . . he doesn't like it. . . . Was scouring inside with a spoon, picked everything open. Afterwards stopped the hole with iodoformed foundation muslin.

June 14.—It is four weeks exactly today since I have been laid up here, and as yet cannot think of walking. It is a good job, though, that the bone is intact and the ischial nerve unbroken."

June 16.—Took a few steps on crutches. Am tormented by mosquitoes and changeable weather. Now it's hot, now a cold draught. Catching frequent colds, which makes things much worse."

(Of course, this could not have been so—even at night the external temperature seldom fell below 73° F—and these complaints about catching colds must be put down to my general weakness and overwrought system.)

June 18.—A marked improvement has set in. Left toe very annoying. Wound and slit (made at the operation) have healed up, but big toe is very sensitive, and I am at a loss to know how I shall ever be able to put on a boot."

From that day (June 18) onward my diary settles again into the old regular groove and assumes its ordinary aspect. Every incident and event, however insignificant, of my everyday life and surroundings is recorded briefly, but with sufficient accuracy to allow for the subsequent reconstruction not only of the general impression, but also of details.

It is true, a good many things were written in *précis*, and others were only hinted at ambiguously, for fear lest the Japs, who kept a watchful eye on all our movements, might come to read these jottings.

This constant spying, this suspicion, weighed upon us beyond endurance, the more so, as it could hardly be justified by the "necessity of war."

I want to say a few words in general on the subject of this "convicts' leper-house" *régime* that we were being subjected to.

All through the war the Japanese papers, and more especially the "pro-Jap" ones, assiduously cultivated a whole romantic legend about the chivalrous treatment that all the war prisoners met with on the part of our enemies, to say nothing about the wounded, and I trust therefore that this brief digression will not be found to be misplaced.

Strictly adhering to my hard-and-fast rule—to rely upon personal observations only, to take those facts alone for granted that I have seen with my own eyes and, moreover, have recorded on the spot—I shall not repeat here all the evidence that I have accumulated from others about that "chivalrous treatment" enjoyed by those prisoners who had surrendered without being wounded. They themselves can, if they feel so inclined, tell their own tales of woe, and more eloquently, no doubt, than I could do for them.

I shall speak about the state of affairs only which existed at Sassebo, whither I was brought after the Battle of Tsushima, and whence I vas released only after the peace negotiations had been actually concluded, that is, during the period occupied by the ratifying of the treaty. During this period many petty comforts and liberties were indulged in by prisoners and many little breaches of hospital discipline were winked at, so that it never fell to my lot to go through "the real thing" in the war prisoners' *régime*; but how the wounded officers fared, let the readers see for themselves from the following truthful statement of bare facts:—

Five officers of the general staff, twelve superior commissioned officers, one non-commissioned officer, and two "conductors"—twenty men in all—were confined in a single ward, usually occupied by the common Japanese sailors, and this was by no means through lack of space. To say nothing about the empty separate rooms, intended for the seriously wounded, a whole series of the so-called "officers' wards" were absolutely empty. In these wards the beds were separated from one another by adjustable partitions, and each of the little sections was lighted by its own window, and, generally speaking, the accommodation was incomparably superior to that of the "sailors' wards."

In our ward, the beds stood about a yard apart. At night-time there was no rest from the incessant groaning and moaning of those who had been badly wounded, and from the mutterings and incoherent ejaculations of those who were raving; in the daytime the constant chattering of the lighter cases disturbed the more serious ones just brought from the operating theatre, depriving them even of a short rest. . . . The authorities of the hospital would not furnish us with screens even; although everybody knows that such things are common enough in Japan, even in the poorest households. . . .

"But why did not you complain?". . . you may ask me.

"Why, simply because refusal would be certain; and what is more, there would be malicious relish in this refusal, a triumphing over helpless men who had the cheek to complain and ask favours."

In the Middle Ages, when knighthood flourished at its height, every violence inflicted on a prisoner, captured in a fair fight, was considered to be a disgrace. The term itself, "a fair fight," signified an encounter of two belligerents who believed in the honour of war, who were ready to fight to the very last, but who also esteemed each other as equals.

In Japan this rule was utterly unknown.

In Japan, the business of a spy, which the most impoverished tenth-rate lance-knight would shrink from in utter disgust, was, from time immemorial, considered highly valorous. The object of war was not only victory and conquest, but revenge and enslavement.

In the eyes of a European knight, the braver the resistance offered by an enemy, the more he rose in one's esteem, and *vice versa*. According to the Japanese tradition, the more persevering was the enemy in his fight, the more terrible were the tortures that awaited him.

Richard Coeur-de-Lion considered Saladin "his brother in arms;" but Cheedayosee (the Japanese Napoleon, as he is called) brought home, as trophies from his invasion of Korea, 40,000 Korean ears and noses, and over this gruesome pile he erected a monument. Can these "ears and noses" call forth anything but disgust? are they not a hundred times more abominable than the pyramids of human skulls, piled up by Tamerlane, which provoke general horror?

Long ages of history, full of sanguine cruelty, imbued with but one motto: "*Woe to the vanquished!*" could not pass without leaving their effect, without stamping the soul of the nation with that stigma of barbarity, only the outer crust of which could be washed off by a paltry thirty or forty years' contact with European culture.

"The authorities have ordered that these war-prisoners be treated in accordance with European customs, for otherwise Japan would be unable to enter the circle of the great Powers. This is indispensable. Do you understand?

"Aye, aye. For the benefit of our country we are prepared for any sacrifice—even to the extent of foregoing our sacred privilege of getting our fill of well-earned revenge upon these wretches who have fallen into our hands, and ought really to be torn limb from limb, broken upon a wheel, skinned, quartered, and thrown to the dogs."

Yes! I will say this openly and consciously!—we were treated like criminals, who, so far from being sent packing, were chosen by the authorities to be cured and waited upon. And these orders were being carried out externally; but it seemed as though the very atmosphere of the hospital was permeated to satiation with rancour and malevolence. It found expression in endless stinging pricks to our honour and self-respect, in petty annoyances and vexations which made our lives a burden to us.

In this country of the quintessence of etiquette and decorum—in this country of elaborate traditional courtesy, where, in course of conversation between two persons equal in rank, education, and social position, no pronouns are used, but by allusions to the "great mansion" or the "highly honourable lady," the dwelling and wife of the other man are understood, and the speaker's own home and wife are referred to as "the filthy hut" and "the miserable woman"—in this country where a whole cult of "ceremonies" has been preserved through scores of generations—the personnel of the hospital, in addressing us wounded officers, called us simply by our names, cutting out the rank, and even the plain *san* ("mister"), without which even servants are never addressed by their masters.

You should have seen the interpreters, who spoke a little Russian (picked up in Vladivostok and Port Arthur, where most of them had been employed as shop-assistants, cooks, messengers, and servants)—performing the ceremony, especially relished by them, of distributing the mail. They would appear in the ward with a batch of letters in their hands, and call out with gusto:

"Bardin! (a sailor orderly) Letter!"

"Philipporski! (colonel in the army) Letter!" and the letter was thrust in his face with studied insolence.

A propos of the letters. What could we divulge, in our helpless condition, from the hospital beds, in our letters home, that could possibly be of any military import? And yet not only were all our letters censored, but even their dimensions were strictly limited—no more than two postcards per week.

And the letters, papers, and periodicals from home were censored so painstakingly, that this function took from a month to six weeks from the day of their arrival.

This is not all. Even papers published in Japan (in English) were not all allowed, even though paid for; and those that were permitted passed a second censorship by the authorities, and many numbers were confiscated.

Well, if this is not the *régime* of a convicts' leper-house, I wonder what is!

As if to complete the likeness, even the exercise of the patients (many of whom were able to move about from the outset, and stood indeed in great need of motion) was confined to given hours and to a little clear space of ground in front of the barracks.

One more circumstance, which plainly characterises all this malevolence: all the wards in the hospital, except ours, were attended by nurses. We had male hospital attendants, and even these were furtively watched. Directly the authorities noticed that some assistant surgeon or attendant was beginning to get on good terms with a patient, and began to give him a little more attention than the barest necessity required, he would instantly be removed; and thus, within three months, the staff of attendants was changed completely more than three times. Nothing of the kind took place in other wards.

To resume: upon reviewing, in my mind's eye, the various hardships and vexations that we had to go through, I come to the conclusion that if, instead of having our noses and ears cut off, we were even cured, it was done for the sheer advantage of it, and not at all out of the chivalrous feelings which would be in vain looked for in the military past of Japan.

Needless to say, all that I have said applies but to the general run of the Japanese: such good Samaritans as doctors Tvassaki and Oki, or such perfect gentlemen as the naval officers Nomoto, Tanaka, and others, who used to visit us in the hospital, are of course exempt from this generalisation. But all those mentioned above have dwelt so long in the centres of European culture, always moving in very good society, that they have not only acquired refinement and education, but were also enabled to combine in their characters, on the common background of the cult of courage and self-denial, Christian ideals and the traditions of our "knighthood."

Of course such a metamorphosis is quite possible for individuals, but exceptions only prove the rule.

CHAPTER 17

Peace Negotiations Commenced

Up to this point I have never once mentioned the impression which was produced upon all the wounded in general, and upon me in particular, by the intelligence of Admiral Nebogatoff's surrender with four ironclads; and this omission is not due to any special considerations, but solely to my desire to stick to my diary.

There is no doubt that this news was imparted to us on the day after the event; but all through the first month or so of our confinement in the hospital not a word was mentioned on this subject in my diary; and if my memory does not deceive me, I had accepted the information with perfect indifference. My attention had constantly been absorbed by the momentous and *painful* question as to what they would do with me at the next dressing.

June 20 was a day of joy.

"Today washed myself at the tap, standing up."

This meant that I had reached the lavatory alone, and managed my toilet without help. But . . . from the lavatory window a corner of the harbour could be seen, and I was obligingly shown . . . *Nicolas I.* emerging from the docks. . . .

". . . Gone somewhere under her own steam . . ." I could hardly keep back tears of bitterness. . . . Japanese flag—Name *Tki.* Merciful God, what a disgrace!—and right in her wake *Apraxine* . . . going to test her engines. . ."

So only now, a month after the blow was inflicted, did the pain make itself felt! To such an extent had everything been overshadowed by the question as to whether there would be more operating on me today or not.

June 21.—No changes (meaning the wounds). Worry and more

worry. . . . What awaits us upon our return?—Regeneration of the navy, a living spirit in the training, live men instead of bureaucratic officials, fulfilment of duty instead of mere getting through the "red-tape" routine. . . . Good words these. . . . But who will effect this?—Those who have created the mess in which we now are, are sitting securely in their easy-chairs . . . the war has not touched them. . . . No! it's no use . . . oh, if I could shake all this off, and go away and plunge headlong into some hard work! . . .

Yes, it was hard lines.

June 25.—The day before yesterday I went upstairs again to the admiral and spent two hours with him. The sitting position is obviously bad for me. All night through after that visit, and all through yesterday, there were violent shooting pains at the bottom of the wound. Must be the *ischial* nerve. I am lying about slack and exhausted.

I must have felt very bad, but still I could not resist going up to see the admiral again. It was not I alone—all of us, officers and sailors, were cherishing the hope, that "he" would recover and would "pull through." Hardly anyone of us had any definite conception of what we meant by "pulling through," but we all understood each other; all clung to this hope, for we all knew what a difference there was between that brilliant admiral who left Libau and that chief who was leading us to face death at Tsushima. He—the chief—suffered in all the sorrow and trials of this fateful voyage more fully and deeply than any one of us. It was he who led us into the battle, about the issue of which he had reported, five months before, with a warrior's straight-forwardness, that he entertained no hopes of success.

"Do you remember the first message of the *Czar?*" the younger ones among us urged passionately. "And the subsequent ones? Those inquiries about his future fitness for work? Has anyone had more opportunities of personally experiencing the evil effects of the old unbending and stereotyped routine? He won't leave a single stone unturned under the spire,' [1] when he gets back, you may be sure. Let him get about again, that's all!"

How touchingly naive were all these young midshipmen, and even we, with our wider experience, who had seen a thing or two already, were not much better, for we had forgotten the old adage: "*Favoured by the Czar, but disfavoured by his dog-keeper.*"

---

1. The building of the Admiralty in St Petersburg is remarkable for its tall golden spire—"the needle of the Admiralty," as Poushkine calls it.

Still, I paid another visit to the admiral on the 25th, and was rejoiced to find him "in good humour; wounds getting on very well; temperature normal." But my pilgrimages to the second floor did not let me off scot-free. The next one I could undertake was only on July 1, and in the intermediate time I was pretty bad, judging by the brevity and general appearance of my notes.

July 4.—The big wound partly healed . . . very painful. . . .

July 5.—This night we had some fun. A fresh breeze sprang up from the west (possibly a typhoon is progressing further down to the south) and blew down the scaffolding of the barracks, that are being built alongside of ours. Wound very painful to touch. It used always to be very comfortable after a dressing, and now I have to lie still, like a mummy, without shifting the leg at all. Wind stiffening. Almost a regular gale. Raining. Oh, for a good ship in mid-ocean! Wrapped up in a "sou-wester," raincoat, and top-boots . . . pouring in torrents from above, seas dashing across the deck. . . . But who cares! The ship is ploughing ahead on its course; bearings are known; course kept correct. Fullest confidence and . . . blow, ye winds! lash, ye torrents! rage and rave, ye seas! You won't scare me—I know I am stronger than you! And I shall go where I will!

What exultant moments those are, full of proud consciousness of one's own power and command! Will this ever come again? And when?

Forgive me, if these extracts from my diary lack polish, but let it be remembered that all this was written on a hospital bed.

July 6.—Yesterday, all day long a storm was raging . . . leg gave me no rest, may be owing to the weather. Dressing very painful ... walking or sitting impossible. And even lying is not much better. . . . Hang it all! Only a week ago it seemed to me that everything was well on the way towards recovery.

July 9.—Even Tvassaki (and he is always encouraging) said today: "No good." What's the matter? Can't make all this out. Lying most of the time. Hopping about (when necessary) on crutches.

I was not the only one who experienced this severe check in the progress of convalescence. It seemed as though some sort of an epidemic was sweeping through our ward. Quite a number of those who long before had been walking about and had even ventured outside, were laid up again. Everybody evinced a peculiar nervousness and irritability. All kept snarling at the attendants, and quarrelling with each other.

It was Tvassaki who found out the microbe at last. It was the first batch of back numbers of the *Novoye Vremya*, wherein Mr Klado was unravelling day by day, before the Russian public, an utterly fantastic story of the battle, based for the most part upon sundry odd bits of information—sensational telegrams of American correspondents, and such like—strung on to the erratic thread of Mr Klado's own flighty imagination. And it was upon this flimsy foundation that Mr Klado was reconstructing all the circumstances of our defeat. And what a monstrous, outrageous concoction all this was!

It was the very same Mr Klado, who, writing in this same *Novoye Vremya* but four months before, was proving scientifically and as plain as daylight, that the squadron, pining away in weary suspense off Mada-gascar, had still "fair chances of success," even after Port Arthur had fallen; and if only it should be "reinforced" by some old, furbished-up scrapiron (the "self-sinkers" of Admiral Nebogatoff), then it would not be "chances" any more, but a dead certainty! Well, now he was nonchalantly evolving, by strictly logical methods, the "self-evident reasons" of a defeat unparalleled in the history of war. And the reasons were, of course, incapacity, utter ignorance, and lack of warlike valour in those who were simply and unostentatiously going to die.

Imagine a situation like this: that, travelling somewhere on the outskirts of the world (say, in Argentina), you happened to be run over by a motor car, horribly mangled and laid up in a hospital; and in the meanwhile, at the other extremity of the world, far away in St Petersburg, a man, who had risen to a prominent position and enjoyed social esteem and confidence, was circulating in a systematic manner among your friends and acquaintances a rumour—oh, nothing defi-nite, it may all be gossip, don't you know—but still, there are current *very persistent* rumours, don't you know, that Mr N. had not been run over at all, but—so people say—had been caught red-handed at a club, card-cheating, had been badly knocked about, and finally thrown down the stairs.

"I am surprised at N., really I am; I wouldn't have believed such a thing of him, would you? He always gave one the impression of being such a decent sort, don't you know! It only shows you how careful one must be in choosing one's associates," and so on.

Now imagine, in addition to this, that the man knew all along, when doing this, that, owing to certain special conditions you were bound to absolute silence, until that very remote and problematical day, when you were released and returned home. Then you will have to struggle against a firmly established, and already deeply ingrained popular conviction, and will have to attempt to dissuade people who cut you dead, or who only listen to you with an air of bored politeness.

And this was exactly the situation that, upon the arrival of the news, we realised ourselves to be in.

"*Calomniez, calomniez! il en restera toujours quelque chose!*" the Frenchmen say; and this rule had the wider scope and more propitious conditions, because the victims of the slander would be enabled to raise their voices against those who slandered them behind their backs only after many months had elapsed (how many they knew not), even if they lived to do so at all.

And this is why, to the extreme dissatisfaction of the chief surgeon and the "man-ripper," our officers' ward presented a picture in the first half of July, that differed very little from the end of May.

July 10.—Have been laid up all yesterday. Apparently peace of mind is just as necessary as rest of body. Dressing was a regular torture. Now (even after two hours) I can hardly keep from howling! The effort to contain myself throws me all into a sweat.

4 p.m.—Exhausted by these exertions, I fell asleep quite unexpectedly, and so soundly, that they hardly managed to wake me up towards the end of lunch. When I lie quite still there is no pain.

July 12.—Was not tormented particularly this time, but owing to cauterization with chloric zinc, there is such a maddening burning, that I am literally and incessantly wriggling about on my bed.

2 p.m.—Thank God! The admiral has been able to undergo the operation at last. (Hitherto fears were entertained that he would not live through it), and a piece of bone has been successfully removed that had got jammed under the edge of the broken skull.

Night.—The admiral bears up famously (so they say)—no pains, no fever, no exhaustion. What a triumph! All the time the thought was lurking in the background—what if he succumbs? In that case would it not have been better for him to perish in the fight, than to go and meet such an ignominious death—a prisoner in the enemy's hospital!

228

July 13.—Were probing my wound mercilessly today. Tvassaki says: "Can't make head or tail of this wound; it's quite a puzzle to me; some of the holes get cicatrized, others open up again."

Dull, continuous aching. Weather wretched—rain, wind, and awfully desolate. Just like autumn. And the same miserable weather inside my soul. Such rot is written in the papers about what is going on in Russia. I hope to God that all of it is not true. . . . Discussions spring up ever and *anon*—all about the future. Cheerless talk. . . . We want Peter the Great, that's whom we want! Heroic, sweeping measures! . . . . Who up there, on top, will attempt a sharp "switch-off" from the old groove! To "sidetrack" those who have attained their commanding positions chiefly owing to connections, relationships, etc.? One cannot expect them to acknowledge of their own accord the necessity for their own removal and for filling their places with the right kind of people. . . .

July 14.—Poor, hapless Russia! Even the English are looking on in consternation, and cry: (*Nagasaki Press*) "If one could imagine a nation that is bent on burying itself in its own ruins, that spectacle would be presented by Russia."

July 19.—Last night I again risked going upstairs to see the admiral.

(My diary is here filled with nothing else but details of dressings and progress of the wounds. I will pass them over as being devoid of any interest.)

July 23.—All's well. Good news from Russia; that is, not from Russia exactly, but about Russia. It is reported in the *Nagasaki Press*, that there is going to be no peace, as the emperor has telegraphed to Commander-in-Chief Linievitch: "Neither surrender of territory, nor indemnity." And here the Japs have already printed maps, with Manchuria, Korea, Saghalien, and the whole of the Primorskaya province marked as their possessions, not to speak of all the Russian battleships dismantled in the neutral ports and a war indemnity of five *milliards*.

Thank God! all have bucked up wonderfully.

True, it's hard lines to be dragging on this wretched existence, but . . . sooner die in captivity, if that's part of the price of an honourable peace for Russia.

July 24.—All goes well. I am promised a quick recovery. Time goes by so wearily, especially in view of the impending peace negotiations.

I wish I could fall asleep and wake up in, say, three weeks' time. . . . What's the worst about it is—there's nothing definite. Surely we can't believe all that's being said in the papers?

It must be said here, that we all earnestly believed (or would have liked to believe) in the declaration of General Linievitch about his readiness to take the offensive, and we were very hopeful that, perchance, even when the negotiations were in progress, he could have some successful encounter, and thus put some kind of a trump card in our diplomats' hands. . . . But further developments, which we were looking forward to with feverish impatience, shattered our hopes. Linievitch persevered in his inactivity. Mistshenko suffered a set back in his raid. . . . And Saghalien? Here is what I have written about Saghalien, summarising the general opinion of the whole population of our ward:—

> A new disgrace on top to finish up with. If it had been decided to give up defending Saghalien, they ought to have evacuated the island. But as the troops stayed there, their duty was to fight. The Japanese acknowledge themselves that, what with the lack of roads and an intersected country, Liapunoff could have given them a very nasty time with the force at his command.

On July 26 an incident took place, which somewhat stirred up the monotony of our existence. A typhoon came our way, whereof the centre passed just a little north of Sassebo. From early morning a stiff east wind set in. At 3.30 p.m. the two-storied barracks that were being built alongside of ours, and the scaffolding of which had been blown down three weeks ago, collapsed. Now it was already covered up with a roof (the Japanese build the wooden framework of a house first, surmount the skeleton with a heavy roof, and then start filling in the walls). The avalanche was a fearful sight. I was slumbering on my bed, when suddenly I was startled by a cracking noise and the shriek of Midshipman D——, "It's falling!"

I turned round and looked out of the big window, close to which my bed stood, and lo! I saw the gigantic wreck actually crashing right down upon us. . . . I forgot all about my wounds and bounced off to the opposite wall with the lightness of an antelope, But all came off right, as I had misjudged the distance.

Our barracks were only struck by a few detached logs. At 5.30 p.m. the wind shifted almost due south, always stiffening. Quite decent-sized trees were being uprooted and dragged along the earth. Piles were torn off the roofs and flew about in mid-air like a flight of jack-daws. In the central two-storied building, a wall was blown in by the pressure of the wind; crowds of workmen rushed to prop it up. At 6 o'clock serious fears arose, lest the two-storied barracks, where the Admiral's room was situated, should collapse. He was brought to us on a stretcher, dishevelled by the wind and considerably wetted by the rain. The storm reached its culminating point about 7 p.m. At 10 the wind shifted S.W., and commenced slacking off. The total result was, that all the two-storied houses of the hospital were considerably damaged, and three of them had had their roofs blown off altogether.

On July 27 my big wound was completely filled up and cicatrized.

"Thank God," I wrote in my diary.—High time, too. No less than seventy-four days have elapsed since it was inflicted.

August 4.—No desire to write at all. Peace negotiations are under way. The newspaper reports are very vague and ambiguous. Still, what was Linievitch bragging for? Feeling wretched.

August 6.—Took a walk. Moving very slow, and only for half an hour, but was completely tired out.

Chapter 18

Peace Concluded

Those only to whose lot it has fallen to live through a heavy and dangerous illness, and one made worse by incessant pain, will be able to understand fully my experiences of the subsequent few weeks. I felt, or at least I thought I did, how, with every hour, the ebbed tide of strength and health was steadily coming in again, filling the gaping hollows, bringing out the colour in the sallow, morbid complexion, and life into the lustreless, sunken eyes. . . . And how anxiously and painstakingly I followed all the doctor's prescriptions concerning the gradual extension of the time of my constitutionals, watching the working of my leg, and training it to obey my will—to keep within even tracks, to make no "sallies" outwards . . . (the *ischial* nerve had been affected after all).

Towards the end there were but three of us, out of the whole population of the ward, with wounds as yet uncicatrized; and now but two remained. . . . I confess frankly that when these two used to be carried off to the operating ward, I could not refrain from relishing the pleasant thought: "And I don't have to go any more!" and this thought made me happy. It may have been unworthy, unholy glee: but I could not help it.

And simultaneously with this, my intellectual activity, hitherto concentrated entirely upon the progress of the wounds, seemed to break loose from these narrow bonds, and burst out with unprecedented vigour and brightness. In the course of a few days I had compiled, *in extenso*, all the brief notes I had been jotting down since being bedridden in this ward, and already, on August 9, I laid before the admiral a circumstantial report wherein I exposed to a searching and thorough investigation all those conditions which had been slowly, in the course of many years, preparing for this inevitable annihilation. In this report I did away with asterisks for real things, and used proper names in their definitions. After all I had suffered personally, I deemed myself not only entitled, but obliged to speak my mind without any more self-restraint.

The admiral never alluded to this report at our subsequent meetings; but in St Petersburg, where it was printed and circulated to all the higher officials of the Naval Department, it proved a great success, and took immediate effect in raising the whole closely united population of the Admiralty up in arms against me.

To return to my diary.

August 13.—Got up rather early—the clock has just struck five. Just been out on the *piazza*. The rain has ceased; a few ragged little clouds are hanging still, scattered far and wide in the sky. The western part is still immersed in semidarkness, the eastern half is suffused with a mellow glow, and, all along the horizon, a purple radiance is reflected from underneath. The air is dim with the mists of dawn. The harbour and the slopes of the hills are enveloped in a vaporous veil. Nature is still fast asleep. Not a leaf rustles in the drowsy calm, not a blade of grass moves. A deep awe-inspiring calm reigns supreme ... a calm so absolute that even through the closed doors the sounds of snoring within are distinctly audible. How deeply, how yearningly the breast expands, drinking in the intoxicating freshness! What a feeling of lightness and stirring strength pervades the body! Oh, for a pair of wings! ... And suddenly—crash!—and all is dark and blighted around ... it's the terrible fatal word, "captivity."

August 14.—A heated debate has been going on since early morning on the subject of the manifesto of August 6.[1] My God! What an absolute ignorance of the forms of representative government in all other States! And it might be imagined that all this idiotic nonsense was talked by young midshipmen only, who have never been lectured, of course, on international law in their training schools, but the same ignorance was evinced by men who had become grey in the service of the State.

About the electoral systems in different countries nobody, as a matter of course, had any definite notion; the majority had heard that

1. Concerning the primary scheme of a very limited popular representation, drafted by M. Buligine, which was never carried into effect and was ultimately superseded by the manifesto of October 17 (30), under pressure of disturbances throughout the country.

233

in England there existed a House of Lords and a House of Commons, which sometimes got at cross-purposes, but how and in what manner these squabbles got smoothed over, they had no idea; the Senate of France was thought to be analogous with ours. [2] while about the Upper Chambers of Austria and Germany, and about the Senate in Italy, complete darkness prevailed. And the result was that some were jubilant, imagining the *Duma* to consist of deputies, elected by the popular vote, whose decisions were submitted immediately to the supreme authority of the land; while others, fearing the dangers of thus "going the whole hog," were dead against any representation at all.

All this would be funny, if it were not so sad.

August 15.—Bitter thoughts now occur to me about our navy. Not only a thorough cleansing is required up above—it is necessary to start all over again with education down below. And to re-educate is so much more difficult than training the virgin mind. . . . I am writing this fresh from the influence of a heated controversy which broke out today in our ward. Someone received a letter from Kioto, where the bulk of the naval prisoners are kept. It was said in the letter, that among our officers a series of lectures had been organised on the sciences of navigation, gunnery, and mining, and also a game of naval strategy was being conducted—and that, generally speaking, the prisoners endeavoured to utilize as much as possible this period of compulsory inactivity.

Someone among us started teasing our younger comrades, by pretending that, after being turned out from the hospital and joining the prisoners, they would have to fall to books, attend lectures, and, what was more, pass exams, in conclusion.

Everybody laughed, of course, but one of our middies took the matter in earnest, and declared point-blank that he wasn't going to attend any blooming lectures, not he.

"Yes, you will, if you are ordered to."

"Oh! and who is going to order me about, I should like to know?"

"Why, your superior authorities, of course! "

"Superior fiddlesticks—there are no authorities here, except the Japanese!"

"To my utter astonishment and disgust, all his colleagues took sides

---

2. The governing Senate of Russia is a purely bureaucratic institution, composed of a few of the highest officials of the State.

with him and energetically upheld this statement. There was no arguing with them—their reasoning was simple to the verge of obstinacy.

"Let the admiral himself tell me: 'Go!' and I *won't* and there's the
end of it! Now then, how's he going to *make* me go?"

From this, it follows that the fulfilment of commands is only necessary when in default of compliance, punishment can be meted out
immediately. If you are unable to punish for the time being, then you
can't give any orders. A fine idea of discipline and duty that!

August 16.—After a spell of nasty weather, we are enjoying sun-
shine and warmth. After dinner I walked for more than an hour in
the courtyard. I was dog tired and broke down completely. There is a
dull aching in the bottom of the wound. I imagine that the severed
parts of the muscle have grown together somewhat awry. When I was
returning, my leg was continually giving way under me—weak both
in the hips and the knee.

The Japanese newspapers say that the peace negotiations are progressing well, and that the Japs have agreed to evacuate Saghalien on
condition of receiving a large war indemnity, which means that they
intend to get possession of, above and beyond our Port Arthur-Dalny
railway, South Manchuria, Korea, and a large sum of money into the
bargain. What on earth is Linievitch doing? Linievitch who only two
months ago was consumed with eager longing to fight! If only he had
harassed the Japs a bit, they would have become more tractable. But all
his bragging was evidently only "bark," not "bite."

August 17.—The *Peresviet* steamed out of the docks and went off
. . . . . painful spectacle . . . and, as if to rub in the impression, music
is playing today on the esplanade in front of our barracks, and such
familiar tunes all the time, too—marches—"The Double-Headed Ea-
gle," and "Kronstadt-Toulon." Hang it, I can't get rid of the importu-
nate thought that all this music was from our battleships.

About 9 p.m. a telegram was brought in, printed specially on a slip
of paper:

Peace has just been agreed upon.

Everything stirred up. The first impulse was, of course—joy. Peace!
Why, yes, but at what price? and all the faces frowned as if by magic.

August 18.—I have been tossing about restlessly in my bed all night
through. Peace has been concluded. Two roads are stretching ahead of
Russia: the new one just faintly marked out—the road of reform; and

235

the old, deeply-rutted one, among the familiar swamps and jungles.

Just before dawn I fell asleep, but awoke soon. Sky suffused with redness. What a glorious dawn. Who is it breaking for? Could it be for the Japanese only? Oh, for them day has broken long since, and today every Japanese arises from his night's rest, filled with hope and confidence in the future, imbued with the deep consciousness that the sacrifices offered on the altar of his country have not proved futile. A glorious peace has concluded a victorious war, and Japan now occupies her indisputable place among the Great Powers.

And thou, my beloved, far away country? Like the Ivan Tsarevitch in the fairy tale, thou art standing, irresolute, on the fatal crossing of the ways. . . . May God help thee to choose the right one, which ever it is. . . . Bitterness ineffable I feel for thee,—hapless, beaten, and humiliated beyond measure, and my heart yearns madly and mutely to serve and toil for thy happiness. . . . What an ocean of gloom and sorrow is left behind! I feel both like crying and praying. . . .

August 19.—It is said in the Japanese papers, that we have given up one-half of the Saghalien, and have to pay 200 million *roubles* [3] "for the upkeep of the war prisoners and wounded." A masked war indemnity. A lamentable peace.

August 20.—The Japs are evidently dissatisfied with the terms of the peace. What have they to grumble about, I wonder? No papers at all reach us any more.

August 21.—Still no papers, but the assistant surgeon says that throughout the country indignation is running high; monstrous petitions arrive at the capital, with requests to refuse the confirmation of the peace treaty; Komura is being threatened and warned from returning to Japan.

August 22.—After prolonged and pressing demands, and applying to all grades and descriptions of officials, we have at last obtained the papers. No wonder they were being hidden from us. Japan is being swept by a storm of rebellious discontent. It appears that the Japanese Government, not content with the actual reports of their victories, were constantly "stretching "them to a sensational extent (was it to keep up the people's spirits, or what?), and naturally, by this time the people of Japan considered Russia to be completely crushed, sprawling beneath Japan's raised heel, and beseeching mercy. And now comes

---

3. About 20 million pounds.

the inevitable sobering down and disappointment. No festivities any-where. Not a single flag to be seen, and the Japs are so fond of beflag-ging their houses. On the contrary, they say that on the occasion of the return of the delegates from America, flags will be flown half-mast everywhere. The papers are printing the terms of the treaty framed in mourning.

August 23.—My leg still obeys very indifferently, especially in the mornings, before it has warmed up to its work. The scab hasn't come off the wound so far, and is awfully painful to the slightest touch. I am afraid lest it should burst open afresh. The big toe on my left foot is also very troublesome.

August 24.—Our approaching departure seems to be the only top-ic of conversation. The Japs are all in a bustle. The hospital authorities are evidently eagerly intent on delivering us to the General Commit-tee of War-Prisoners as quickly as possible, although it would seem to be much the simpler course to release us direct from here? More es-pecially as many are still in need of medical treatment, while two, not to count the admiral, have their wounds not even cicatrized yet.

A new inquiry came today from St Petersburg about the state of the admiral, his ability for work in the future, etc., etc. The flag-captain would not undertake to draw up a report on the admiral's condition in his own words, so he committed the task to the chief-surgeon, re-questing his full and unreserved diagnosis.

August 25.—Today the actual preparations for the departure have begun in earnest, and the day after tomorrow we are sailing for Ki-oto.

I feel now just like standing in front of a locked door, which is going to be thrown open at any moment. And what is behind? I have no idea. There's a passionate longing to get back home as soon as pos-sible, and yet the very prospect of return seems so strange and fearful after all, for us who come back beaten, from captivity. . . . How long will it take to show up those who are really to blame for this crushing defeat? The only thing that is inspiring us with hope, is the messages which our admiral received during the first days following upon the battle. But since then a long time has elapsed; many things may have become changed, and, indeed, such appears to be the situation, judg-ing by the papers; the gentlemen from "under the spire" have taken measures to bring themselves out dry from the mud-puddle and leave us in the lurch.

August 26.—Rain and stormy. Had a touch of fever during the night. The most painful of the critical moments which I have lived through flashed in my mind, and so realistic, so life-like were the sensations, that I could not tell whether they were dreams or waking hallucinations. Especially that fateful one of the surrender. . . .

Well, did I not hasten on deck as soon as I had been roused, and told about the "smokes" sighted, and did I not insist upon steam being got up in the boilers, and didn't the flag-captain agree with me and give his orders? Everyone remembers this, and all confirm it. Am I to be blamed for again dropping into a state of coma? that I did not crawl up on the bridge after him, that I trusted to his resolution?

Could anybody demand this from a man wounded in both legs, utterly exhausted, shivering with fever, whom every step costs superhuman efforts and suffering?—Of course it is impossible, and nobody would think of casting a slur upon me.

But I myself? No—there was an error! I ought to have asked somebody—that sailor who had helped me downstairs—to carry me up on to the bridge! The situation was too serious and too much was at stake, and didn't I know our flag-captain's lack of backbone, his weak point of giving way to persuasions and changing his mind. . . . Relied on others? healthy and strong ones, who were but spectators in the battle? Expected them to work this time? that their turn had come?

Rubbish! Had no right to rely on anybody. You have given way to physical weakness; you failed to gauge the paramount importance of the moment! That's what it was. . . .

The papers bring us news of the disturbances at Tokio. The mobs were bent on demolishing the building of the Ministry of Foreign Affairs, and engaged in a pitched battle with the police, burning down several police stations. Two chiefs of the police, five inspectors, and sixty policemen were wounded; the mob's casualties are five killed and two hundred wounded. Troops are being hurried to the capital, martial law has been proclaimed, and the press has been muzzled by temporary regulations.

August 27.—Our departure did not take place, owing, as I have heard, to the delay in sending up clothes for our bluejackets, of whom many were rescued all but naked.

August 28.—The day passed in bustle and packing. At 7.45 p.m. the procession started from the hospital. The admiral was being drawn in a *jinrickisha*; two were carried on stretchers; I was recommended to take my crutches, in case of emergency, but I got reckless and went as I was, with a stick only; anyhow, it was not far to the harbour. Alongside the quay a tug was awaiting us, and carried us to the steamer *Yenkai Maru*, formerly a passenger boat, and evidently, previously to the war, plying on a line especially favoured by the tourists, as the first cabin saloon and staterooms were got up in quite a European and even luxurious style. We were all installed very comfortably. The chief of the local military staff, Rear-Admiral Sakamoto, came to see us off, talked a lot of complimentary rubbish, bade us a happy voyage, etc., etc.

At 5.30 we weighed anchor. Then we were all invited to the saloon, doors were shut and window blinds let down. This was in order that we should not be able to see the outlet from the port, nor remember the disposition of the coast defence forts. At 6.40, when we were already well out at sea and could not spy out any secrets, we regained our liberty. I could not help thinking of the good old customs of our own naval bases, where every casual visitor has everything open before his eyes, as plain as can be.

The leave-taking at the hospital turned out rather dry, and who could have expected that the parting should be cordial and *sans rancune?* From whom did we meet with humane treatment? We could count them on our fingertips. The surgeons Oki and Tvassaki, the superintendent of the hospital, Assistant Surgeon Matsano, and Hospital Attendant Miagee (there were others, but they were being replaced constantly). There were others who did not ill-treat us so shamelessly, but it was only because of the express injunctions of the authorities; and in their hearts they were imbued with the firm conviction that a war prisoner is a slave and the property of the victor.

At sunset the weather broke up. The sky clouded over; the sea assumed an ashen grey tint; a swell sprang up from somewhere. Just like our autumn. . . . But many hours had not elapsed, ere it cleared up again and a glorious moonlit night set in, such as can only be observed in Japan towards the end of August and the beginning of September.

I am standing on the poop-deck. Propeller throbbing and knocking underneath. A white, winding ribbon is trailing from the stern. Very still. At regular intervals the dry, sharp clicking of the automatic log is heard. Ever and anon the rudder chain rumbles faintly. We are going through the Great Hirad Straits—10 p.m. We have shaped our course E.N.E. for Shimonoseki. I get my bearings by the moon and the outline of the coast. To the south the mountains of Kiang-Sion loom sharply outlined on the moonlit background of the sky. Between us and the shore the surface of the sea is dotted with hundreds of lights. It is the Japanese fishers. They are now quietly engaged in their occupation along their shores, as indeed they were all during the war. . . . They know they are safe. . . . Their fleet rules their seas. ... It ruled them before, and will rule. . . . For how long yet! I don't know what it is, that is so painful within me. Is it real pain or imagination only? Woe to the vanquished! And why did that confounded doctor poke his nose in? I think I will go and turn in.

Can't sleep. A guard is passing my window. I accidentally glanced at a mirror, and a strange, dark, bearded, tired face looked out at me in blank surprise. . . . True—I am very tired—these last days with their tormenting thoughts. . . .

August 29.—About 6 p.m. stopped at the quarantine station, and at 8 put to shore at Diry, where we sent ashore the bluejackets, who were going on the same boat. They are going to Kamaoosta.

About 9 a.m. cleared out of the Straits into the Sea of Japan, and shaped our course for the S.E. quarter. All of a sudden I remembered that in 1898 the *Vladimir Monomach*, under command of Prince Uchtomsky went aground somewhere about here in a fog, but got off safely without external aid. Now *Monomach* is resting in peace at the bottom of the Korean Straits, and its commander is in captivity. . . .

We are being accompanied from Sassebo by Doctor Tadzuki and Lieutenant-Captain Kimura.

By the way, when turning in last night, I got into my berth and thought that I had fallen through, so completely unused had I become to a decent bed. No wonder; three and a half months' lying on a straw mattress as hard as wood, and under my head a tiny rubber pillow which I bought at the hospital shop—for the hospital only accommodated us with canvass rolls stuffed with sand.

I remember what tortures I suffered from this roll during the first few days, whilst I was not aware of the fact that I could send an attendant to buy me this pillow! What with fever, and the necessity of keeping in the same position (prone on the back), the neck gets stark stiff and cramped, and continuous, splitting headache follows, so that it seems as though the cursed roll is pressing not on the skull, but on the very brain.

Hot. Early in the morning a faint southeaster was indeed blowing, but now in the afternoon it has calmed off completely. The whole surface of the sea is dotted with the sails of the coasting ships. There

seems to be no end of them. This is where the Japanese fleet is re-
cruited from, and draws on its inexhaustible reserves of real seamen,
and not of clumsy rustics fresh from the plough.

At 6.45 we dropped anchor at the quarantine station situated on
the little island of Ninoshima, where we are to be delivered into the
charge of the General Committee of War Prisoners.

CHAPTER 19

Arrival at Kioto

Scarcely had we cast anchor, when the commandant of the island, with the medical officer of quarantine, came alongside. They at once entered into a lively altercation with our escort, Captain Kimura and Dr Tadzuki. From what they told me, it would appear that the colonel had demanded that we should undergo all the formalities of disinfection, vaccination, etc., just as if we had come fresh from the seat of war, although we had come direct from Sassebo, where we had spent three and a half months under constant medical supervision.

It was with great difficulty that they persuaded him to give up his claim. When we learned later at Kioto, from the prisoners who had to go through this process, what it meant, we thanked heaven for having removed this cup from our lips. I will return to this subject in due course later on.

It was no easy task to persuade the colonel to change his mind, as he would see nothing beyond his instructions. Poor Kimura perspired freely in the effort.

We went ashore at 7 p.m. to a village composed only of wooden shanties, of which the two nearest the entrance were set apart for the admiral and the three officers of his staff.

The admiral's bed was separated by a curtain from ours, which were close alongside each other and under one mosquito net. The furniture consisted of a small table, three stools, some bedsteads of rough woodwork, with a few cross-bars and planks of timber which had scarcely been planed, and were covered with thin and much-worn mattresses. Sacks of sand served as bolsters, and there was no trace of any sheets. Three woollen coverlets completed the equipment, none of which was by any means fresh.

Without uttering a word the admiral gave one look of inspection, sat down by the door, and sank into a deep reverie.

Kimura, who had followed us, appeared much put out, and began to pour forth excuses, consoling us by assurances that this state of things would only last one night.

"Could we not, at any rate, have a pair of sheets for the admiral," said I.

"Unfortunately, I am afraid, there are none here."

"Perhaps the colonel has some."

A faint smile appeared on Kimura's face.

"I doubt if he even knows what they are. All the *bona-fide* officers have gone to the front, and only the leavings of the army are here. They know nothing of European customs. I will go, however, and see what I can do for you."

Finally they unearthed an almost clean cover, which they offered the admiral as a sleeping bag. This was all the linen that Kimura and Tadzuki could find; and having done this, they hastened aboard again, after ironically wishing us a goodnight.

Neither the admiral nor we could sleep a wink. Our shanty, which was only some 20 or 30 feet from the beach, was close to certain primitive structures which I need not define, and as the wind shifted about midnight and blew off the sea, we were overwhelmed with foul smells in spite of closed windows.

At early dawn, therefore, we were all up.

A bucket of water was brought us for our ablutions, with a wooden slop-pail and a small zinc basin, which was so dirty that none of us would touch it. We preferred to go and wash by turns in the courtyard, using the slop-pail, which was relatively clean, as our basin.

When the colonel and the interpreter came to pay their respects to the admiral and to ask if he was satisfied, Rojëstvensky told them quite plainly, that in Russia pigs were better treated than we had been in Japan.

The colonel, in much confusion, blundering out excuses, abruptly departed, and we did not see him again till we were on the point of leaving. The interpreter did his utmost to explain to us that the poor man, who was a thorough Japanese, had endeavoured to treat us in a European manner, but that ignorance of our customs had frustrated his efforts.

It is true that in hospital our food was not of an appetising kind, but it was sufficient in quantity, and if it was not always well dished up, it was at any rate eatable: here everything was different.

There were no table-cloths or napkins, the knives and spoons were dirty, and the prongs of the forks were filled up with various kinds of leavings. These, however, could be cleaned at a pinch, but not so the plates on which our portions were served. Judging by the repulsive appearance of the edges of them, we had reasonable cause for serious misgivings as to the middle of them. The bill of fare consisted of a sort of broth made of oats and sugar and flavoured with curry. We realised that we had no choice but to be content with tea and dry bread, when to our delight a refreshment seller appeared on the scene, and from him we were able to purchase some American canned food, such as ham and bacon and a preparation called *pâté de gibier*, as well as some Californian fruit: this was washed down with some *café au lait*. At mid-day another meal was offered us, consisting of greasy water claiming to be called broth, and a dirty yellow omelette redolent of onions. Three-quarters of an hour later we were still seated at table, when the shanty began to move with a grating noise, and all the plates and dishes were set dancing.

This was an earthquake, which lasted ten seconds. Three minutes afterwards there was another and less severe shock, which lasted five seconds.

At four o'clock the table was again laid—if I may use the expression—and the oat and sugar broth reappeared, followed by a liquid in which small pieces of bacon and meat were floating. Even the least fastidious among us turned away from this preparation with disgust.

When we asked the interpreter why this meal was taking place so early, he told us that we were going away, that there would be no means of getting dinner *en route*, and that we should have to wait till the following morning for our next feed. In vain did we appeal to the refreshment seller; his stock was sold out, and there was not time for him to go to the town and get a fresh supply for so large a body of customers as we were. Besides the admiral and three staff officers, there were five junior officers, two petty officers, and one cadet.

However, there was a rosy side to all these hardships. When, during the last days in hospital, and even more on the steamer, when in fa-miliar surroundings and good company, we had time to reflect on the past and think about the future. Then the misery of it all overwhelmed us, and we had moments of such despair, that a very little more would have made us throw ourselves into the sea. When I look back on the state of my feelings on board that steamer, I must own that if any-thing had gone wrong—if we had struck a floating mine, or had a collision—I would not have lifted a finger to save myself, so utter was my depression. Death would have been welcome, and I desired nothing more. Now we had other distractions: we had to pull ourselves together to avoid dying of hunger—we had to make a pillow out of a tunic rolled up in a napkin, to clean our own plates, knives, and forks, and such-like.

These sordid cares left us no time to brood over our miserable reflections.

There! they are calling us—we must be off. At 4.30 p.m. we left the quarantine station in a harbour tug, and half-an-hour later we were at the little town of Odzena.

The admiral and two of the midshipmen, whose wounds were not yet healed, went to the station in *jinrikishas*, the rest of us walked. Although there were many people in the streets, no one took the least notice of us. I do not know whether this was in obedience to orders, or was due to familiarity with such a sight, as more than ten thousand prisoners had already passed through Odzena.

There was no escort: the interpreter marched at the head of the party with a very young official, then came the admiral's *"rickshaw,"* and the notorious colonel, who had no doubt reported to the authorities the snub he had received in the morning, and had already received instructions accordingly.

In Japan, affairs of this sort are no joking matter. He kept at a respectful distance from the admiral, and never took his eye off him, so anxious was he to anticipate his least wish. He lighted a match the instant he saw him take out his cigarette case; rushed forward with a chair if he saw him leaning on a railing on the platform; and kept asking him if he would like some tea, soda-water, beer, etc.; but as he did all this, his face became purple with confusion, or anger at the part which he was compelled to play.

The train was late, and we did not start till 5.40. Our carriage was not very comfortable; it consisted of two compartments, a first and second class, with a lavatory between. In the first class were three cushioned seats divided into three places each, two running the length of the carriage, and one across. The admiral, the three staff officers, the interpreter, and the escort took possession of this. In the second class there were only two seats with eight places in each, running the length of the carriage; in this, were the eight other members of the detachment and the civil interpreter. They were very closely packed, but consoled themselves with the belief that the journey would not

245

last long, and that at Hiroshima, where we were to leave the branch line and join the main line, a more comfortable carriage would be provided. But the interpreter soon disposed of this hope, by telling us that there would be no change till we reached Kioto.

At 6.15 we arrived in the station at Hiroshima, where the commanding officer, his *aide-de-camp,* and the deputy governor (the governor himself was at Tokio), with his chief secretary, met us in full uniform.

After an interminable amount of shunting, our carriage was detached and joined on to the Kioto train, when the admiral was saluted by Lt. -General Manabe, commander-in-chief at Hiroshima, and all his staff. Of middle height, thick set, and with an intelligent and well-bred face, he had more the appearance of a Provencal than of a Jap. He had a dignified air and the manners of a European. Round his neck hung the Order of the Hawk (which is equivalent to our St George's Cross). On his breast he wore the Order of the Rising Sun on the right side, and of St Stanislas with crossed swords on the left.

Accustomed as I was to Japanese customs, I was much puzzled to understand how it was that a general with all these decorations was not at the front. Lieutenant Martinie, the French naval *attaché,* explained to me afterwards that there was a woman in the question, as generally is the ease.

In Japan the women's patriotic associations have much influence, and ladies of fashion are not above taking the lead in them. They occupy a place something between the *Soeurs de Charité,* who live in the hospital, and our lady patronesses who condescend, like the sun, to make occasional appearances there, as sufficient to ensure the welfare of the "poor devils."

The Japanese women attend the sick themselves, take an interest in them, and devote all their time to them.

During the Boxer War, when the general was winning his laurels under the walls of Pekin, his wife, while engaged in her usual works of charity, won the hearts of the sick and wounded French committed to her care, and was in consequence awarded a medal. Unfortunately the French representative was guilty of a serious blunder in giving a medal to Mme. Manabe, who was an ordinary member of the staff, and nothing to the lady president, who like a thorough Jap was mortally offended; so the lady president, who happened to be the wife of the general in command, resolved to take a notable revenge. When General Manabe, covered with well-earned decorations, returned home, he found a party of officials examining, under a search warrant, the walls, and turning over everything in his house and garden. The general had casually mentioned in his report that he had heard that General Manabe, who was in charge of the Chinese palace, had seized the opportunity of carrying off all the most valuable objects, and hiding them in his house.

In a matter of this kind the Japanese will not stand any joking, for they consider that the national honour is at stake. It is a matter for real regret that all European nations do not share their point of view. Martini did not know the actual result of their investigations. Be that as it may, the star of the general waned from that day, so that he was not even chosen to take part in the war against us.

I beg the reader to excuse this short digression, and now return to my journal.

Before the admiral had time to get out of the carriage—even before the train had stopped—the general jumped in. After the members of the two staffs had been introduced to each other, and a few civil commonplace expressions spoken concerning the uncertainties of war, and the victors of one day becoming the vanquished of the next, we all sat down round a table, and tea was served in European fashion. At this juncture a little comedy, which had evidently been rehearsed, began to be played.

Manabe asked the admiral whether he had been comfortable at Hiroshima, and if he had any complaints to make. In reply, he very quietly, but also very definitely, gave him his candid opinion; whereupon the general, with an air of astonishment and vexation, severely blew up the colonel, who stood at attention, hand to cap all the time, as red as a lobster, and streaming with perspiration. When this was over, he became profuse in his apologies, throwing all the blame on the hospital authorities at Sassebo, who had turned out the wounded with unaccountable haste, and without giving any notice. But for this, he would have considered it his duty to go in person to Hiroshima and place himself at the disposal of his honoured visitors.

"What a clever liar he is," said I to myself when this incident was over. The conversation was carried on for some minutes in a genial and informal manner. The general declared, with much iteration, that the Order of St Stanislas was the decoration which he prized most highly. Only four of them had been awarded to Japanese after the war in China, and as the Marquis Yamada was dead, there were only three holders left, of whom he was the youngest.

After much saluting, the train started again at 7 p.m. Two hours later we began to feel the pangs of hunger. I found it necessary to draw up my knees in to my stomach to suppress the pangs of famine, and there was not the slightest sign of a refreshment-room at any of the stations.

At last, at 10 p.m., we stopped, and I saw for the first time some of the members of the local ladies' patriotic society, for we were travelling in a hospital train full of sick and wounded. I wish that some of our Russian lady patronesses could have been there; they would have seen and learned some very interesting things.

With much rustling of their silk kimonos and clattering of their "*gata*," or high wooden sandals, these ladies set to work, quickly, but without any fuss, to visit all the carriages, and to hand round cakes and tea, saluting and smiling all the time. They were not above washing up the cups and saucers and running to fetch boiling water, etc.

When we examined our allowance of provisions, we found it somewhat scanty. It consisted of a tiny box of ham, six pieces of bread, and half a pound of chocolate. The admiral urged us to be patient, and to make the best of what we could get; but there was so little conviction in his tone, that we knew that he was as famished as we were; we decided to eat half our bread and the ham, and to keep the rest to eat with the chocolate later on. As there were in the box five very minute slices of ham, we each had one and a quarter, but we most imprudently ate all our bread, trusting to getting some boiled rice when the time came to eat the chocolate.

We had to sit bolt upright all the night, as there was not room for us to lie down side by side on the seats. In the evening we had implored the admiral to occupy one of them for himself, but he steadfastly refused, and we knew him too well to imagine that he would ever go back on his word.

The moonlight was magnificent, and the country through which we passed was of singular beauty, but nobody paid any attention to them. Clouds of a peculiar kind of mosquito, which flies close to the surface of the ground, bit our ankles and stung us through our socks. One of our party declared that he could hear them sucking and smacking their lips. After midnight reinforcements came, but these were of another species; they were very small, and only went for the exposed parts of one's face, neck, and hands. It was like being tickled with stinging nettles.

There is a French proverb, that *he who sleeps dines*, but as we had not a wink of sleep, we began, about 4 a.m., to feel the acute pangs of hunger. Even the admiral, being unable to bear it any longer, awakened our escort, and called upon them to tell him at once when and where we could get breakfast. The colonel explained through the interpreter, that a European breakfast would be ready for us at Simedzi, where we were due at 11 a.m. The admiral was much annoyed.

"Since we left the steamer you have given us nothing to eat, for I prefer to say nothing about the pig's food provided at the quarantine station. You will, please, telegraph at once to the next station to have five hardboiled eggs ready, each, for twelve persons, with some bread and tea.

We thought the colonel would have had a fit. He protested that the breakfast was to be a European one, and that as his superior officers had arranged the route and the hours of the meals, he could not make any change. The admiral would not listen to him, but stuffing some Japanese banknotes into his hands, he shouted: "Quick, quick; I tell you to send off a telegram before the train starts."

This all occurred at a small side-station. "Your Excellency," pleaded the interpreter, "he can do nothing, and cannot accept the money without government authority."

"Cannot! what do you mean?" and the banknotes, rolled up into a ball, flew out of the window. The interpreter hurried at top speed to pick them up.

At 6 a.m., at Okayama, an agreeable surprise awaited us; all that the Admiral had ordered was there in readiness. When we caught sight of a large basket full of eggs, and a still larger one of bread, jokes began to fly all round. There seemed to be enough to victual a whole battalion; this, however, did not prevent the baskets from being emptied as if by magic a few moments later. Their contents had been washed down by cups of tea, which, in spite of the early hour, the good ladies had brought us. We would have been content with green Japanese tea, but they had had the consideration to prepare for us Chinese tea, in European cups, with saucers and even spoons. The president, an elderly lady, did the honours to perfection.

Hunger gave way to good humour and yawning, and as the mosquitoes had disappeared in the daylight, each of us curled himself up in his corner and went to sleep.

At 11 we reached Simedzi, where we were in expectation of the famous European breakfast which the colonel had dinned into our ears, but which, as it turned out, had nothing European about it save the knives and forks. At each place was a little box of white wood containing a minute slice of fried meat, rolled up in a bit of bread, three others of smoked tongue, and a tiny potato—all cold.

The ladies (always these admirable ladies) poured out for us some soda-water and beer in addition to the tea. When this so-called "square meal" was over, the admiral took the matter into his own hands, and without consulting the colonel, he slipped some money into the interpreter's hand, and told him to telegraph to Kobe, ordering them to have twelve good beefsteaks, with potatoes, ready for us on our arrival. With much trepidation the interpreter referred the matter to the colonel, who merely shrugged his shoulders, as though to say, "so be it—I can only be hanged once for a double offence."

At 1.20 we found ourselves seated like true sybarites round a table covered with a spotless tablecloth, and with napkins on our knees. The consequence was that when we arrived at Osaka well fortified with this extra meal, we treated the Japanese food, which under the guise of a "European meal" had been provided for us there, with some indifference. So we sat down at table merely as a matter of politeness.

From a newspaper which we bought here, we learned that on the very night when we left Sassebo a fire broke out on the *Mikata*, and that this fine cruiser had been blown up and sunk. The admiral at once sent a telegram of sympathy to Admiral Togo.

We reached the station at Kioto at 5.40 without any fresh adventures, and were met on the platform by the commanding officer, Major-General Okama, a major who is inspector of war prisoners, and the lieutenant in charge of the temple set apart for the admiral's residence, as well as by an interpreter. Several of our comrades who had gone ahead were also there.

The colonel, who had accompanied us, took his leave, and he did so with an air of delight which seemed genuine. We got into a carriage, not a jinrikisha this time, and the admiral and the senior officers proceeded to the temple of Chidsiaken, the others went to that of Honkokudsi.

CHAPTER 20

Details of Our Daily Life

September 1.—For the admiral and his staff there has been reserved a separate house, or, to be more exact, an annex of the temple, to which it is connected by an arched wooden bridge built over the narrow branch of a pond, laid out in the shape of a U. As a rule, this pavilion, which is fitted up altogether in Japanese style, is kept for travellers of distinction who visit the city.

It is divided into two: in the first part, there are three rooms, or rather one room which can be partitioned off into three by means of movable screens, which are easily folded to admit of their being taken away altogether if desired. This room constitutes the admiral's quarters. The remainder of the accommodation is separated from it by a broad corridor, on to which two rooms destined for his suite, another room for servants, and a storeroom, open. I was told off to lodge in one of these rooms, in which there were already two other men who had arrived before us, whom I hardly knew, and for whose society I did not care particularly. Fortunately, however, the admiral, whom nothing escaped, at once noticed my annoyance and invited me to take up my quarters in his third room. I protested feebly, but, as I have related before of the incident of the sleeping accommodation in the railway carriage, I knew that it was useless to argue with him.

"This room is yours; it is no good its staying empty, and whether you live in it or not, I am not going to make any further use of it."

All this happened yesterday evening. The admiral was given a plain iron bedstead with a mattress and two pillows, while the rest of us were given wooden couches, like those in the Ninoshima Quarantine Station, with the pleasing addition of a hard straw mattress and a bolster filled with sand! As I had not closed my eyes for two nights, I slept like a log. When I woke up in the morning, I had the greatest difficulty in the world to recollect what had happened to me and where I was. At 9 a.m. General Okama and his chief-of-staff arrived. The details of this visit, which I noted down on the spot, were highly characteristic of the behaviour of the Jap when he tries to play the European!

All the newcomers, from the admiral down to the most junior midshipman, were invited to make their way to a hall, in the centre of which was a table surrounded by chairs.

When all were assembled, the door opened, and Okama, still followed by his *aides-de-camp*, appeared in the doorway, and began, by way of welcome, to address us through his interpreter as follows:—

"It is in my capacity of military commandant in charge of the prisoners of war that I am here today."

Then he took a paper which had been respectfully handed to him, and began to read us a lecture in Japanese, stopping from time to time and remaining quite still at the end, while the interpreter translated it into Russian for us.

I, Major General Okama Masansero, Commander of the Garrison of Fushimi, address you, Gentlemen, naval officers recently arrived, as prisoners of war under guard of the garrison which has been placed under my command. You left your country last year and accomplished a long voyage in the face of countless storms: you have endured privations and misfortunes and have undergone trials of all kinds. You have nobly fulfilled your duty to your country. Eight up to the time when unkindly Fate, falling upon you, caused you to be taken prisoners, you remained resolute and unmoved, and fought with patriotic energy and courage, to which I cannot but do homage. That is why, considering your present situation, I express my condolences and heart-felt sympathy with you in your misfortunes.

Up to this point the speech was suitable enough and even courteous. If certain phrases seemed to us a little odd and some of the expressions slightly awkward, we put it down to the desire of the interpreter to translate word for word.

Then we came to business—

1. During the period of your captivity you must observe strictly all the regulations and conditions laid down by the Imperial Japanese Government, and under no circumstances must you deviate from or transgress them. The maintenance of military discipline and good order is absolutely indispensable for sol-

diers and sailors, and you are well aware that it is the same in all countries of the world. I desire, therefore, Gentlemen, that you will attach special importance to keeping the laws of this discipline.

2. The orders of the commandant, transmitted through his officials, must be carried out to the letter, as coming from the supreme Japanese Authorities.

3. During your stay here you must remain on the most friendly terms with each other, and above all you must abstain from all intemperance, for exemplary behaviour, in raising the dignity of the soldier, causes him to deserve well of his country. For the present, it only remains for you to wait patiently for the signature of peace.

4. It is in my official capacity as your commandant that, at our first interview, I feel myself obliged to speak these words of admonition.

During this lecture I looked at the admiral furtively. He was standing with his hands behind his back and his eyes cast down as if listening attentively, and it was only his habitual nervous twitching of the jaw, close to the ear, so well known to us, which betrayed his inner feelings.

If addressed to young middies, these "words of admonition" on good behaviour, might not have been altogether misplaced. But senior officers, with hair already turning grey, and above all an A.D.C. to the Emperor and Vice-Admiral Commander-in-Chief, did not feel altogether at their ease when thus receiving, standing, side by side with midshipmen, the admonitions of a Major-General who was recommending them to abstain from all intemperance!

I should have liked to believe that the Japanese only countenanced such ceremonies as these, owing to sheer artlessness or because they did not really know the rules of politeness and decorum commonly used in Europe; but I found it very hard to be convinced that it was so. To the Japanese, above all people, this part of European civilisation ought to be most intelligible and most congenial, because, of all countries in the world, it is in theirs that the spirit of etiquette has been best kept; that is to say, the outward forms of the relations, one with another, which should be kept even among members of the same family.

It was obvious to us that Okama was delighting in the task with which he was charged.

The interpreter having finished the lecture, Okama, with a solemn inclination of his head, invited us to sit down. When we were seated, he took his place in his chair; then, still by means of the interpreter, he embarked on the following conversation:—

The interpreter.—"The general wishes to express once more the deep respect he holds for your great services and your personal courage. He hopes that the doctors here will prove to be not inferior to those at Sassebo, and that the serious wound on your head will soon be completely healed up, especially as the climate here is better than at Sassebo."

The admiral.—"Tell the general that I thank him."

The interpreter.—"The general is much troubled about the condition of your wounds, especially as your arrival, of which he had been notified long before, was postponed day after day; and so he is delighted to see you here at last."

The admiral.—"Thank you."

The interpreter.—"He regrets being unable to offer you here the comforts which are customary in Europe, but he will be glad to do anything he can to make up for the deficiency."

The admiral.—"Thank you."

The interpreter.—"He instructs me to ask whether you are tired after your voyage, and how you are feeling today."

The admiral.—"Very well."

The interpreter.—"He regrets that his military occupations do not permit him to continue this pleasant conversation, but he feels obliged to depart, and wishes you good day."

The admiral—"Goodbye."

Soon after the departure of Okama, the major who was accompanying him, came to offer us for signature, each individually, a declaration form to give us the right of moving about freely outside the temple from 8 a.m. till 6 p.m.

The signer pledged himself not to try to escape, nor to send off letters or telegrams, nor to pass the prescribed limits, nor to enter into communication with other prisoners confined in the neighbourhood, nor to make his way into private houses, etc., etc. This curious document began thus:

> I give my word of honour as a sailor and a Russian officer, that
> I pledge myself before Almighty God . . .

When the major presented his paper to the admiral, he (the admiral) merely answered, "Quite unnecessary," which was as brief as it was to the point, and turned his back and walked out of the room.

Considering that the plenipotentiaries signed a treaty of peace a fortnight ago, and it only needs formal ratification, it would be equally stupid and useless to try and escape; but as the Japanese found this time appropriate for playing this farce with us, I determined, for my part, to pay them out. Therefore, with an appearance of great candour, I declared to the major that I had not given my word of honour, but had been taken prisoner at a time when I was very seriously wounded, and so I was cherishing the firm hope of escaping on the first possible occasion.

The admiral's flag-captain and A.D.C., who had come with him from Sassebo, followed my example, and, together with me, refused to sign. As a matter of fact, it caused me but little privation. During all my time on board the *Suvorof*—that is from October 14, 1904, to May 27, 1905—I only set foot on land on three occasions: once at Vigo, and twice at Nossi-Bé, and then only on official business, and for an hour at most. Here, the temple and its magnificent garden are far more spacious than a man-of-war, so that not to go outside them is a matter of entire indifference to me, considering that thus I owe neither thanks nor gratitude to our conquerors.

September 2.—All the rest of yesterday was spent in household cares and purchase of things which were absolutely necessary.

There is in the temple a small cook-shop, whose owner, a Jap, speaks Russian pretty fluently, and is willing to undertake to see that the things which we order are sent us from the town—of course, after deducting a very large commission as his share in the transaction.

The admiral and his staff (eight persons) are not the only inhabitants of the temple; there are, besides us, an officer of the *Osslyabia*, representatives from the *Vladimir Monomach*, the *Sissoiet* and the *Ural*, and finally twenty-three or twenty-four of those who surrendered with Nebogatoff's division, and who make a clique apart and refuse to keep not only the military discipline which Okama preached to us with such fervour, but even the most elementary rules of good behaviour. Sub-lieutenants of the Reserve and some young men who favour the modern "smartness" cultivated of late years in the Naval Training School, set the tone, and, although they certainly do not form the majority, are certainly the most conspicuous.

The serious-minded and well-bred among us, who take account of past events and appreciate our present position in a more rational manner, do not put themselves to the front, and, above all, take good care not to brawl on all occasions.

We have learned today what annoyances we were saved at Ninoshima by the energetic declarations of Dr Tadzuki, who, as Director of Sassebo Hospital, held himself guarantee for our not carrying with us the germs of any infectious disease, with the result that there was no pretext of keeping us in quarantine. The others were treated as follows. Directly they arrived, the members of each detachment were gathered together in a shed promiscuously, with no distinction of age or rank; then everyone had to strip entirely and put all his clothes into a canvas bag marked with a number which tallied with that on a copper ring which each man had to put on his finger.

Whereupon, this troop of naked men was conducted to a neighbouring shed, where were large wooden tubs of water treated with antiseptic. There they were immersed, several at a time in the same bath, while the attendants watched to see that each man put his head well under the water, and deluged with buckets all those who resisted. When the bath was over, the whole crowd was sent into an adjoining hall to be vaccinated, and had to wait patiently until the lymph dried, after which they were allowed to exchange the ring for their clothes, which had in the meantime been disinfected. To finish up, they had to endure a fortnight's confinement in the quarantine barracks.

It is only fair to admit that the Japanese, who had no information as to the sanitary condition of their prisoners, had every right to try and prevent infectious diseases being brought into their country, but they might have enforced their sanitary measures in a more agreeable way. My informant laid special stress on the words, "They pushed us about and herded us like cattle," and then he grew pale and blushed alternately at the remembrance of what he had undergone, for it was obvious to him that the conquerors could not resist the paltry satisfaction of treating Europeans in the same way as a native crowd just arrived from a country ravaged by plague.

September 3.—I awoke this morning at daybreak, before 6 o'clock. The temple buildings, with their quaint roofs, trellised galleries, arched bridges, gardens, ponds, variegated foliage of the trees, and ornamental and artistically trimmed shrubs, blended together in a wonderfully attractive picture. From all around floated up sweet smells and freshness, which caused an extraordinary increase of courage and energy to spring up within me. I suppose that all who are recovering from serious illness experience this.

I began to wander about the corridors, and saw there sights singularly out of keeping with these beautiful surroundings—groups of men, huddled round a table, who had evidently passed the night in playing cards; their faces were flushed, their eyes bloodshot, their voices hoarse—and I felt a wave of immense pity for them sweep over me, and passed on.

What wonderful masters of the art of miniature these Japanese are! The more I walk about, and the more I explore the recesses of our enclosure, the more I admire the artist (for he is no mere gardener) who, in so small a space, has been able to create the impression of a large and ancient natural park, by making use of every knoll and every small fold of the ground. Here is a craggy slope, and reaching down from it what to all appearances are not steps built by the hand of man, but merely a passage hewn out of the piled-up rocks. Here is a path barely visible in the bushy grass; yet I only have to push aside a few branches to find myself on a trim lawn, in the middle of which stands a tiny moss-grown temple dedicated to some god or other. Here is a long, flat stone, which seems to have rolled down from the rock, and to have come to rest right across the stream, which connects the two branches of the pond, so as to make a bridge. Instinctively I cast my eye round to look for the place from which it has broken off. To think that all this is not the result of the caprice of nature, but of the well-planned work of human artists!

September 4.—It is obvious that our refusal to pledge ourselves in any way, has caused the Japanese astonishment as well as some anxiety. The major came to find the admiral this morning, while a lieutenant came in to us to persuade us that, after so long a period in hospital, some distractions and walks were essential to us. This manoeuvre having failed, the lieutenant, who was not easily discouraged, came back in the evening to beg us to persuade the admiral to sign the document, which, he said, was really nothing more than a mere formality. We only laughed.

September 5.—Yesterday evening while we were having tea with the admiral, the conversation turned on . the difference which exists between real active service and the "red tape" conditions and regulations in vogue at our Naval School—conditions which are absolutely contrary to those presented by practical service. The admiral grew hot over it, and told us that it is absolutely necessary to reform the service education of our officers and men from the very bottom, together with the organisation of our arsenals and the Admiralty. He added that we had always followed the wrong track, and had finished by falling asleep lulled by the song of "All Goes Well." Our ignorance might perhaps serve us for an excuse for the past: if we had been culpable, we had at least been sincere, and people might forgive us at a pinch; but for the present, when the war has opened our eyes, if we persist in following the old road and not profiting by our bitter experience, we shall be committing an absolutely deliberate and wilful crime which will debar us from pleading any attenuating circumstances.

I do not pledge myself that those were the exact words which the admiral made use of, but I do declare that what I have just written contains the essence of his opinions.

September 6.—The general commanding the division, Lieutenant-General Ibaraki, has arrived at Osaka; he is coming to inspect, even more solemnly than Okama on the first day, the newly arrived prisoners. Everyone, from the admiral down, was ordered to attend in the dining hall. At the last moment, however, there was a counter order, as the authorities were afraid lest the admiral might refuse to leave his room. In any case, Ibaraki knows how to behave himself better than Okama.

Directly he arrived at the temple he sent his A.D.C. to ask whether the admiral would be willing to receive him, and on receiving an answer in the affirmative, he came hat in hand, as for a visit of courtesy.

Moreover, his good manners won him a welcome during an audience which lasted for a quarter of an hour. When he left, the admiral accompanied him as far as the door, and took leave of him in a most cordial way, whereas he had taken no more notice of Okama than if he had not existed. All the officers, gathered in the dining-room, were formally presented to the general, who did not make any tactless speech, but confined himself to expressing in a few simple words his deep sympathy and hope to see them soon at liberty.

September 7.—For three days now we have had bad weather. Every morning our linen and our clothes are wet through and through. The food is more abominable than ever, but that is not the fault of the superintendent or of the cook, but of the system.

I ask you—How, with a grant of only 1s. 3d. a day per officer, could it be possible to give us three good meals—breakfast, lunch, and dinner, especially with the price of meat at 11d. per lb.? Each officer receives, besides his food, 6 *roubles* (12s.) a month, to keep his clothes and boots in repair, buy tobacco and soap, and meet various other tri-fling expenses. The upkeep of the rank-and-file prisoners is estimated at 6d. a day, all told.

Taking these statistics and the numbers of prisoners of war (ad-mirals, senior and other officers, sailors and marines) published in the Japanese newspapers, it is not difficult for the numerous unemployed mathematicians whom we number among our ranks, to calculate what entertaining the prisoners of war will cost the Japanese, supposing our release to be complete in November. The results only differ because we cannot all agree as to the exact date of departure and the numbers of the detachments; but all the statistics approximate to £500,000 or £600,000, to which something might be added for transport, erection and upkeep of the huts, medical expenses, etc. Reckoning 100 *roubles* (£10) per head (an excessive estimate) for these supplementary ex-penses, we must add £700,000, and thus, after great thought, we arrive at a total, in round numbers, of £1,500,000, allowing, in addition to the above details, a good sum for unexpected expenditure.

I wonder, therefore, why the Japanese exacted £20,000,000 on the above count, and I am absolutely convinced that their demand was only agreed to in order to mask a war indemnity, and it was that which humiliated me more than anything else.

We cannot even make a pretence of appeasing our hunger with such meagre rations. Those who have availed themselves of the per-mission to go outside the temple grounds, go and have lunch every day at the Miako Hotel and take there one square meal, sufficient to last the whole day. Our position is less advantageous because only the admiral, after much difficulty, has obtained permission to have his meals brought in from outside.

The rule on this point is rigid, as the authorities are afraid lest we might manage to have secret communications from outside brought in to us in our provision baskets. We are able, however, to make some arrangement with our cook, who, for a very moderate remuneration, is willing to eke out our daily fare a little; but he, unfortunately, very soon reaches the limit of his accomplishments, and can hardly get be-yond beef-steaks and omelettes. Occasionally the canteen man gives us a ham or a case of preserves, and we have provided ourselves well with all the necessaries for making tea, coffee, or chocolate.

I have been able to get hold of the *Nippon Kai'tai-Kai-sen*, the description of the Battle of Tsushima, compiled from the reports of Togo, his subordinate admirals, officers in command of ships, and various other people who took part in the fight, and even of mere spectators. It makes two big volumes in Japanese, and I have begun to translate them today, which will help me to kill time.

At the same time, I am giving a rub up to my Chinese characters; formerly I used to know 2500 of them, but want of practice has made me forget many of them; but now as I study them, they almost all come back to my memory quite easily.

I must confess that there are but few students among those lodged in the temple; two or three officers, it is true, like playing the naval war game, but it is always the battle of Tsushima which provides the subject. They have tried every kind of combination, but the result is always the same—it is invariably the Russians who are beaten.

On the other hand, the majority do absolutely nothing except loaf about the town all the day, or rather, bury themselves in refreshment bars, restaurants, and tea-houses. In the evening and at night they play cards, and it is very seldom that these parties end without scenes of drunkenness and quarrelling.

September 8.—The rain has stopped, but the cold has come: in the mornings it is only 55° Fahr. and everything is drenched, because the mist is just as thick inside the room as outside. That is not astonishing, for, of the three partitions which separate me from the open air, one is of cardboard, and the other two of very thin and transparent oilpaper.

September 9.—I got chilled in bed last night and have got a cold—also I am coughing like the d——, and have a sick headache into the bargain.

September 10.—The French Vice-Consul at Kobe has been to see us. Why? We are lost in conjecture. Probably it is to discharge an unpleasant, but necessary duty, for he has been appointed intermediary between us and the Japanese authorities. After this he will be able to say: "I have been to see them and get personal knowledge of their wants." I tried to speak to him of the food which they are giving us, but he merely shrugged his shoulders and said: "That all comes of their being unable to understand your European tastes."

Tanaka, who has just been appointed captain of a cruiser, came in this morning to enquire after the health of the admiral, on behalf of the Minister of Marine and the Chief of the Naval Staff, and to bring him, in the name of the International Committee of 'Red Cross ' ladies, five boxes of Egyptian cigarettes and five cases of champagne, which the admiral sent at once to our mess. I am very much taken with this Tanaka; he reminds me of my old friend Nomoto.

September 11.—It is almost as if summer had returned, so beautiful and warm is the evening.

September 12.—Nebogatoff had already paid two pretty long calls on the admiral before today, but I had not met him. The Japanese Government, having been notified officially that he and the commanding officers of his division have had their commissions suspended, and are therefore no longer on the active list, has made haste to set them free, and they leave tomorrow.

Nebogatoff came this morning to say goodbye, and by chance we met in the verandah, and he stopped me, and we talked for a while. I confess that my first opinion of him is a bit shaken, in spite of its having been so firmly rooted. I did not wish to speak to him of the surrender of the officers who had been placed under his command—it was too much of a burning question. What good would it do to open up old wounds? His position is not so very agreeable even without that.

The circumstances certainly were desperate: the Japanese, who were masterly in their choice of range, kept about 6¼ to 6¾ miles away from him, and shot at his ships from this safe distance without running the slightest risk, owing to their superiority in speed and the longer range of their guns, just as if they were at target practice—and it is of this that we ought to be most ashamed of all. Nebogatoff assured me that he was making haste to get to Russia in order to demand to be put on trial. He wants all the world to know wherein his guilt really lies. As he was incapable of inflicting any injury whatever on the enemy, he might at least, some critics have said, have sunk his ships and tried to save the men in the boats; but as he was certain that 75 out of every 100 would certainly perish, he could not make up his mind to hoist a signal condemning to death 1500 of the young sailors who had been entrusted to his charge.

Yes, I had not the courage to do it, and to this alone I plead guilty. I am sure you will believe that it was not to save my own skin that I acted thus: I was the admiral, and means would always have been found of saving me. Even if I had wanted to drown myself they would have taken good care to fish me out by force; the Japs first of all, as I represented a trophy of war to them. Oh no! it was not for my sake, but for the men's. My heart failed me—well, let them put me on trial!

That was, indeed, the only argument which could have justified him. It is quite clear that he had nothing to fear for his own life, and that it was not to save himself that he surrendered his ships.

September 13.—Warm and wet.

September 14.—This morning Monsieur Armand, the French Minister, and his naval *attaché*, Martini, arrived with Okama and the major. As always, the admiral ignored the existence of Okama, and explained the reason of his conduct to the minister. He could not permit a mere major-general to preach him a sermon in public on military discipline and good behaviour. No! he could not forgive him for that.

Armand invited us to dinner this evening at the Miako Hotel; he had also invited some Japs.

September 15.—Nothing new.

September 16.—At 10 o'clock this morning, there was a slight earthquake shock.

September 17.—Cold and gloomy weather.

September 18.—Same as yesterday.

CHAPTER 21

Politics

September 19.—The great toe of my left foot is very troublesome. About a fortnight after the operation it apparently healed up, and soon a new toe nail began to grow in place of the one that was torn off, and now I have a fresh annoyance. For no obvious reason the toe has become swollen and inflamed. The doctors shrugged their shoulders, and said it was caused by the scar not allowing the new toe nail to grow normally. They ordered it to be bathed in hot water three times a day. For a short while this treatment relieved it, but afterwards the pain began again. I accomplished the journey from Sassebo to Kioto in loose slippers. At Kioto the doctor's advice was the same—that until the nail grew, the toe was to be kept in hot fomentations. I dared not doubt his opinion, but was very much worried as to how I was to put on boots on leaving. The right leg was slowly but surely growing stronger and becoming manageable, although occasionally when I walked, and was not paying particular attention, it would suddenly give way. It only hurt when there was a change of weather.

September 20.—The thermometer stood at 55½ degrees Fahrenheit in my room this morning.

Our seclusion here does not differ much from confinement in prison. The only difference is that there is plenty of light and air. There is an ample supply of the latter, but it is cold and damp.

September 22.—The treaty of peace reached Japan to-day for ratification.

A copy of Apuchtin was found somewhere or other, and we arranged a literary evening with him. D—— does not read badly. How keenly one realises that Apuchtin wrote, not for the sake of work, nor even for the sake of glory, but simply because at a psychological mo-

263

ment he felt inspired. He did not compose, he did not seek subjects: they flowed from the depths of his soul, giving an accurate picture of the frame of mind that possessed him at the time. How extraordinarily characteristic is the farewell letter of a suicide to his lawyer; the carelessly jesting tone which hides such infinite despair, such unbearable pain, and the knowledge that all is in the past, and nothing in the future.

Where art thou, my cruel scourge, who dost chasten and oppress?
Where art thou, my radiant star, whose glowing rays caress?

After poetry came prose. *The Diary of Paul Dolsky* brought strange thoughts into my head. Here indeed is what a typical man of our time and society thinks (or ought to think) on discovering that old age is upon him, that life is spent, is spent in vain. Nothing useful has been done. But is it only the fault of Paul himself? Involuntarily one recalls another childless, solitary man, who lived twenty-five centuries ago, and died at the age of forty-five—that is, approximately, at the age at which Paul wrote his own obituary. When the friends of Epaminoudas complained that he was dying without leaving any posterity, he answered them, full of pride and happiness: "I leave to Greece two deathless daughters, Leuctra and Mantinea."—And how about us?

September 23.—I try to have no dealings with the Japanese, and therefore personally have nothing to complain about. But others enjoying the right of "free promenade" are very much dissatisfied. According to them, the Japanese deliberately try to take advantage of the remaining days of their power to make life unbearable by petty annoyances. Yesterday Lieutenant B—— was five minutes late: he returned from the town at 6.5 instead of at 6 p.m.; and they took away his pass granting the right of exit. The most insulting thing of all is that, *de facto*, similar orders—the right to punish or pardon—emanate from none other than a police sergeant, who speaks a little Russian, and is placed at the disposal of the subaltern in charge of our temple. This is not done by mere accident, but is a regular system, which is acutely felt by us in our position. Orders are given to the prisoners by a person ranking considerably below them in their service capacity. A major comes to an admiral with orders, a subaltern to staff officers, a non-commissioned officer to his senior officers.

September 24.—A bright, hot autumn day.

September 25.—Some English officers and sailors from the squadron that has arrived at Kobe, came to Kioto today. They are honouring their allies. Our men have been advised to refrain from walking out, to avert possible misunderstandings.

Judging by the papers, the treaty of peace has already been ratified, but we are still under guard.

September 27.—Nothing fresh.

September 28.—I read in the *Strannik* (Pilgrim) yesterday (it is sent us from the clergy mission) an interview with L. N. Tolstoi, on the eternal subject of life and death. Tolstoi considers death the awakening, and life a sleep, with dreams, in the midst of some other existence, infinitely broader and more vital than that of the immediate reality surrounding us. Why has a man fallen asleep? This question he leaves unanswered, but further on gives an exceedingly alluring example. A man sleeps soundly, unconscious that he is asleep, sees a vision and thinks it real: such a man leads a purely animal life. Another one sleeps badly—feels, though uneasily, that it is only a dream: a man like the last seeks a solution of the deepest problems, and on waking is dissatisfied when he tries to recall them.

A quiet death from old age means that a man has slept enough, and does not wish to sleep any more. An early death means an awakening, from external causes; suicide, a desperate effort with which one awakes from a nightmare. A harmonious and beautiful hypothesis, only it is a pity that there is no experiment which could test it. For instance, those friends and comrades (I do not speak of thousands of unknown people) who were suddenly "awakened" at Tsushima! Can it be they all slept so soundly that they quite forgot their dream, and not one of them enquired after myself or anyone else? It is strange!

There is one thing I feel certain about: judging by what is heard of our naval ministry, and by what I see around me, there is little hope that in the near future there will be an improvement and real efficiency in the service: and not the endless drudgery of "notching off points." If that is the case, according to Tolstoi's theory, I have slept enough, and in justice to myself should be awakened—or is this a nightmare, and must I do it myself.

My nerves are so shattered, my frame of mind so gloomy, that after tea at the admiral's I attacked X—— like a wild beast, and took him to task severely. He is a typical Transundian, who already anticipates the joys of returning to the parental roof, and swells with pride and self-confidence. What the Japanese did at Port Arthur is better known

265

to him than to me, because at Transund everything was verified by scientific experiments. "Ah! betrayers of the fleet."

September 29.—Martini, the French naval *attaché*, sent me a letter of four pages. He says that nothing is known at the embassy as to when, or under what conditions, our liberation will take place. They are informed (from Paris) that a special Russian Commission for taking over prisoners of war will arrive, which will be furnished with the necessary instructions and full powers, and to which they are to render every assistance. The news from Russia in the papers is so contradictory and incoherent that it is sickening to read. However, they are only local papers.

We are having the same clear moonlight nights that we had when we first came here. All this beauty of nature and climate is for them! Why is it? Perhaps it is that although we have many patriots willing to devote their lives to our fatherland, the Japanese are always ready to die gladly for theirs. Perhaps this is only justice.

September 30.—According to the papers, the treaty of peace was ratified on the 27th, but the severity towards us is worse than it was before. In my opinion, the Japanese are acting foolishly by harassing us in this manner.

Many of those returning from captivity were formerly friendly to Japan, and are now her enemies. I repeat that I personally have no intercourse with them, but I cannot help seeing and hearing. I was always a warm advocate of the idea of a union with Japan (and even published several articles in 1900-1901 in which I showed that we could very well amicably fix the boundaries with our neighbour), and the Japanese as a nation were much inclined towards it, but I now swear that if there should be a fresh war with Japan, I will certainly take part in it. If on account of inefficiency I am retired, and they will not accept me on service, I shall beg to be a passenger (correspondent or anything). If they refuse, I shall enlist as cook. I long to get back there, if it is only to see how our guns will fire on them.

October 1.—*Pokrov.* [1] Exactly a year ago, on a dull rainy day, the fleet came out of Libau Harbour. A service for those about to travel was held, and the priest of the *Suvoroff*, Father Nazare, prayed "that the noble lord Zenovi" and all his company might have "health, salvation, victory, and mastery over the enemy." How far off all this seems.

---

1. A Russian feast of intercession to the Virgin.

We have a large dining-room, where a travelling church is arranged. An orthodox priest (a Japanese, Father Simeon Mia) celebrates Mass in Russian. A trifling incident gives a clear example of the conduct of the Japanese towards their prisoners of war. A Japanese *gendarme* is obliged to be present at the service, in order to watch (the devil knows what he is to watch. Perhaps they are afraid that letters and telegrams will be handed to the priest unknown to the censor). Movable screens forming the outer wall of the dining-room were altogether taken away, so that it was only separated from the veranda by a few pillars. This *gendarme* would bring a chair, place it in the veranda directly opposite the doors of the altar, sit down, cross one leg over the other, push his cap on to the back of his head, and smoke a cigarette.

The senior of those present (the admiral was not there, as he was not yet able to stand for any length of time) pointed out to the gendarme the impropriety of his conduct, and received the reply, that he was there in discharge of service duties. The flag-captain, at the request of those present, handed in a report of the occurrence to the commander of the garrison. It will be interesting to know what will come of it. [2]

October 2, 3, and 4.—I have thought it best to omit these pages of my diary, and will only say a few words on the cause of the events noted in them. The news of the political agitations that were going on in Russia could not fail to find an echo among the prisoners of war. This news was gathered from papers edited in English, but under Japanese censorship, and of course represented the position of affairs in the darkest light. The inhabitants of the temples (not only ours but others), with that political ignorance which I had already noticed in Sassebo (on account of the manifesto of 6th August), divided themselves into parties of the most extreme views. There was not only no centre, but not even a modified right and left.

To tell some of them that you rejoice at the institution of the Imperial *Duma*, and find it desirable to broaden its legislative rights, was to earn the title of agitator, revolutionary, and even anarchist. Talk to others on the advantage of the Imperial Council, reformed into the likeness of existing upper chambers, and they turn from you with disgust and condemn you as a member of the "black hundred." Especial indignation is called forth from both sides by the statement that the

---

2. What happened was "that with a view to avoid misunderstandings," it was ordered that in future service was not to be held in the travelling church.

army and navy should be outside party politics; that this rule is universally recognised; and that nowhere have men in the services the right of a vote at elections.

More than once this question has led me into a quarrel. I pointed to the example of Poland, where the nobles formed an army, and at the same time occupied themselves with politics, established a confederation, and brought the kingdom to ruin. Another example: Spain is a kingdom arising from the ruins of her colonies with their "*pronunciamento*" proclaimed by military circles. "What should be the creed of a service man, in your opinion?" was a question once propounded by a certain vehement partisan of the constituent assembly. "Yes, that would be interesting to hear," chimed in another, who knew nothing beyond autocracy, orthodoxy, and nationalism.

"It appears to me that this creed was brilliantly formulated more than a century ago, by a man—not in the services—but no fool."

"Who was that?"

"Ostermann. You remember how they awakened him in the night and asked him the fateful question: 'What emperor do you serve!' and he, with deep conviction, answered: 'The one now happily reigning.'"

From that time I was equally obnoxious in the eyes of both parties.

"And you, forgetting your duty to your country, are prepared to serve the old *régime!* to defend the government that is leading Russia to shame!" exclaimed someone.

"So it means that if, when we return to Russia, a Convention is sitting, you are ready to serve it?" joined in others.

This method of arguing is an old and purely Russian custom. It is just as it was at the time of the schism, when no one was asked the crucial question, "Do you believe in the power of the Sign of the Cross?" without fulminating anathemas at one another. They even burnt each other at the stake for such questions of dogma as to whether two or three fingers should be used in crossing themselves. However, all these discussions were a mere passing mental phase, and the majority of my comrades recovered their balance of mind, and on returning to Russia, former revolutionaries; gave up visions of a constituent assembly; and I furious "black hundreds" made peace unconditionally, with an effective Imperial *Duma*.

In some cases the metamorphosis even went J so far (again the adaptability of our nature), that the reds of yesterday turned into Conservatives, and former absolutists dreamt of a ministry responsible to the Imperial *Duma*. And we are all still in the service!

I have considered it right to publish these pages, in order not to place in a somewhat false position those whose opinions and declarations were written down by me at that time. There was something infinitely more serious, alarming, and even outrageous, about which I cannot be silent, but which I shall refer to later on.

CHAPTER 22

Freedom

October 5.—The formal ratification of the treaty of peace is officially announced in today's papers. We were informed that for the future the guard on the temple remained only for the protection of the late prisoners of war from possible attacks on the part of the ignorant populace, who were dissatisfied with the terms of the treaty—that we were perfectly free; but in the event of any distant excursion beyond the town, they begged that we would give notice, in order that the authorities responsible for our safety might take the necessary precautions. Our Japanese subaltern appeared with a joyful face and handed me a piece of pasteboard (rather like a large-sized visiting card), on which was written in Japanese that so and so (my name and rank) is permitted to visit all places that he wishes to see. In a word, it was a kind of passport.

I thanked him, and wished to avail myself of my privilege today, but suddenly discovered that the authorities (intentionally or unintentionally I do not know) had blundered. It appeared that it was necessary before going out, to present the card that had been brought to me in such triumph by the subaltern, to the police sergeant, and to inform him at what hour I should return. If this hour were after sunset, then it was necessary to obtain permission, ostensibly from the commander of the garrison, but in reality not from him, but from the major, the subaltern, and in the end from the very same police sergeant, who would begin to question why you wished to return at such a time, where did you intend to go, etc. I gave up the idea of the excursion, and, calling for the subaltern, returned him the card and explained that according to our ideas, it was unbecoming for a staff officer to request permission to return at a certain time, from a junior, with the risk of receiving a refusal depending on his judgment. A similar case actually occurred today. "Why do you wish to return at 10 o'clock?" asked the sergeant. "I intend to dine at an hotel, and play billiards," answered the good-natured Russian. "You can go till 9 o'clock: I will write it down at that," was the reply.

October 6.—How has the feeling of self-respect—I will not say the feeling of one's own worth—been corroded out of these people? They have apparently forgotten everything, and are prepared to fraternise with the Japanese. It is disgusting. Let us take a living example— (this is an explanation of the "disgusting"): I do not refer to the time immediately after the Franco-Prussian war, but to the present day, thirty-five years later—a Frenchman (especially a service man) will not look at a German if he can help it. It makes him uncomfortable. He thinks that everyone he meets will stare and look upon him as one of the "vanquished"—and how can he resent this? But look at our people—No, evidently I was born either too soon or too late.

By the kind permission of a Japanese *gendarme*, our people run about the town, and on returning, gleefully recount how the street urchins (so brave) put their tongues out and cry, *"Tse-u-tsin"* (foreign devil); how they were received in a Japanese eating-house (of course for money), and taught to eat with chopsticks; how (overcoming their repugnance) they ate raw fish to avoid shocking their table companions, and found it excellent. They seemed to forget (perhaps they never acknowledged it) that defeat was an insult that could only be washed out by victory. They forgot the sacred resentment which they should carry in their hearts, in the hunger for which future generations must be educated. They forgot the shameful destruction of their fatherland—and perhaps, too, they forgot their fatherland itself, Russia. Can this word have lost its meaning for them?

"God with us!" Are we still entitled to bear this proud motto? Will not every European who sees a Russian officer fawning on a Japanese, say, "God with you?" The glorious invincibility of Russia, heaped up during centuries, has crumbled away. How shall we resurrect it? Evidently a cataclysm is necessary—not war—but the extermination of empires and nations, in order to restore our lost prestige.

October 7.—Okama came today and announced the ratification of the treaty in a triumphant speech. I suspect that though he read the announcement from a paper, he composed it himself. It would have been done better by an official order.

It is raining in torrents. Three days ago was the festival of bringing the first ripe ears of grain into the temple; but the rice remains green, and it is useless to think of the harvest. It is a consolation. (I am not ashamed of rejoicing at the misfortunes of others.)

October 8.—I cannot tear myself from the same old subject. Yesterday Z—— drove to Osaka and returned at night, not having had permission (he had driven out with several others). This morning, when they made a fuss about it, he was very brave—said that as peace was concluded he was a free man, and that if anything happened, he knew how to stand up for himself: but at eleven o'clock in the morning, having learnt that in spite of his friendship with the gendarmes, his late return had been noted in a book, he immediately cringed to the Japanese subaltern. He walked arm-in-arm with him and invited him to dine somewhere. The subaltern was captious at first, but afterwards allowed himself to be persuaded, and promised not to report him.

October 9.—There were 50° F. in my room last night. It is not much positively.

October 10.—The French Ambassador telegraphs that yesterday General Daniloff, President of the Commission for the Transfer of the Prisoners of War, left Vladivostok for Nagasaki in the *Bogatyr*.

October 12.—The last days of captivity are the most trying. It is cold. The devil take all my writing!

October 14.—A major came to the admiral today on a highly diplomatic mission. He announced that the chief of the division and other commanders proposed to entertain us (the former prisoners of war) at a farewell dinner. The admiral of course thanked them, but replied that though such an invitation was undoubtedly made with the knowledge and approval of the highest Japanese authorities, we were deprived meanwhile of the possibility of obtaining in good time the sanction of our own government for its acceptance, and therefore it would be better not to raise the question at all. A refusal—but in such a form that the major could only express his thanks. I will again make a comparison. Would some German general in charge of French prisoners of war, after the Franco-Prussian war, have proposed something similar? Certainly not.

The Germans could not fail to respect their enemy. They would be afraid of placing both themselves and the French in an awkward position by such a proposal. Why did the Japanese run such a risk? Was it on account of their *naiveté?*—hardly that—it was simply because they have no respect for us—and not without reason. We ourselves give them sufficient cause—to say nothing of X—— and Z——, who are ready to admire a common log of wood because it is "genuine Japanese." These are cranks.

A little while ago, today, as I was passing an office, I witnessed the following scene: Three Japanese soldiers, one of them a non-commissioned officer speaking a little Russian, and a Russian staff officer were sitting at a table smoking and conversing amicably together about the curiosities of Kioto which were worth seeing. No wonder the Japanese treat us in an offhand manner.

October 15.—This morning there were 48° F.

October 16.—The admiral received a telegram from the French Ambassador, to the effect that flag-officers with their staffs, and captains of ships, are permitted to return at their own convenience.

October 17.—The admiral positively declines to return in a roundabout way on board a foreign steamer. Unlike General Stössel, he telegraphed a request to General Daniloff to be allowed to sail for Vladivostok in the *Voronege*, which would be one of the first ships to leave Japan. I fully understood him.

It was characteristic of General Daniloff that he did not pay the admiral a visit in passing through Kioto, nor send any one of the numerous members of his commission to confer with him; nor did he even deign to address a single word to him, either by post or telegraph. I am loath to believe the newspapers. They are publishing such queer news of the state of affairs in Russia.

October 18.—I prevailed on N—— N—— , as the senior officer resident in the temple (not counting the admiral), to intercede with the Japanese authorities on behalf of our youngsters, whom the Japanese *gendarmes* are deriding for their surrender.

October 19-20.—(*These are the pages I have decided to omit.*)

October 21.—The Japanese, notwithstanding the courteous but categorical refusal of the admiral, are evidently bent upon trying to arrange a dinner ... and not without good grounds. It is a fact that the majority (not only here, but in the other places of confinement) made a grateful and polite refusal, influenced by the motives expressed by the admiral; yet, some were to be found who accepted the invitation. Do you know why? In order to prove their independence, to show that they were not influenced by the admiral. Who can fail to be angry with them? But as for our crank Japanophiles—I can only clench my fists. They nearly wept at the thought that a real Japanese dinner with *geishas* might fall through. I rejoiced with all my heart (and up to now I have not repented of this feeling) when information was received that, on account of the small number of those accepting the invitation, to the great distress of the commander of the garrison, the dinner could not take place.

October 22.—Feeling depressed. Absolutely nothing doing, and no news from anywhere. The autumn wind is moaning dismally; dead leaves are whirling in the air and fall against our cardboard walls; trees, half-bared of their foliage, swing and twist their branches in a grotesque manner. The pond is covered with rubbish and is dirty. It is not a pond but a muddy puddle: even the fish have buried themselves in the slime. My spirits have gone down to the depths. Oh, if only I could bury myself too . . . deep, deep, ever so deep, head and all.

October 23.—The temperature at 8 a.m. was 45.4° F. My hands are freezing.

One of our midshipmen, Prince G——, returned from Tokio, whither he had been dispatched to make investigations. He tells such stories that we are loath to believe them. For some reason the brave General Daniloff had been appointed President of the Commission for the Transfer of the Prisoners of War, straight from the front, where he was threatening the enemy. The general inquired what he should do in Japan? They replied: "The French Ambassador will inform you, but you are, in the first place, to choose six staff-officers as members of the commission, an *aide-de-camp*, a secretary, and clerks." No sooner said than done. They went on board the *Bogatyr* and sailed. The authorities had enrolled the captain of the *Bogatyr* as a member of the commission, but he was boycotted, as he was inclined to be caustic and was frankly bored by the talk of what was customary in international communications.

Upon arrival at Nagasaki they left him behind (under a specious pretext), and proceeded themselves to Tokio. At Tokio a new difficulty presented itself; the general, his *aide-de-camp*, and the members of the commission knew only a few words of domestic and gastronomical import in any of the foreign languages, and whenever the Japanese tried to approach the commission in French or English, they positively affirmed that they did not understand Japanese. It proved necessary, even for the correspondence with the French Ambassador, to engage a Japanese interpreter! At a luncheon at the French Legation in which the midshipman took part, he found himself in the role of dragoman, and could not help overhearing the general encouraging his *aide-de-camp* and urging him not to lose a chance, and to find out all he could from him. M. Armand had informed the admiral that he was expecting the arrival of a commission, the president of which would be furnished with the necessary instructions and authority, but that this president was asking him: "Where are the prisoners? How many are there? How are they to be discharged to their homes? Please give me instructions."

The result was that the Japanese took the initiative in their own hands, and the brave general was left with no alternative but to carry out their orders. Through ignorance of languages, he was not always successful in doing this.

Oh, my beloved fatherland! I recognise your hand in this. Could they really not have found a single general, and a half-score of staff officers who could speak foreign languages? How many such there were with the active army. Why was this low comedy necessary? What confusion, what embarrassment, what lack of organisation! Did not a great soldier (I forget who it was) say, "*organisation is the mother of victory.*"

I was so much annoyed, that I went to bed at 7 p.m. The devil take it; there is not much sleep to be had in 41° F. I was awakened by the cold and went to have tea with the admiral.

October 24.—The temperature at 8 a.m. was 36.4° F. My hands were like hooks, as the proverb says. I can hardly scratch these lines. I walked round the temple. There were pictures similar to "The Retreat from Moscow," or "The Russians at the Shipka Pass."

People sit huddled up, wrapped in blankets, and squeeze themselves as close as they can round the "*khibatches*" (coal pans).

Admiral Viren was here today. My sympathy is with him, although at Port Arthur he energetically contended that by transferring our guns on shore we should prove of more service to the defence. Recalling the Battle of Shan-tung, I am now, perhaps, prepared to agree with him. Could real seamen have backed out of a fight already half won, because the commander of the fleet was killed and the flagship had left the line! And if there are no sailors, then can we hope for successful actions at sea?

The admiral, who had already received a somewhat frigid permission from General Daniloff to go to Vladivostok in the *Voronege*, invited Viren to go with him. The latter, of course, was very much pleased, as he was not at all inclined to be a target for the Kodaks and pens of war correspondents for the next two months.

Midnight.—It is bitterly cold. I burnt a whole bottle of methylated spirit in a saucepan in trying to warm the room. It was no use.

October 25.—I woke at 7 a.m.; the temperature was 35° F.

October 26.—I have installed a gigantic "*khibatch*" in my room. It warms me, but I have a bad cold and a headache. No matter what the coal is, it gives off fumes.

October 27.—The orderlies were drunk today and created a disturbance which ended in a fight. We can only control them by words of reproof, which is not worth much in their eyes, and the Japanese emphasise the fact that spirits are allowed for all those living in the temple.

October 28.—(*I omit this.*)

October 29.—We received official notice that we are to be released on Monday, 31st October (13th November). The captain of the *Voronege*—an old acquaintance of mine—came to report to the admiral that he is awaiting his arrival.

October 30.—The last day of captivity; hasty preparations. Many people came to wish the admiral a pleasant journey. Deputations came from the wardrooms of different ships. Is it through conscience or through fear? God grant it is the former.

Welcome dear fatherland! How much have I endured physically and mentally . . . Must I repeat it? We failed. We did not know how to gain a victory. What then? Were we not willing? Were we afraid? Did we not go? But if we did not know how to win, have we not paid for it with our blood? Receive us, saved by a miracle from certain death. And believe that every throb of this still beating heart belongs to thee. It was not I, it was not my will—fate herself preserved me and did not allow me to perish as I wished. Not wantonly. Why? . . . To serve thee! No, I have no other wish. . . . An oath, a fearful oath I swear: for thee—the whole remainder of my days, all my strength, and all my blood. For thee—everything! . . .

In a French novel I came across the sentence: "*Mon Dieu, si je ne suis bon à rien, que je meurs!"* This is a justifiable wish which ought to be granted if a supreme justice exists at all. And here am I unscathed. At a time when men were falling like flies, in the turrets and in the conning tower, I, wandering about the decks and bridges, remained untouched. Three times were the fire parties who worked under my direction annihilated, and I was only wounded. I was captured; I might have been tried and punished as a fugitive from the *Diana*. I narrowly escaped. Was it at random? was it all chance?

October 31.—I had to rise at dawn. The dawn of freedom. And oh! how cold it was. Everything is collected and packed. The train leaves at 9.38 a.m. Okama came to say goodbye and wish us good luck. There was another parting at the station, where all the chief officials had gathered. The train started. At a sign from the general all the Japanese waved their caps and shouted "hurrah." Thank God, it is over. At Osaka, General Ibaraki, the divisional commander, with his staff, fulfilled the pleasant duty of wishing us a happy journey. On, on! At Kobe station we saw General Daniloff with his *aide-de-camp* (a captain, I forget his name) and the captain of the *Voronege*, who was evidently directing the movements of our men, who felt themselves lost in a Japanese crowd.

I cannot omit to state that as it subsequently transpired, only the interference of the captain spared us from a very unpleasant ordeal. The general having completely surrendered the initiative to the Japanese, who have everything so wonderfully ordered, was preparing to take over the admiral and his staff as he would the lower ranks, *i.e.*, by counting them on the pier when entering the boat, in the eyes of the curious crowd. The captain of the *Voronege* convinced him, not without difficulty, that such a parade was out of place and unnecessary, as the Japanese did not at all insist on it.

Thank God! Once more on Russian territory, under a Russian flag! Although it is not customary on board a merchant ship (the Volunteer fleet fly the merchant flag), as we stepped on deck from the gangway everyone saluted as if it were a warship.

November 1.—With difficulty I was aroused at 9 a.m. On the day of our transfer to the ship, the big toe of my left foot gave me great pain, though I hardly walked at all. As soon as I came on board, I hastened to pull off my boots and put on slippers. Today, by special order, some lace boots of American make were brought to me from the shore. They were of such dimensions, and so wide across the foot, that my bad toe was installed as though it were in a reserved cabin.

Evening.—I cannot refrain from a previous remark: at Kioto, in the midst of dirt and petty cavilling, freezing with cold, and tormented with hunger, life was easier than it is here now. A multitude of small worries obscured our chief sorrow then. Now that the first raptures of our freedom have subsided, and everything around is so pleasant and comfortable, oppressive thoughts are again disturbing me. It is hard.

In spite of all the cabins being fully occupied, we had to take another passenger—Major-General S———. He came here and went straight to the admiral. "For God's sake take me with you," he said, "for I don't know when I may expect my turn to leave, with this blessed Daniloff Commission." The admiral answered that he was not in command here, but as the captain had given up his own cabin to him, in which there was a sofa besides a bed, he begged him to make use of it; however, he was not allowed such self-denial. The captain had a brilliant idea: he proposed that I should move into a common cabin usually occupied by a stewardess, and that the general should have my berth in the double cabin. I agreed with pleasure. True, instead of a luxurious bedstead I only had a very short and narrow bunk (they must choose exceptionally small stewardesses in the Volunteer fleet), and I could hardly turn round in my new quarters, but then I had it all to myself—a great advantage.

The wound on my left foot has reopened and is suppurating. The ship's doctor examined it, and decided that there must be some foreign matter in the wound—either a fragment of shell or piece of bone that had been overlooked. He did not advise me to have an operation during the journey, but recommended me to change the bandages twice a day till we came to St Petersburg. I of course agreed. It would be very offensive to be sent again to a Japanese hospital from a Russian ship.

November 2.—Today they embarked the rest of the men; and the last passengers, Rear-Admiral Viren and his flag-lieutenant, arrived on board.

At 3.30 p.m., the Orthodox priest, Simeon Mia (a Japanese), who had come from Kioto, held a farewell service.

M. Martini (the French naval *attaché*), the French consul at Kobe, and even General Daniloff with his adjutant, came to say goodbye.

The admiral looks vigorous, though he has grown thin from hardships and worries (during the last days at Kioto). He is a mere skeleton;

the doctor says that that is a trifle, his nerves are of iron; they will sustain him so that he will outlive all of us. If only they do not give way. I agree with him. If he is employed again in St Petersburg, he will live and put on flesh, but if he is retired he will not last long. [1]

---

1. The commander's shrewd prognostication verified itself. Upon his return to St Petersburg, Admiral Rojëstvensky was rapidly and skilfully shelved "out of mischief's way," and this wonderful man's heroic and humble martyrdom was ended by death during the year 1909.

CHAPTER 23

In Sight of Our Native Land

November 30.—They were prepared for sea last evening, but were detained by the fouling of the cables. I waited until I could wait no longer, and went to bed. A bad omen. At 2.15 a.m. I was awakened by the noise of the propellers. I looked out of the port; we were turning. At 2.20 we went ahead and lay on our course. In a good hour, thank God! The weather is calm; there is a bright moon, though it is cloudy.

Evening.—We are steaming well. At noon a fairly fresh north-easter was blowing. It was rather cold. Now it has gone down and it is warmer. We eat and sleep as we have not done for some time. During supper the men made a disturbance on account of the bad quality of the food. Someone climbed on to the top of the fore hatchway, and made an inflammatory speech. It ran as follows:—"Gentlemen, they do nothing but rob us men, whose sweat and blood is held cheap." (I omit expressions not fit for publication.) With much satisfaction I consider it my duty to remark that the captain of the *Voronege* rose to the occasion. He went straight to the crowd, and begged them not to cry out all at once, but to state clearly what was the matter. They told him that the porridge was musty—"Look here," they said, "your own stewards would not touch it—why won't they look at it? Besides, it is not boiled, and you can't eat it raw."

"Well, how was I to guess that the stewards wouldn't eat it," said the captain. "I have tasted it with jam, and find that it is musty and not fit to eat. I shall order another supper for you. But why make a fuss? I am no more to blame than the stewards." Then followed an explanation highly convincing to the lower ranks, but little to be understood by readers unacquainted with naval jargon.

"That is so! he is quite right," they exclaimed. Murmurs of approval were heard after he had finished.

This first time the mutiny miscarried, and tranquillity was restored—will it be for long?

The leaders did not consider their point gained. A non-commissioned officer of some railway battalion came up to the bridge as spokesman, and talked to the captain on behalf of the others, not only about the events of the present moment, but also of things in general. Among various other questions he propounded the following. The allowance for the upkeep of a soldier for a year is 600 *roubles*; but only 50 are spent on him. Who has stolen the remaining 550?

He was evidently repeating something he had learnt by heart, not knowing what he was talking about, but taking it for the truth. I could stand it no longer and interfered. I asked him if he knew arithmetic. He was positively offended. "Well," I said, "then here you are. The peace establishment of our army is more than a million, and it means that if, for the upkeep of one soldier, 600 *roubles* a year are set aside, the total will amount to 600 millions. But what about fortresses, barracks, warlike stores? they will cost as much. The total will then come to 1½ *milliards!* Can you suppose the War Office spends as much? Do you know the estimates?" The non-commissioned officer, somewhat confused, hurriedly ended the conversation and went away, but was not convinced. I heard him audibly grumble as he went down the ladder towards the group of comrades awaiting him. "We know these figures, it is easy to juggle with them."

At 9.5 p.m. we anchored at the entrance to Shimonoseki Bay. The pilot did not undertake to pilot us by night.

Midnight.—Outwardly all was quiet. There was a report that meetings were being held in the hold and resolutions being carried. A guard of our *Suvoroff* sailors was posted by the captain's cabin where the admiral was quartered. Unfortunately they were unarmed. There were only 56 officers in the steamer, and only five revolvers among them. A few (of whom I was one) enjoyed the right of obtaining them from the moment of the official liberation. It was reassuring to feel that I had one in my pocket, even though it was an inferior one, and to know that in case of attack they could not hit you over the head with a stick, or seize you unceremoniously by the collar and throw you overboard. In the wardroom of the steamer a notice is nailed up:

On going to sea all the ship's company must be on board, etc.

Of course this, is absurd. The men are not impressed by these notices, but ignore them; anyway the prevailing frame of mind on board is not reassuring.

November 4.—About 3 a.m. (the sentry either did not suspect or was asleep) a drunken soldier crept into the admiral's cabin, and demanded that he should instantly be given vodka. He said: "We have spilt our blood. You ought to feel for us, and make much of us now we are free again." The admiral lay in bed completely defenceless. Fortunately the sentry heard a noise, the guard ran up, and the drunkard was led out; but they could not arrest him. He immediately disappeared among the half-drunken crowd awaiting him on the forecastle.

In the morning, just as we had begun to weigh anchor, a Japanese cutter approached us, and handed the captain a secret dispatch:—

Detain steamer, as there is a military mutiny at Vladivostok.

At 10 a.m. we crossed to Moji, lay there, and hoisted the quarantine flag. The official explanation of the cause of detention was— "On account of plague at the port of our departure." As a matter of fact, there were two cases of plague at Kobe, one of which had been brought there from Hong-Kong. However, thanks to communications with the shore, through merchants who came in boats, the men were quickly informed of the truth, and the disaffection increased.

At 1 p.m. the *Yaroslav* (which had left Kobe a little before us and was also detained here) left for Nagasaki. About 4 o'clock the *Voronege* went there too.

I am obliged to say a few words on account of occasional remarks interspersed in my diary. The subject refers to all kinds of revolutionary propaganda countenanced by the Japanese among the lower ranks of the prisoners of war. The private correspondence of the latter, their intercourse with their country, and with their nearest superiors (the latter often to be found in the same town), and even with the lower ranks who were confined in the neighbouring camps, was made difficult and hedged round by a mass of formalities. So widely opened were the doors of the barracks, for the importation of leaflets and books issued by various committees in America and in Japan itself, that the preachers of revolutionary (it would be more correct to say anarchist) ideas did not need either the co-operation of the French Legation or the special permission of the War Office for free entry into the camp of the prisoners of war.

Both literature and preachers were welcomed by the Japanese. I came across some of these books and leaflets: *Organisation of masses for national revolts, Street fighting, Types of barricades against attacks of cavalry and infantry, How to act if tyrants have artillery at their disposal*, etc. Later on (at Vladivostok) we saw a living example of how the principles laid down in the manifesto of October 17 were interpreted by the populace.

The activity of the Japanese in this direction, or more truly their open protection of the preachers of anarchy, was so apparent that even the French Minister, notwithstanding the dislike of diplomatists for a scandal, considered himself obliged to go and make representations. The answer he received (printed in the Japanese newspapers) was inimitable in its candour, not to say cynicism. "Our rule is, '*Injure your enemy in whatever way you can.*'" Thus retorted the Japanese Minister of War.

Among the troops were several musicians, who had formed themselves into a band (God knows of what kind); at first they used to play their marches, *polkas*, waltzes, and galops, under the windows of the captain's cabin during lunch. The admiral thanked them for their kind trouble, and ordered refreshments for them at his personal expense. The musicians accepted it as their due, not without pride. Suddenly a disturbance arose. They were reproached as being "glad of a sop," and that their servile fawning was treason to a free proletariat, etc. As a result there was no music at lunch today, and when it was over, the band gathered in the bows of the steamer and for two hours played the "*Marseillaise*" and the "*Carmagnole.*"

What next will there be? Involuntarily I remembered how I quarrelled with the chaplain of the *Suvoroff*, Father Nazare, proving that in a man-of-war it was futile to pray for a Christian ending of our lives. "Painless, shameless, and peaceful," that for men going to death only one of these three words need be left—"shameless." What could be more shameful now—the fear of death at the hands of our own men.

November 5.—The ship's crew (a trustworthy crowd) are in two watches. To help them we have organised our own watch; two officers and one sailor keep watch on the cabin occupied by the admiral. Four other officers are spread over the upper deck. The revolvers are transferred from hand to hand. There are in the steamer thirteen rifles, and cartridges for them packed in a case; but unfortunately they are kept in a compartment, access to which is through the living deck. An attempt to get them might cause an explosion.

At 3 a.m. I went on watch in my turn. A well-known place. The captain was keeping close to the islands and cliffs, in order that in case of open mutiny, he could run the ship ashore at once. He was quite right. The Japanese would not pardon the criminals—although they themselves had provoked them—in order to show that they were "top dog." On going on watch I learned that at about 2 a.m. a meeting was held in the first after-hold. It broke up at about 3 a.m. Detached groups wandered about the deck. Evidently they noticed that on the quarter-deck, spar-deck, and forecastle, there was something in the nature of a guard. They began to disperse in a shamefaced manner. (Apparently they were not aware that we were almost unarmed.) About 6 a.m. we arrived at Nagasaki. The captain of the *Bogatyr* came on board. He told us little that was good news. There was a senseless, drunken revolution at Vladivostok. In this harbour (Nagasaki) were the *Mongolia*, and some Norwegian vessel that had collected fugitives who had escaped from the rebels. The ship's company state that in the steamer a red flag is carefully kept, by which the people sworn in at Hamadera were led astray.

5 p.m.—The situation became more acute.

In the morning the senior engineer, profiting by the delay, wished to send a pump to a factory for repairs. He was not allowed to do this until it had been inspected, and the managing committee (of the mutineers) had given its decision. They were afraid he might send part of the machinery to the factory, without which it would be impossible to go to sea. They examined it and gave permission. Among the troops were thirty Cossacks (trans-Baikal troops) who had been captured, together with their officer S. M———. From them the latter received warning that at a meeting today it was decided, that if, by to-morrow evening, we did not leave Nagasaki, the mutineers would throw overboard both admirals and all who sided with them; take possession of the ship, and it would be seen what further. . . .

A direct demand has just been presented by the executive committee:

If you do not go to Vladivostok tomorrow we will go ourselves.

The Cossacks could not be persuaded to enter an open protest They said there were too few of them. Six troopers of the Daghestan brigade begged us to buy them Japanese daggers, and promised to "cut off the heads of anyone and disembowel them rather than that the admiral should die." A curious offer on their part. Is it worth it? Not a great reinforcement, six men against a crowd of two and a half thousand, of whom (by the evidence of the same Cossacks) about a hundred have revolvers and a good half are armed with hunting knives.

9 p.m.—After supper, in spite of rain and darkness the upper deck was full of men. The band was playing the *Marseillaise* incessantly, and orators making speeches on the forecastle. A large and fairly melodious choir was singing, "Arise, exalt yourselves, oh working men," on the quarter-deck. The spar-deck and poop, joined by a fore and aft bridge, were in our possession (we had to abandon the forecastle in order to concentrate our strength). The ship's company were on our side. They were accused of behaving like mean tyrants, and threatened with the same fate as ourselves. My leg was very painful, it may be from the weather. I was unable to walk about much. What are they (the mutineers) waiting for, if they have decided.

Meanwhile the captain had informed them on shore of the doings in the steamer. A police inspector has just arrived. He announced that there were no troops in Nagasaki, but the governor had summoned them from camp, and they would arrive tomorrow at 10 a.m. They had telegraphed to Sassebo to send a man-of-war. In the meantime all the police had been mobilised, and two echelons would soon arrive. "Are there many?" I inquired the admiral.

"About 70 men, who will occupy the spar-deck, and the rebels will only pass into the cabin (where all the officers and crew were assembled) over their bodies," categorically explained the Japanese.

At 11 p.m. the police arrived, and it seems imperceptibly, noiselessly, and without attracting any attention, proved to be masters of the spar-deck. Evidently our men, having listened to all sorts of nonsense at Hamadera, supposed that the Japanese authorities would not only take no measures against them, but would even be ready to give them support, and suddenly—such an unexpected turn of affairs—an extraordinary effect resulted. Music and singing stopped instantly; the upper deck was deserted; the ship's company met not the slightest opposition in the fulfilment of their duties. (Before this the artificers had been driven from the engines, and they had even placed their own men at the electric light stations.) However, it is reported that in the holds, into which the Japanese decided not to penetrate on account of their small numbers, burning debates were being held and a call to arms made—but unsuccessfully.

November 6.—About 1.30 a.m. the flag-captain came up very much agitated, and requested us to go on to the poop, promising to show us something very interesting. It was decidedly curious. Three ropes had been paid out over the stern, and some Japanese boats had made fast to them not far away. The flag-captain assured us that he had seen our officers lower the ropes and summon the boats. What utter nonsense! Now, when the rebels had hidden themselves in the hold, at the sight of some tens of armed police; when one could sleep in absolute security, can it possibly be so? But no, I am loath to believe it. The night passed in perfect quiet, and in the morning, five officers were missing. It is sad to relate, but, "You cannot leave a word out of a song." . . .

At 11.30 a.m. four Japanese torpedo-boats arrived from Sassebo, and with the covers of the torpedo tubes thrown back, began to cruise round the steamer. The mutineers were completely cowed. Delegates appeared, and assured the captain that it was all folly on the part of some desperate wretches who did not know what they were talking about. There was a disgusting scene, from taking part in which I was spared, thank God.

November 7.—Although I have written a good deal it is not worth recalling.

November 8.—General D. arrived on board the steamer at 10.30 a.m., and very nearly wrecked the whole business. He summoned one man from each company and retired with them on to the poop. He admonished them for four hours, and in the end proposed that they should swear that they would mutiny no more. He also proposed that they should give up the ringleaders, but received the stereotyped answer:—"*There are no ringleaders, we acted in unison.*"

Having decided that his four hours' harangue had fully convinced men who, for eleven months, had been under the influence of experienced agitators, the general explained that everything was now satisfactory, and we could go to Vladivostok: but—he stumbled against the protest of the ship's company. The captain of the steamer respectfully informed him that not only he and his officers, but also the crew, refused to go to sea with men who threatened to throw them overboard, as he had no means of preventing them carrying out their threat. Thunder and lightning! The general would try him by court-martial—take away his command; telegraph to St Petersburg—and I don't know what more.

With difficulty the captain of the *Bogatyr* managed to explain that the personnel of the *Voronege* was serving voluntarily, and the mutiny of the troops, in the absence of means for its suppression, would be force *majeure*, and give them the right of breaking their contract. The result was, it was decided to distribute the troops in the *Tambov* and *Kieff*, and to send others to the *Voronege*. The general's thoughts were turned in another direction. It transpired (and was said almost openly) that all these disturbances were owing to the presence on board of the two admirals; and therefore it was proposed, in order to avoid further unpleasantness, that they should go on board the *Yakut* which was leaving for Vladivostok on the following day. (This was the first occasion that we had met with such hostility on the part of official Russia. They were no doubt well informed here how the wind was blowing in St Petersburg.)

November 9.—They have finished the transfer of the troops to the *Kieff* and the *Tambov*.

November 10.—Both admirals, the staff, and General S., who never left us, were transferred to the *Yakut*. Of the latter (General S.) it may be mentioned that he quickly ended his warlike career. He reached the army before Mukden, having been appointed commander of a brigade, but, before he was able to take up his command, and never having seen it, he was taken prisoner. At midday we weighed anchor.

We left Nagasaki in magnificent weather. Towards evening it blew from the north; the *Yakut*, 730 tons burden, began to pitch and toss considerably.

November 11.—Towards morning the wind freshened. They had to lessen the number of revolutions on account of the cross sea. We ploughed along all day at five knots. The rolling was horrible. The blows of the waves against our counter were just like cannon shots. It was impossible to sit down in the saloon without being thrown out of one's seat. It became quieter in the evening.

November 12.—The weather has improved, and they have increased speed. Even the general, who had lain like a log, arose hearty, gay, and witty. It's a strange business: he doesn't seem at all depressed by the fact that he is returning from captivity, and is wholly absorbed in speculations as to whether there will be a vacant brigade for him, or if be will have to wait until his turn comes. Why is it that oppressive thoughts torment me so. By the evening it was quite calm: even the swell had gone down. D—— sat down at the piano—it was an old battered instrument and out of tune, but yet how soothing the long unheard notes of a favourite opera sounded on it. It would melt the iciest heart. How good it would have been to have died to the sound of such soft, tender music—to fall asleep and wake no more.

November 13.—It is nearly dawn; the top of Foggy Hill is visible. The sky is overcast and it rains occasionally. Today is Sunday. Mass was said. No doubt everyone prayed with all their heart, both joyfully and yet with pain, so it seemed afterwards. To port and ahead of us is the Russian coastline . . . and after a few half-score miles—a Russian port.

12.20 p.m.—All the places are familiar to me: on the left Cape Brussa darkens the horizon, on the right are the islands Durnova and Hildebrand. Welcome, my native land! Welcome, Russia!

CHAPTER 24

With Linievitch and Kuropatkin

November 14.—Yesterday at 4 p.m. we anchored in Golden Horn Bay. In the harbour were the *Jemchug, Aleut, Terak,* some torpedo boats, and some unknown steamers under the naval flag—all that remained of the Russian fleet. On shore were the burnt buildings of the officers' quarters, blackened columns of chimneys where had stood the naval club (what a library they had there!)—ruins,—and the sites of burnt houses.

Rear-Admiral Grevé, commander of the port, was flying his flag on the transport *Aleut.* From thence came Captain A—— to offer congratulations on our happy arrival. "Commander of the flagship—*c'est moi,*" he said, endeavouring to be witty, greeting us nervously and hurrying on to go to the admiral. The jest failed, and everyone—he also—seemed rather sad. Then Grevé came and quickly made his official call, and took both admirals on shore to his house.

Since this morning there has been a fog as thick as milk. Someone came on board the transport. Stories were told of the recent events. Carefully estimating and comparing these narratives, I came to the conclusion that strictly speaking there had been no mutiny during the first days of *pogrom* (devastation) and incendiarism—it was only a drunken orgy, which the perplexed and ill-informed authorities did not know how to suppress at the time, but allowed it to grow until passwords were used amongst the rebels. The authorities expected and feared that something would take place. Troops were sent to protect government buildings and establishments, but with a strict order "only to protect."

The following sketch is drawn from life. Half a company of soldiers stood guarding the house of the military governor. In the street was a crowd of the riff-raff of the port. Opposite was a two-storied house, in the lower storey of which was an eating shop and wine cellar, and in the upper storey a restaurant and confectioner's shop. The crowd was aggressive, but could not make up its mind to start an attack.

Every movement towards the governor's house failed of itself, and did not even get as far as the grey wall of men whose pouches contained cartridges. But the other side of the street was practically free. A heavy cobble stone flies through the plate glass window of a shop, and the same moment the mob rushes away helter-skelter, but the grey wall stands immovable, only the officers confusedly confer together, and orderlies run off somewhere (no doubt to the telephone). The dispersed crowd again collects. It still cannot believe that it "may."

A second window is broken, and again there is no interference. More and more; "Come on boys," they cry. The lust of destruction overpowers them. They break the glass, cutting them selves in forcing their way through the windows, although the doors had been broken some time ago and the entrance is clear—they pillage—it is not so much pillage as destruction. Smoke curls up from somewhere and tongues of flame flash out. More irrepressible becomes the pressure of those from outside, who have not yet been able to get in, and are afraid they will be too late. The two streams collide, there is a fight, and already there are some injured and burnt . . . but the grey wall stands immovable.

The drunken crowd (not so much from wine as from the lust of destruction) creep closer and closer to this wall. Bottles taken out of cellars, and expensive meats, are kindly thrust into the silent ranks, and their regularity is broken. First one goes, then another, as though they were unexpectedly tempted by the turbulent crowd. The grey wall crumbles and wavers: in vain the officer begs for instructions (by telephone) either to put a stop to the disorder, or to take his men away, of whom only a mere handful would soon be left. He was ordered to follow the instructions he had received to the letter. This was related to me: I did not see it myself. I was even told that in Aleutsky Street a sub-lieutenant with a section of soldiers did not allow any pillage, and was at once removed from his post almost under arrest. Towards evening the town was on fire in many places, and a drunken crowd, with whom were mixed soldiers and sailors, burnt and devastated because the "strong arm was wanting."

Local residents (those who did not give way to panic) categorically confirmed the fact, that it was not the hundreds or so Cossacks entering the town on the third day of the disorders who restored tranquillity, but that the people had come to their senses. The first day they were intoxicated, and on the second they recovered from their excesses and slept them off. The real tumult only broke out later, and was caused by the recollection of how they were allowed to do as they liked, and annoy the authorities with impunity.

For the same reason, too, the "Port Arthurites" who had returned from captivity filled with revolutionary propaganda, might have plotted their foolish but real mutiny. If the first spark at Vladivostok was not accidental, but burst forth under someone's direction, then one could not refuse to grant a patent for absurdity to the directors. They should have awaited the arrival of the *Yaroslav, Voronege, Kieff,* and *Tambov* from Japan, with several thousands of men, who positively believed in the possibility of the creation of a Yussuri republic.

November 15.—I went ashore, as it was necessary to buy some warm things for the railway journey. A strange scene met my eyes—burnt houses, devastated shops, and yet the town was full of people. The general impression was that they wished to ignore the traces of the late debauch—and rightly too; there was something to be ashamed of.

November 16.—A cold N.W. wind was blowing, but my heart was warm. Here, in Vladivostok, are many Port Arthurites who escaped capture by breaking through to Chefoo, before the surrender of the fortress. The people here themselves expected the fate of Port Arthur if the war had continued. Their feelings towards us are very different to those of D—— and his suite.

I in particular understood and appreciated this when an old chum of the Naval Academy came up and nearly smothered me in his embrace.

They all, too, with the same interest, asked, almost importunately: What of the admiral? How is he?

I say, without exaggeration, that every one hopes that he, the only one of the whole list of admirals who experienced and outlived the crusade of our fleet from Libau to Tsushima, was saved by a miracle from the lost *Suvoroff*, solely in order that with the fearless hand of a man who has endured to the utmost, he might build up our fleet again. Not the sham that we considered a fleet, but a fleet—a real fleet. It is not only we who think thus, but landsmen as well.

November 17.—We left Vladivostok at 10.45 a.m. Though there were no officials present, there was a crowd to see us off. They came regardless of their manner of dress: they had heard that "he" was leav-

291

ing, and hurried to see him. It was a hearty send-off—sailors, lands-men, civilians. I felt touched.

November 18.—Today we dined at Haichen-tze. A bottle of very nasty Kahetin wine costs 4 *roubles* 50 *kopecks*; it was poor stuff: four bottles wouldn't make a man drunk, and at that rate he might soon be ruined. At night there were 10 degrees of frost, but it was warm in the carriage.

November 19.—We arrived at Harbin at 7.30 a.m. Naval Surgeon Lisitsin was travelling with us on his return from the war. At Vladi-vostok he was attached to the admiral's staff. He would reach home sooner with the admiral, and the latter would benefit by his services (the wound in his head required bandaging daily). I, too, took advan-tage of this event. I received the same advice as in the *Voronege*, to keep my toe in hot compresses until we reached St Petersburg, and there it would be seen to. I limped, but was cheerful. The admiral had al-ready communicated with Linievitch from Vladivostok. They decided to meet. At Harbin we were detached from the train. During our stay our men strolled about the station and its vicinity. I looked out of the window. There was a dense crowd—many were drunk. Their garb was most fantastic. A soldier could not be distinguished from a work-man. Everywhere there were traces of fires. (Here, too, there had been drunken riots). Not much like a place under military law. Those who had gone for a ramble outside formed the same impressions.

At 8.10 a.m. we were conveyed south. It was very noticeable that the nearer we were to the advanced positions, the better order there was. Patrols were moving about, and there were no disorderly crowds. There were even baggage trains moving in good order. There was nothing of the devastation nor the crowds that were to be seen at Harbin and near it.

November 20.—Yesterday we reached the station of Loushagoy where Linievitch was quartered. We lunched and dined with him. Nearly all the time between lunch and dinner the admiral sat alone with him. It is not known what they talked about. After dinner in the evening the staff seized on me, demanding particulars of various details of the cruise and fight. At 7.30 a.m. today we went north. I could not refrain from asking the admiral about Linievitch's telegram. Why did he not take advantage of the fact that there was no armistice? Why did he not attack? Everyone is now crying out that the peace is shameful, that he had a million troops, and the Japanese many less. The admiral was silent at first, but afterwards remarked sharply: "What sort of million had he! He told me himself he had scarcely 370 thousand between Samara and Loushagoy."

"Well, then, is it surprising?"

At 10 a.m. we arrived at a station (I cannot get the correct pronunciation from anyone, they all say it in a different way), where Kuropatkin's train was standing. Here we lunched. The admiral alone with Kuropatkin (evidently for a confidential talk), and we with the staff. Kuropatkin accompanied us to the station and (evidently he had more to say) sat down with the admiral in his compartment with closed doors, for a good quarter of an hour. My compartment was close by, and when the door was opened I involuntarily heard the last words he spoke in taking his leave . . . "on you alone was there hope . . . if only it should not be so again in the future. . . . I say again, that all hope lay in your coming . . . tell the truth, the whole truth . . . if only they will listen."

We remained at Harbin for over two hours. I didn't understand what the matter was. The admiral became angry and summoned the traffic manager and the stationmaster, but they had decided not to tell him the truth (as we learnt later), and made an evasive reply. In substance, the affair was about the possibility of letting the special train ordered by Linievitch pass while permission had not yet been granted by the strike committee.

November 21.—We passed through the Hingansky tunnel at 12.45 p.m. North, or more truly north-west, of Hingan, it is quite winter. Snow and sledges.

At 2.30 p.m. there was a demonstration at —— Station. A crowd of soldiers and workmen gathered round the carriage. The railway officials hid themselves. The conductor ran up, pale as a sheet, saying that they were going to break into the train. It turned out to be nothing dreadful—only a deputation of three men who had come to inquire about the health of the admiral. I announced that he was "pretty well, thank God," although not yet quite recovered from his wounds, which were severe. They were satisfied, but begged, if it were possible, that he should come to the window, because the people having heard of his arrival, had assembled to greet him. I told the admiral, and he went out on to the platform at the end of the carriage, just as he was (in his ordinary coat).

The oldest of the deputies (an artillery n.-c. officer) began to make a speech to the effect that—at his age he had not spared himself, and shed his blood, and therefore they wished him good luck, and God grant . . . but here he grew decidedly confused, and those around cried "hurrah!" and they all stepped forward. Taking advantage of the moment's quiet, the admiral cried out: "Thanks for your kind words. This is your representative, eh!" and leaning down towards the soldier standing on the footboard, embraced and kissed him.

A roar came from the crowd. I looked at the deputy in perplexity, and at the tears streaming down his broad black beard, and felt as if something had choked me . . . it was all so unexpected. "These are all the wounded who are being sent home," explained the conductor, who had now recovered from his fright. "Ah yes," now it was all clear. These men of course knew the "price of blood." The train slowly steamed away, and they ran alongside it. A loud hurrah! was thundered forth, and hats and caps flew into the air.

November 22.—At midnight we arrived at Manchuria station and stopped. The railway was on the verge of a strike. The committee had already manifested their activity. They did not recognise special trains. The admiral telegraphed to Linievitch, but apparently the telegram went no further than the nearest station. At 2.30 and at 6.30 a.m. I was awakened by the jolting of the train, and was under the impression that we were going on. A bitter disappointment—we were being transferred from one line to another.

9 a. m.—Nothing fresh. A clear, frosty morning, 1.75° F. below zero.

According to reports, only military trains with reserves who have been discharged to their homes, are allowed to pass. About 11 a.m. we received a telegram granting us permission to proceed. From whom? From Linievitch or the committee? I could not clearly find out. At noon we went on.

The foreign matter forgotten by the doctors, in my wounded foot, evidently cannot stand the hot compress, and is trying to come out, not through the big hole, but by piercing its own way from behind. That is all right, as long as it comes out and does not delay on its way. I have a bad cold and bronchitis. I swallow quinine and *phenacetin*, and warm myself with hot tea and claret, and wrap myself up in everything I can. My legs suffer severely—they are frozen. Some kind person found some warm galoshes in a shop near the station and bought them for me. I am more comfortable.

6 p.m.—An unexpected discovery—another carriage is attached to our train in which are two travellers. One of them is assistant traffic manager. He told the admiral that he had hooked on with the object of settling misunderstandings on the journey and carrying out an unimpeded investigation. To us in friendly conversation he gave other explanations; he was chiefly to take advantage of the permission to pass the special train (orders had been given not to stop the admiral or cause him any unpleasantness) in order that he might inspect the line. The information he had gained was far from reassuring: two-thirds of the engines had been wantonly damaged; not more than thirty per cent, of the rolling stock was working; we had still to go another section (120 *versts*, 80 miles) with the same engine and driver, as there was no change to be obtained at the railway depot.

What a desolate country!—Sloping hillocks, vast plains (travellers call them brine pans), and for a hundred *versts* there is neither tree, nor village, nor any sign of human habitation. The dried-up pasture, on which a sheep could not exist, protrudes its rough straggling blades from under a thin coating of snow.—It is a desert.

November 23.—Night. The hills are becoming higher and more massive. We sometimes plunge into deep cuttings, and sometimes traverse a high embankment. It is all uninhabited. Indeed, in comparison with this part of Transbaikal, even northern Manchuria is a paradise. We stopped at the Orlofnany station. A military train has been wrecked twenty *versts* ahead of us. The heating apparatus burst. About twenty men were wounded and scalded. The admiral immediately ordered our doctor and some volunteers to go there on our engine. Profiting by our long detention, I took courage and hobbled into the refreshment room, where I ate a roast tree-partridge and laid in a stock of seven. (I am heartily tired of ham and preserves—our usual diet.)

At 6 a.m. we continued our journey. The doctor on his return informed us that the accident was quite trivial. Not only was there no one killed, but there was no one seriously wounded. A wood now came in sight, a herd of cows and a drove of horses. In places Buriatsky villages were to be seen.

The scenery between Aga and Ingoda was surprisingly beautiful. The last time (on my way to Port Arthur) I passed this place in the night and was unable to admire it. It is clear, calm, and frosty, 8 C Fahr. below zero. There was a delay at Chita town station. The assistant traffic manager explained that a crowd of "manifestants," about three

295

thousand strong, was moving along the line and making for the town. It would be dangerous for us to go on and meet them. They might take it for an act of hostility and arrange an "accident." It would be better to wait and let them pass.

At 1.50 p.m. the procession went by us. There were two red flags, and behind them, in proper order, were two military bands: one a Cossack band with yellow shoulder straps; the other, which I learnt afterwards belonged to the railway battalion, wore red. From afar we had heard the strains of the "*Marseillaise*," but when they went past the train the bands were not playing, and a large and fairly good choir were singing something about, "it is time for the working men to obtain their freedom." Among the crowd there were many of the educated classes, both men and women, officials of various departments in uniform, officers, and a large number of soldiers.

At 2.5 p.m. the line was clear. We started. A curious scene occurred. In the station near the train were a group of "grey caps," who had left the procession and assembled on the platform near the admiral's carriage. Seeing the admiral at the window, they cried "hurrah!" and gave him an ovation.

At the next station we learnt from our fellow-travellers, who had wired to Chita, that everything had passed off successfully. The governor (General Holshtchevnikoff) received the "manifestants," and had made a speech to them from the balcony. Yielding to their requests, he had released from the guardroom the officers who had been arrested for taking part in the meetings, and agreed to the establishment of a council of representatives of all classes, of which he himself was president. Jokingly they called him the President of the Chita Republic. He acted wisely. Had they killed him, and the power passed into the hands of some committee or other, Linievitch's army would have been cut off from Russia.

November 24.—We are travelling without any special adventures and fairly fast (an average of 40 versts = 26 miles an hour). About 1 p.m. we arrived at Muisovy station, where we dined off real and excellent "*shtchee*" (cabbage soup), and goose. In the midst of the banquet the assistant traffic manager, who was travelling with us, appeared and announced that a strike would begin at 2 o'clock. Only trains with reserve men would run. But the admiral, it appears, is allowed to pass; he added in a confidential tone, "We shall soon see, however; if they give us an engine, it means we shall go."

His tidings proved correct. At 2.30 they gave us an engine. I wonder how far we shall go! How long shall we benefit by this friendliness? The strike is universal throughout Russia. They demand a pardon for an engineer named Sokoloff who had been sentenced to death at Kushka.

7 p.m.—The assistant traffic manager says the reason that we have not been stopped is solely due to the presence of the admiral. Our train has been declared to be a military train. All others are detained. God grant that we may continue under the same protection.

9 p.m.—On the Circum-Baikal railway. The sky has become clear. It is a glorious moonlight night. The scenery is not only beautiful but awe-inspiring in its beauty. At times it is dreadful; when on the left there is a wall of rock, and on the right a precipice invisible from the window; and the train rushes along high above the mirror-like surface of the lake, inclining as it rounds the bends, and looking as it were into an abyss. At the station near the southern extremity of Lake Baikal, we obtained some Petersburg newspapers of the 10th and 11th November. It is a long time since we saw one. We read them, and cannot believe our eyes. Like a train Russia herself seems to be rushing somewhere, leaning over an abyss; should an axle crack, or a sleeper be broken, everything would go to ruin.

At the same station we changed the engine and the men in charge of the train. The traffic examiner, who had been stranded here, came in. I happened to be the witness of a curious scene.

Traffic examiner (going towards a carriage and turning to a group of railway servants and workmen), "How now? Shall I get to my destination? Shall I be alive! "

A voice: "Drive on, Alexander Alexandrovitch! meanwhile keep calm, we have not yet received the order." At 11.25 we arrived at Baikal station. For the last three hours I have not been able to tear myself away from the window, admiring the view.

November 25.—At Baikal station yesterday we fully appreciated the circumstance that the railway strike has not spread to the refreshment room. True, instead of a first-class waiting-room there was a dirty shed, but what dainties! I have seen nothing like it for two years.

When I went back to the carriage I slept like a boa-constrictor. I heard neither the arrival at Irkutsk, nor the whistling and jolting when they were changing our carriage from one line to another.

We can make nothing of the strike. It is—and it is not. In any case the ordinary traffic is suspended, although they promise that the last express will leave tomorrow, and our carriage will be attached to it.

The passengers have dispersed to look at the town, to hear the news, but chiefly to have a good lunch and dinner. Only cripples are left in the carriage. An attempt to obtain food from the station refreshment room through the conductor, did not meet with success. The station was literally filled with passengers and their luggage. My messenger was told that "You have no business here, let them come themselves." I was obliged to walk. My appearance was very homely. I wore a lambskin cap bought at Vladivostok, a wonderfully cut sac coat made by a Japanese at Sassebo; on my feet were warm galoshes like sea boots; in addition, my hair had not been cut for a month, and I walked with difficulty, leaning on a stick.

I successfully reached not only the waiting-room but even the refreshment bar. The barman evidently took me for a pensioner; we quickly made out a menu together, and when I, after drinking a glass of vodka and tasting some dried sturgeon, wished to pay, the barman clapped me on the back and said, "We won't quarrel about the account." Towards the evening (it was already dark) the wife of the governor (Maj.-Gen. Kaigorodoff) came and had a long talk with the admiral. She was evidently much agitated. I don't know what they talked about.

November 26.—Our fellow-travellers relate some of yesterday's impressions. No one knows in the town what will happen tomorrow, and cannot even count upon where they will find themselves—whether in the Russian Empire or in a state of an all-Russian Federation, or in a completely independent Irkutsk Republic.

The admiral (again at dusk) was sent a carriage (probably the result of yesterday's visit), and drove to the governor-general's and then to the governor's. On his return he told us that both of them were completely deprived of all authority, while their sole support, a battalion—I don't know of what regiment, but with blue shoulder straps and the number 36, sent by Linievitch—was becoming restless. The officers were taking part in meetings, and the men did guard duty unwillingly. They said that if by the 30th they were not sent home, they would not be answerable for order. The local troops are not worth mentioning. Telegrams go through the censor of the strike committee. The authorities are completely cut off from both St Petersburg and Linievitch. It's a pleasant situation.

Today is the feast of St Innocent, patron saint of Irkutsk. All the vodka was bought up last night. This forebodes a great debauch. They are afraid that there will be an uprising on that account.

At 8.32 p.m. we successfully continued our journey.

CHAPTER 25

"The Price of Blood"

November 27.—At 2 p.m., at Tulun station, a crowd of soldiers and workmen again gathered round the train. They sent deputies to beg that the admiral would show himself to them, if it were only at the window. He (in spite of the frost—8° below zero, Fahrenheit—came out on to the end platform. They asked him if it were true that the authorities did not wish to send him reinforcements from Russia. Was it true that "Nebogatoff's Division took no part at all in the fight, but remained far astern." The admiral answered them shortly and resolutely. "Was there no treachery?" a penetrating voice suddenly called out. Instinctively we felt that this question tormented the crowd the most.

"There was no treason; our force was not sufficient and God gave us no luck," firmly replied the admiral, and bowing he retired.

Sympathetic cries followed him. "God grant you good health." "May you live for a century." "You are an old man, but have spilt your blood: we are not the only sufferers—you are wounded in the head." The train started, accompanied by a thundering "hurrah!"

November 28.—At 1 p.m. we arrived at Kaimsk. It is clear and frosty; there are 17.5° below zero, Fahrenheit.

About 5 p.m., at the siding at Uriask, we overtook a mutinous battalion of reservists, who would not allow us to go ahead, explaining that their need was the greater. The station authorities were terrorised. They told us it was worse yesterday. The battalion had damaged an engine. They demanded that the engine should be detached from a mail train that had overtaken them, because "there are more than a thousand of us here, and we can carry all before us." At 6.45 p.m. we went on.

November 29.—We are crawling behind a train of reservists at a speed of 18 *versts* (12 miles) an hour.

November 30.—The night before last, by a trick, we overtook several detachments at the sidings; but by stealing a march on them in this way, we were nearly stranded in the open *"steppe"* for lack of water. It was an eventful journey.

At 12.30 p.m. we crossed the bridge over the Obi. On the right bank of the river, near the station, a large town and cathedral had risen up; streets were laid out regularly, and there were *isvostchiks* with numbers. I remember how I drove through here ten years ago in a post sledge; it was then a desert.

December 1.—At Omsk, 9 a.m., we obtained some newspapers, and only read of military revolts. However, well informed people warned us that all telegrams had to pass the censors of the "committees." The news is mutilated and is often pure fabrication. There is some consolation in that, as otherwise one might think that there is not a sound spot in Russia.

We are continuing our journey, and, except for the revolt of the reservists, have had no further experiences.

Through being absorbed by the news in the papers and the talk about them, I forgot to change my compress. In the night it dried up. In the early morning I woke from the pain. I had to moisten the compress and draw it off. Today I could hardly walk. The great thing is to bear up till I get to Petersburg and not break down on the way.

11 a.m., Tcheliabinsk.—All is quiet to outward appearance.

December 3.—9 a.m., Ufa.

7 p.m.—We have already crawled a hundred *versts* behind the train with reservists. They won't let us pass. There are a whole series of similar military detachments on ahead. We succeeded in passing one of them, thanks to the cleverness of a station watchman; but the poor fellow paid for this dearly (we were informed afterwards that he was nearly beaten to death). It is becoming all-absorbing.

December 4.—Last night we stopped a long time at the station of Kinsel. The station authorities had received a threat by telegram that they would be burnt alive if they did not allow three detachments to pass ahead of us. (They were the same that we overtook by trickery.) At 12 noon we arrived at Samara. The situation is hopeless. The line is completely in the control of the reservists. Travellers only shrug their shoulders when we ask at what approximate date we may reach Moscow. There is complete anarchy. The commandant of the station nearly wept in telling us how absolutely helpless he was. Suddenly there was a miracle. It came out that Admiral Rojëstvensky was in the train (our carriage was attached to the last express). A crowd gathered round and they made an ovation. Three times the admiral was obliged to come out on to the platform and bow. The line was cleared. At 12.30 p.m. we went full-speed ahead.

About 2 p.m. we were approaching a wayside station. Having been warned that two whole military detachments were waiting here, we decreased speed, fearing that they might detain us (by changing the signals). The conductor ran up pale and agitated, saying that there was a large crowd on both sides of the station, and that it would be better for us to stop. We are scarcely moving, but the signal stands correct and the line is clear. Suddenly from right and left was heard a "Hurrah!" More than 2000 men climbed on to the embankment stumbling, running after the train, shouting and throwing their caps into the air. It appears that the Samara detachment telegraphed to their comrades that the admiral was travelling by the express, and therefore we need not fear any delays in the future. It was touching and flattering, though curious.

December 5.—We are running as fast as an express ought to go.

6 p.m.—Tula.

11.15 p.m.—Moscow.

December 6.—Our carriage was attached to a passenger train, and at 12.15 we started on the last stage of our journey.

At 5.30 p.m. we passed Luban. We are approaching St Petersburg. Alas! I never thought to return thus! It weighs on my spirits.

At the best, my remarks are not of such general interest as to be worth recording literally every day, but for the completion of the sorrowful tale here related it appears to me to be necessary to give the contents of my diary in short general lines for the following six months.

On arrival at St Petersburg, it became evident that the real instigators of the coolness shown us at receptions, were General D—— and his satellites, and not the representatives of the Vladivostok garrison or the active army (not to mention the rough masses of reservists), who, knowing the "price of blood," treated us so sympathetically. In St Petersburg we were met by enemies, who were the more dangerous because the majority at the outset had played the part of the most devoted friends. And when it became clear that the Admiral not only wished, but had the strength to work, and was anxious to leave no stone unturned in his efforts at reforming the navy—he considered that "a repetition of the past was an unpardonable transgression"—then a powerful coalition was formed against him composed of that class of society who consider the Admiralty their own private property.

A few days after our arrival in St Petersburg, the admiral presented his last report—about the cruise of the squadron from the China Sea into the Gulf of Korea—the first contact with the enemy—the circumstances preceding the battle of Tsushima, and the development of the latter up to the moment when he (Rojëstvensky) was put out of action and lost the power of giving an account of the events that occurred. In a short time he also presented a full report, which made its appearance in the press, verified and confirmed by captains and officers who had escaped from the destruction, and a plan of our and the enemy's manoeuvres. Not one of these documents (like all Admiral Rojëstvensky 's reports of the voyage) was published, although the papers were full of apocryphal tales about different moments and episodes of the battle, written clearly from the accounts of eyewitnesses.

In saying "clearly," I do not wish to be accused of mere verbalism. In my hands are documents proving that the newspaper *Novoe Vremya* (*New Times*) received for publication several letters of Lieutenant Vuiroboff, who perished in the *Suvoroff*, but only printed some of the letters received, and in those they took the liberty of making omissions and of editing them in such a way that they served a definite purpose.

I am firmly convinced that the letters of the Constructor Politovsky (whom I knew personally and always considered a thorough gentleman), published in a book under the title *From Libau to Tsushima*, were also edited in the same way. My readers must not think that I wish to show up people who were conducting a slanderous newspaper campaign against Admiral Rojëstvensky, as villains in a melodrama. Nothing of the kind. These were gentlemen who did not profess the idea "evil for evil" so much as "nothing succeeds like success." Their aim was to "flay" the admiral and make him the scapegoat. At all costs, they had to adhere to the reports of the battle published immediately after it took place, which had been hastily gathered from telegrams from American correspondents which were not reliable.

If only the reports of the admiral had been published at the end of the year 1905, in which he with business-like brevity stated that neither with the forces which he then disposed of, nor with the "weight" which they had decided to attach to him (Nebogatoff's Division) could there have been hope of success. If only it had been made clear that there was no lack of talent, or, what is more, courage and self-sacrifice, but that the complete inefficiency of the weapons with which men, true to their oath, were sent, not into a battle, but into a massacre, was the cause of the unheard-of destruction.

If only it had been clear to everyone that it was not the survivors who were guilty, but those who had sent them to inglorious defeat: what would have happened? What might have happened? With what consequences would such a moment of common knowledge have been fraught for the gentlemen living so peacefully beneath the Admiralty spire, [1] or even outside it?

For me, with my still open wounds, a semi-invalid, full of the bitterness of enforced silence, and of the impossibility of replying publicly to the calumnies organised by the press, utter silence was intolerable.

I brought out a series of articles in which by statistics and documents I tried to prove (and I daresay did prove) that the creators of the third (Nebogatoff's) squadron which detained Rojëstvensky in Madagascar, deceiving the public by an account of mythical war, coefficients of ships that might be sent to reinforce the second squadron, were guilty of a crime against Russia.

Having finished this question, I promised in the following articles to give my readers a true description of the battle, and the events preceding it; but here I was summoned by the Minister of Marine, Admiral Birilieff, who gave me a categorical order, that I was not to write anything about the late war, unless it was censored by the authorities. It was pointed out to me that such a prohibition could easily be circumvented by finding a suborned editor, who would write in my words; but the minister would be quite satisfied by my word (of course, if I agreed to give it). As an inducement, it was explained to me that a special court had already been appointed to inquire into all the details of the misfortunes we had undergone, and premature disclosures by individuals would only have the unpleasant character of being attempts to influence public opinion; that it was inadmissible

1. The spire of the Admiralty chapel.

from a service point of view, etc. I was then still in the service, and so, having received the order, I strictly obeyed it, and did not betray the confidence reposed in my word.

Is it necessary for me to explain that by this mode of action *my* mouth only was closed, while the *Novoe Vremya's* "knights of the pen" vociferated all the louder without fear or reproof.

Just at this time, the doctors definitely stated that unless I went to some warm climate for rest, away from the slough of gossip that irritated and aggravated me, in all probability I should not live to see the triumph of the truth. They drew up the medical certificate required by the regulations (I forgot to mention that a piece of bone was drawn out of the big toe of my left foot, without difficulty—it almost came out of itself—and the wound began to heal quickly).

As regards the affair of the surrender of the *Bedovy*, a Special Court of Inquiry had already been appointed. (For some reason this was separate from the court for the surrender of the ships in general). I went to the president of it, and begged him to examine me early, as I could testify very little, and that little was not worth much credence, as being the evidence of a severely wounded man, who might easily confuse, in his imagination, delirium and reality; things seen personally, and things heard of afterwards. I well knew the value of such recollections from personal experience, when I was convinced that autographic and readymade (but afterwards forgotten) remarks appeared in contradiction to the clear picture formed much later, under the influence of the accounts of those surrounding me.

They examined me and let me go.

A few days later and I, installed in the Hotel "Cap Martin," between Mentone and Monte Carlo, on the shores of an azure sea and amid the groves of Alpine pines, secluded myself from the world. Russian papers and journals were not taken in here at all. The *Figaro* and *Gaulois* devoted twenty or thirty lines to our affairs, and to those I endeavoured to pay no attention.

The only work which I undertook, and decided to finish, even though it were beyond my strength, was the Battle of Tsushima.

In accordance with my given word not to print anything unless it passed the censor of the authorities, in my writings I refrained from the least criticism on questions of strategy and tactics, from all analyses of operations; but with greater impulse I devoted myself with photographic accuracy to the reproduction of details, ruthlessly rejecting everything that might awaken in me even the shadow of a doubt as not recorded in my note-book, or substantiated by living witnesses. It is curious how tormenting such a work proved. Two or three hours' work, resulting in two or three pages of notepaper, laid me on the sick-bed. I slept a heavy, restless sleep. It was quite conceivable, because I compelled myself to live the past over again. So it went on for more than a month. I thank God I finished and posted it, having addressed it (for security, in order that the thick packet should not be detained on the frontier) to Rojëstvensky himself, with a request that he would give it to my brother, who would undertake to see it through the censor and have it published.

Having fulfilled "a duty confided to me from God," I prepared to give myself up to absolute repose, when suddenly I received a letter from an old friend who did not generally evince an inclination to express tender feelings, and in this correspondence did not make up facts, and treated me in a really friendly manner in this emergency.

I allow myself to quote literal extracts from his letter:—

The gentlemen whom you are preparing to convince, and have partially enlightened, are masters everywhere. They are saying with conviction, that you fled abroad and will not return to Russia because you are chiefly guilty of the surrender of the *Bedovy*, and threaten to have you shot. This is an example to show you how far they will go. The inquiry is officially a secret, but this only contributes to the success of the calumniators, who hint that for them the curtain of secrecy is raised.

It is quite possible (from their coign of vantage), and the easier therefore to believe them, but meanwhile they lie shamelessly. I am personally convinced of this. They are now reckoning with public opinion, and are making preparations. In the highest circles, they are painting you in lurid hues, and in the opposite camp they represent you as a rabid member of the 'black hundred,' capable of anything, including treachery.

It is said that Rojëstvensky, in order to uphold discipline, hanged men by scores, and that you were his right hand in this; but about these punishments they are ordered to keep silence.[2] Be prepared to be blackguarded from both sides. Their aim is to dishonour you personally to the curt, or in spite of it, so that all your evidence may be discredited. I am writing so that you

---

2. Need I say that the whole time the Second Squadron was in existence, there was not one single death sentence, and the admiral himself was the chief opponent of it.

should not be in ignorance. That would be the most foolish thing of all. You had better come back as soon as possible, so that at all events the legend of your flight might be disproved. You also can 'kick,' but I think nothing will come of it. It has been decided beforehand to put you in the prisoner's dock; however, try your best, and let the devil take the consequence.

Four days after the receipt of this letter I was in Petersburg.

The situation, as he thus described it, proved to be truthful and accurate.

I tried "kicking," but nothing came of it. I myself was partly to blame. I could not believe that the respected President of the Court would submit to being prejudiced, but I will not speak about him. Fate has punished him sufficiently, and three months after that he played the part of the unjust steward.

An attempt to appeal through the Ministry of War to an Imperial Order was unsuccessful. By this order, officers captured when wounded, were to return straight to their units. Worse still, I met with manifest disbelief when I spoke about my wounds; especially on the part of the court, not one of whose chosen members considered it necessary to find out what condition I was in.

The *feldsher* (sick berth attendant) who gave me first aid, and the doctor who bandaged me in the *Bedovy*, were not questioned at all, but the decision had already been made.

I was ignorant of all this at the time, because the inquiry was a secret (for those who were interested in it); and I was perplexed and tormented by questions. "Can they have forgotten? Could they have said nothing? "But it was solely that they were not called upon as witnesses. I pointed to the example of the Court of Inquiry on the surrender of Nebogatoff's Division, where, notwithstanding the then existing Imperial Order, that all officers were to be tried, the president insisted on the deletion from the list of accused, not only of the severely, but also of those seriously wounded. But—that was another president. I asked for a medical examination, basing my appeal on the evidence of the *feldsher*, doctor, and others.

The examination was sanctioned, Life-Surgeon Murinoff was called, but in his hands there appeared to be no information except approximate evidence of the scars left on my body, and he gave a very evasive opinion. I could not realise that by the appointment of an expert, the court had disregarded my fundamental request—the examination of witnesses. I repeat that the inquiry *for me* was a secret; but how could he, a doctor of medicine, called for the decision of a question more vital than life, neglect this circumstance? After this expert examination, it was evident to me from the first my case was prejudged, and it was useless to "kick."

My friends from under the "spire" (how could one distinguish who was a traitor) strongly urged that a public court was the best place in which to prove my innocence; and that it was not for nothing that Rojëstvensky demanded that they should try him also. In this business the utmost powers of the Procurator of the Naval Ministry were insufficient for the direction of the inquiry and the composition of the deed of accusation. On January 9, 1906, these powers were augmented by the transfer of A. I. Vogak from the Ministry of Justice, with the title of Major-General. He assumed the role of prosecutor.

On April 8, 1906, a session was held of a curt to decide questions that were already determined; and shortly afterwards an order was issued by the Naval Ministry, according to which, all of us, from the commander downwards, who being in good health and of sound mind, unwounded and unhurt, surrendered an undamaged destroyer to the enemy, having made no attempts at resistance, ought to be placed in the prisoner's dock together with Admiral Rojëstvensky, who was at that moment lying unconscious in a struggle between life and death.

With regard to the sentence, I was perfectly indifferent; no court could make a decision clearly contrary to the evidence. No skill or cunning of accusation could either supply facts that did not exist, overturn the evidence given under oath, or erase from my body the honourable scars from wounds received in the fight.

The fact itself of being court-martialled appeared to me to be extraordinary. I recalled the first days spent in hospital, the anticipation that the Japanese would drag me before a court (that would have been hard, but the Japanese would have been within their rights). I remembered my doubts as to whether it would be decent to plead for the mercy from our victors of changing the rope for the bullet. The following picture rose before me. A court—a Russian Court—formed a year ago, and we being brought on bloodstained stretchers into the hall and laid in the dock. Would the officer of the court have the courage to say, turning to us: "The court is coming, I beg you to rise?" or, on the other hand, would the president confusedly explain: "Gentlemen, respect them by standing." Many strange, many disjointed thoughts came into my head.

Suddenly one wild—not thought—but cry came from my heart: "Is this the 'price of blood?' is it for this we have shed it?"

At once all else was forgotten, appearing too worthless and insignificant to pierce the heart.

My heart bounded as I recalled a half-forgotten phrase. With a tranquillity that astonished me (up to this moment I had been boiling with indignation), I got my diary, sought and found the necessary page.

> *October 30.*—Last day of captivity. Beloved country, I salute you. Fate preserved me—for what? For thy service. An oath, a fearful oath I swear. For the entire remainder of my life, all my strength, all my blood for thee—everything.

I smiled at the *naïveté* of the statement. I wished to tear it up, to trample on it, to throw it into the waste-paper basket; but I thought better of it. I merely ruled it out and wrote across it:

For my Country—yes. But with you I have paid my reckoning.

Appendix

The Hull Affair

On our arrival at Vigo we heard how great and widespread was the stir which the incident with the fishing-boats in the North Sea had caused. The English papers called the squadron simply the "squadron of mad dogs," which ought either to be turned back or destroyed. The incident itself they stigmatised as an "act of open piracy." (This is juridically absurd, since the condition *sine-qua-non* of piracy, that is, sea robbery, is personal gain.) But public opinion in England was above all excited about the fact that "one of the Russian torpedo-boats remained on the spot until the morning and rendered no assistance to the fishermen, who were saving their comrades."

This piece of news, which emanated from the fishermen scattered on the sea, was discussed from every point of view. It was said that even the barbarians of old had spared the lives of those who had become the victims of war by chance, and had reprieved them; after this there could no longer be any doubt that it was a slap in the face for England, an insult which could only be wiped out by blood, unless the Russian Government offered complete satisfaction.

The return of the squadron and the trial by a Court of Law of the admiral commanding, the captains, and all those implicated in the affair, *but above all of the captain of the torpedo-boa*t, was the least satisfaction which could be accepted.

For me, these statements were a complete revelation. My sceptical views could not be upheld against the testimony of old and experienced seamen.

"One of the torpedo-boats remained on the spot until the morning."

This means that as a matter of feet there were torpedo-boats present. Thanks to our good look-out we had therefore escaped from an extraordinary danger. We happily succeeded in repelling the attack.

If in doing so innocent people were made to suffer, this was no doubt most deplorable, but what was to be done? At Port Arthur women and children were killed during the bombardment. Our government should express its regret, pay damages to the families concerned, but that was all.

I will now ask leave to depart from my rule for once and relate now what I only heard later.

As soon as the admiral had received information about the campaign initiated in the English press, he at once telegraphed to our Naval Attaché in London requesting him to bring to the notice of the press the fact that at the time when the incident under discussion took place our destroyers were 200 miles, possibly even more, ahead of the squadron, a fact which could be easily verified, if the time of their arrival in French ports were taken into account; consequently the torpedo-boat which remained on the spot until morning undoubtedly belonged to those which had attacked the squadron, and had, moreover, been badly hit. Evidently the boat was repairing its own damages, or waiting for the other boats.

It is very significant that this well-reasoned and substantiated statement hardly appeared in any paper, and that the well-disciplined (sic) English press suddenly and completely forgot the evidence of the fishermen, which it had obstinately upheld until then. But this is a small matter compared with the fact that at the meetings of the commission in Paris the English delegates expressed their conviction that the fishermen had undoubtedly made a mistake, that there was no torpedo-boat on the spot; that the *Kamtchatka* had passed there in the morning, and that it was this vessel which had been taken for a torpedo-boat. It was possible (according to calculation of time and speed) that the *Kamtchatka* did, in fact, pass the locality in question on the morning of October 22, but the accounts had spoken of a torpedo-boat which had *remained* on the spot until morning.

And finally—I appeal in this to the experienced seamen of the whole world—can one admit that in broad daylight old "sea-dogs" in the pursuit of their calling could possibly mistake the *Kamtchatka*, a peculiarly misshapen merchant steamer with a, high free-board, for a torpedo-boat? Even the child of a fisherman could not make so gross an error.[1] A further very convincing factor was the fact that all those in the squadron who maintained that "they had seen the torpedo-

---

1. And yet precisely this mistake has been made more than once by naval officers.— In this case it was not broad daylight, but a misty dawn.—Trans.

boats with their own eyes," agreed in their statements, *viz.*:—number of funnels and masts, colour, superstructures, etc., etc. And this, moreover, not on board one ship, where one might have assumed that they had all been the victims of the same hypnotic influence, but on board five different ships, which, at the time, had not been in communication with one another.

I believe that even Monsieur Charcot would not have admitted the possibility of such a "thought-transmission"; but that is not all.

Nine months later I was in bed in the Japanese hospital at Sasebo, and heard from brother officers who had also been wounded, but had by then been healed and allowed to walk about the hospital, that in the adjoining hut there was a Japanese lieutenant and former captain of a torpedo-boat suffering from acute rheumatism. At that time the negotiations which were bound to lead up to the conclusion of peace had begun at Portsmouth (America). This was clear to all, and therefore our neighbour probably did not consider it necessary to be particularly secretive as regarded the past. He said quite openly that he had caught his illness during a bad passage from Europe to Japan.

"Your European autumn is worse than our winter," he said.

"Autumn?" I asked. "What month?"

"October. We, our detachment, started on our passage at the end of that month."

"In October? At the same time as our Second Squadron? How was it that we knew nothing of you? Under what colours did you sail? When did you pass the Suez Canal?"

"You are asking too much," the Japanese answered, laughing. "Under what colours? Naturally, not under Japanese. Why you did not discover us?—That you must ask yourself. When we passed through the Suez Canal?—Behind Admiral Fölkersam's division."

"But then—you were probably connected with the famous Hull affair?"

"Ha, ha! That is a very indiscreet question."

More than this we were unable to get from him, but it was, it seems to me, quite sufficient. All the more so, as at that time (October-November 1904) vague paragraphs appeared here and there in the European press about certain torpedo-boats (four in number, built in Europe) which were then on their way to the Far East to reinforce the U.S. Squadron.

Why did our delegates at the International Commission of Inquiry in Paris concede so readily the possibility of experienced seamen mistaking *the Kamtchatka, which was passing at the time, for a torpedo-boat, which had remained the whole night until the morning on the scene of the event?*—I am unable to form a judgment. History will decide.

In November 1904 a Schwartz-Kopf torpedo was found by fishermen on the south-east coast of the North Sea, which had been much battered by the surf. A picture of this torpedo was published in the European illustrated papers. As is known, every torpedo carries, stamped on all its parts, the name of the firm which made it and a number. If one has some of the parts of such a torpedo before one, this suffices to establish with absolute certainty, by means of the above-mentioned marks, to whom and when the torpedo was sold.

Our delegates, as it would appear, did not devote their attention very particularly either to the testimony of the fishermen, as regarded the presence of the torpedo-boat, or to this find. This is perfectly intelligible, since the supreme direction of these negotiations was in the hands of our diplomatists. As regarded these, I had, based on my lengthy experience acquired during my sea service in foreign waters, formed the following opinion:—According to the views of those employed under the Foreign Office, every Russian subject who approaches them with a request for assistance is beyond doubt a suspicious personage, for a respectable individual never and nowhere in the civilised world gets into difficulties.

Whilst, for instance, an English Consul is ever ready to stand out in the interests of any subject of His Britannic Majesty (even if he does not know him personally), to point out possible complications which might arise, threaten with summoning a squadron, with a naval demonstration, possibly with war—"our man," if he has not been able to simply send the supplicant to the right-about, tries to persuade him to drop his request somewhat after this style:—

> Is it really worth the while to make so much fuss over it? Between ourselves, you might as well confess that you yourself are not quite free from blame in the affair. You had better drop it; it will be the best course in the end.

This prejudice against their own countrymen, the firm conviction that our side always have *les pieds dans le plat* ("put its foot in it"), of course played a not inconsiderable part in the settlement of the "Hull Affair."

NOTE BY THE TRANSLATOR.

The Suez Canal records at Port Said have recently been searched with reference to the above statement, and show that no vessel remotely resembling torpedo craft of any class passed through the Canal anywhere near the time when Admiral Fölkersam took his detachment East.

Lightning Source UK Ltd.
Milton Keynes UK
UKHW012311150620
365054UK00005B/1667